Open Content Licensing:

Cultivating the Creative Commons

Principal Editor
Professor Brian Fitzgerald
Head of School of Law,
Queensland University of Technology, Australia

With the assistance of
Jessica Coates and Suzanne Lewis

Sydney University Press

Published in Sydney by

Sydney University Press
University of Sydney
NSW 2006 AUSTRALIA
www.sup.usyd.edu.au

Publication date: March 2007

The material in this publication is based on papers presented at the *Open Content Licensing: Cultivating the Creative Commons* conference held by the Queensland University of Technology (http://www.qut.edu.au) in Brisbane, Australia in January 2005.

This publication is an output of the ARC Centre of Excellence for Creative Industries and Innovation (http://www.cci.edu.au), Queensland University of Technology.

Unless otherwise stated, the law and services represented in these papers are discussed as they existed in February 2005.

ISBN 10 1-920898-51-4
ISBN 13 978-1-920898-51-9

Individual papers are available electronically through the Sydney eScholarship Repository at:
http://ses.library.usyd.edu.au/handle/2123/1559

This work is licensed under an Australian Creative Commons Attribution-NonCommercial-NoDerivs 2.5 License available at
http://creativecommons.org/licenses/by-nc-nd/2.5/au/. For more information contact Professor Brian Fitzgerald, Faculty of Law, Queensland University of Technology.

List of Contributors

Richard Neville
Professor Arun Sharma
Mark Fallu
Professor Barry Conyngham AM
Greg Lane
Professor Brian Fitzgerald
Nic Suzor
Professor Lawrence Lessig
Professor Richard Jones
Professor Greg Hearn
Professor John Quiggin
Dr David Rooney
Neeru Paharia
Michael Lavarch
Stuart Cunningham
Dr Terry Cutler
Damien O'Brien
Renato Ianella
Carol Fripp
Dennis MacNamara
Jean Burgess
The Hon Justice James Douglas
The Hon Justice Ronald Sackville
Linda Lavarch MP
Tom Cochrane
Ian Oi
Dr Anne Fitzgerald
Neale Hooper
Keith Done
Sal Humphreys
John Banks

Table of Contents

Foreword PROFESSOR BRIAN FITZGERALD	1
A Short Overview of Creative Commons PROFESSOR BRIAN FITZGERALD	3
BANCO COURT KEYNOTE	**7**
Introduction THE HON JUSTICE JAMES DOUGLAS	8
Does Copyright Have Limits? Eldred v Ashcroft and its Aftermath PROFESSOR LAWRENCE LESSIG	11
CONFERENCE KEYNOTE	**27**
Welcome THE HON JUSTICE RONALD SACKVILLE	30
The Vision for the Creative Commons: What are We and Where are We Headed? Free Culture PROFESSOR LAWRENCE LESSIG	36
CREATIVE COMMONS WORLDWIDE	**51**
The iCommons Project DVC TOM COCHRANE, NEERU PAHARIA AND IAN OI	52
GOVERNMENT AND CREATIVE COMMONS	**67**
The Government's Role in Supporting Creative Innovation LINDA LAVARCH MP	69
Why Governments and Public Institutions Need to Understand Open Content Licensing PROFESSOR STUART CUNNINGHAM, DR TERRY CUTLER, DR ANNE FITZGERALD, NEALE HOOPE, AND TOM COCHRANE	74

CREATIVE COMMONS AND THE CREATIVE INDUSTRIES 93

Perspectives from the Creative Industries 94
    RICHARD NEVILLE, PROFESSOR RICHARD JONES, PROFESSOR GREG HEARN AND PROFESSOR BARRY CONYNGHAM AM

CASE STUDIES 115

Open Content Licensing Initiatives 117
    PROFESSOR ARUN SHARMA

AEShareNET 120
    CAROL FRIPP AND DENNIS MCNAMARA

Open Digital Rights Language (ODRL) 127
    DR RENATO IANELLA

Youth Internet Radio Network (YIRN) 135
    JEAN BURGESS AND MARK FALLU

Australian Creative Resource Online (ACRO) 143
    DR DAVID ROONEY

POLICY ISSUES 149

Internet and Innovation 150
    PROFESSOR JOHN QUIGGIN

Digital Sampling and Culture Jamming in a Remix World: What does the law allow? 156
    PROFESSOR BRIAN FITZGERALD AND DAMIEN O'BRIEN

LAW AND COMPUTER GAMES 189

Introduction 190
    GREG LANE

Games History, Content, Practice and Law 196
    PROFESSOR BRIAN FITZGERALD, SAL HUMPHREYS, JOHN BANKS, KEITH DONE AND NIC SUZOR

The Future 229
    PROFESSOR LAWRENCE LESSIG, PROFESSOR STUART CUNNINGHAM AND SAL HUMPHREYS

BIOGRAPHIES 239

INDEX 251

Foreword

PROFESSOR BRIAN FITZGERALD

In late 2003 I became involved with the Australian implementation of the Creative Commons (CC) Project along with Tom Cochrane (DVC TILS QUT) and Ian Oi (then of Blakes Lawyers now a Partner at Corrs Lawyers). We were excited by the possibilities that CC might provide. QUT became an Institutional Affiliate and an Australian version of the Creative Commons licence was completed (creativecommons.org.au).

In order to celebrate and launch the Australian version of the Creative Commons licence and inform people about the project more generally we decided to run a conference here in Brisbane in January 2005 on *Open Content Licensing: Cultivating the Creative Commons*. The chapters that appear in this volume are a result of that conference.

The conference would not have been possible without the generous support of QUT Vice Chancellor Professor Peter Coaldrake. Amongst other things Peter sponsored the visit by Professor Lawrence Lessig of Stanford University Law School, the leader of the Creative Commons movement.

The speakers and participants made this conference a truly memorable event and put Creative Commons on the map in Australia. It brought many of the key thinkers of the open content movement in Australia and internationally together for the first time, and provided an opportunity for them to exchange views and research on this increasingly important topic. I am particularly indebted to Justice Sackville, former Qld Attorney General Linda Lavarch, Richard Neville, Barry Conyngham, Tom Cochrane, Stuart Cunningham, Michael Lavarch and of course Lawrence Lessig for providing their support.

Since the conference QUT has been awarded an ARC Centre of Excellence for Creative Industries and Innovation (www.cci.edu.au) under the leadership of Professor Stuart Cunningham, for which I am Chief Investigator and leader of the Law Program. A Creative Commons Clinic and Creative Commons research program feature heavily in the agenda of this new Centre. The Department of Education Science and Training (DEST) has also sponsored a project – known as the Open Access to Knowledge (OAK) Law Project (www.oaklaw.qut.edu.au) – of which I am Project Leader. The 'OAK Law Project' will develop copyright management protocols for Open Access that can be employed by Australian research repositories.

Jessica Coates and Suzanne Lewis have done an enormous amount of work with the 2005 conference contributors to edit the papers provided by them during and following the conference into polished book chapters. Thank you also to Amy Barker, Susan Hedge and Kylie Pappalardo who assisted us with the process. Keith Done and Sian Haigh gave us tremendous support in organising the conference as did conference assistants Nic Suzor, Damien O'Brien, Amy Barker, Michael May, Amanda Campion-Steele, Cher Bartlett and Elliott Bledsoe.

I hope you enjoy reading these papers as much as we enjoyed hearing them. A video archive of the conference is available at: http://creativecommons.org.au/materials.

- February 2007

A Short Overview of Creative Commons

PROFESSOR BRIAN FITZGERALD

What is Creative Commons?

Creative Commons (CC) is a world wide project that aims to make copyright material more accessible and negotiable in the digital environment. To achieve this Creative Commons asks content owners who wish to contribute to the commons to label their material with a CC badge representing the terms upon which the material may be reutilized: (see the website at creativecommons.org) This process of generically giving permission in advance – use my content so long as you attribute me, or engage in non commercial use, or make no derivative works or share your improvements with the broader community – allows users upon seeing content labelled with the CC symbol to know exactly, at that instant, what right they have to reproduce, communicate, cut, paste, and remix. The content owner reserves some rights of control but eschews the common commercial approach of all rights reserved.

Who is behind it?

Creative Commons is a not for profit corporation having its origins at Stanford University now having its headquarters in San Francisco. The Creative Commons concept was given worldwide impetus through the release of Stanford Law Professor Lawrence Lessig's book *The Future of Ideas: The Fate of the Commons in a Connected World*[1] in 2001 and is further reinforced by his latest release *Free Culture: How Big Media Uses Technology and the Law to Lock Down Culture and Control Creativity.*[2] The international development of the basic CC protocols or licences (iCommons) has grown to the point where over 60 countries throughout the world are participating. In Australia, QUT is the institutional affiliate for the Creative Commons and has been at the forefront of the development of the Australian version of the standard CC licences along with Ian Oi of Blakes Lawyers. The international licences or protocols are available online at creativecommons.org.

---

[1] (2001) Random House, New York.
[2] (2004) Penguin Books, New York.

Is anyone using CC?

The CC project has garnered worldwide attention with the BBC announcing it will licence archived material under CC styled licences and popular US magazine Wired releasing a CC licensed CD including well known artists The Beastie Boys and Talking Heads front man David Byrne with their November 2004 issue. For an interesting example of how CC has facilitated remix and innovation listen to the Colin Mutchler song 'My Life' and the derivative works it has generated, many of which are available at http://colinmutchler.com. Worldwide it is estimated that, as of 1 June 2006, over 140 million link backs have been made to CC licences.

Why contribute to the Creative Commons?

A common question is "why would people want to share digital content?" Some reasons are:

- Ideologically and financially this may be acceptable – the most compelling example in Australia is government where information is ultimately owned by and for the people
- Open contenting one version of your material e.g. a draft (E Print) or a chapter may in fact be a strategy for enhancing the commercialised version of your content
- A wish to share with others for creative and educational purposes – peer production
- Publicity – what the free and open software movement calls 'egoboo' or reputation within the open community which in some cases will be exploited commercially down the track
- Negotiability – through technologically implemented generic protocols that can be utilised with the click of a mouse
- 'What is junk to one may be gold to another' – the idea that the off cuts or digital junk of one person may be the building blocks of knowledge and creative genius for another
- 'Indirect appropriation' – money, design and use of end product, pleasure or social profile gained through involvement in peer production[3]

---

[3] See Yochai Benkler 'Coase's Penguin, or Linux and the Nature of the Firm', (2002) 112 *Yale Law Journal* 369.

Does CC mean that Copyright Law is Redundant?

Creative commons draws on the work of the free software movement. 'Free software' means free as in freedom (to access code) not price and has come to the fore in an environment of proprietary software distribution where source (human readable) software code is hidden from public view. The free software model is to distribute software with the source code open and accessible so that the recipient can easily and better understand the software. This in turn enhances further innovation, error detection and/or security testing. However the free software movement requires through its General Public License (GNU GPL) that if you use open code, innovate upon it and then distribute that code in a derivative work you must share all of the code of the derivative work with the person to whom you are distributing the software code (which in many cases will in effect mean disclosure to the whole community). As has been written elsewhere:

> The powerful insight that Richard Stallman and his advisers at the Free Software Foundation discovered was that if you want to structure open access to knowledge you must leverage off or use as a platform your intellectual property rights. The genius of Stallman was in understanding and implementing the ethic that if you want to create a community of information or creative commons you need to be able to control the way the information is used once it leaves your hands. The regulation of this downstream activity was achieved by claiming an intellectual property right (copyright in the code) at the source and then structuring its downstream usage through a licence (GNU GPL). This was not a simple 'giving away' of information but rather a strategic mechanism for ensuring the information stayed 'free' as in speech. It is on this foundation that we now see initiatives like the Creative Commons expanding that idea from open source code to open digital content.[4]

The point being made is that models like Creative Commons rely on the power of copyright ownership and law to structure open access downstream. In this sense CC is not anti-copyright. Rather it uses copyright as the basis for structuring open access. However CC is designed to provide an alternative model for managing copyright in digital content.

---

[4] A Fitzgerald and B Fitzgerald, *Intellectual Property in Principle* (2004) LBC/Thomson, Sydney.

CC as a Model for Making Copyright More Active

There is great concern worldwide that too much copyright material is left inactive in archives (e.g. government, museums) because the process of negotiating the licence is too time consuming or expensive, even where the copyright owner does not want to make money. Now that we have a vast array of digital technology that can present much of this material to the world cheaply and rapidly more and more institutions are considering how they might allow greater access to their archives/knowledge (e.g. BBC). A facility for accessing archived material, especially publicly funded material, will increasingly be demanded as part of the landscape of information management and creative innovation. CC provides a effective and simple way in which sharing and collaborative effort can be facilitated in the realm of digital content and hopefully a way in which inactive copyright material can be given new life.

Conclusion: Copyright More Accessible and Negotiable

In a world where the digital generation feed off a culture of cut and paste, remix and instant Internet access Creative Commons will provide a vitally important facility for sharing knowledge in the name of culture and innovation. While respecting the basic principle of copyright CC allows a broader understanding of information management in a way which builds on the existing system. There can be little doubt that CC will become an important option in any copyright management and distribution strategy from the most sophisticated to the very simple of cases.

- February 2007

Banco Court Keynote

Does Copyright Have Limits? *Eldred v Ashcroft* and its Aftermath

> THE HON JUSTICE JAMES DOUGLAS AND PROFESSOR LAWRENCE LESSIG

Introduction
The Hon Justice James Douglas introduces Professor Lawrence Lessig, and provides background on the Creative Commons movement and the Eldred v Ashcroft *case.*

Does Copyright Have Limits? *Eldred v Ashcroft* and its Aftermath
Professor Lawrence Lessig discusses the 2003 US case of Eldred v Ashcroft, *which challenged the 1998* Sonny Bono Copyright Term Extension Act *and its extension of US copyright terms by 20 years.*

Professor Brian Fitzgerald
(Head, QUT Law School)

Introduction

THE HON JUSTICE JAMES DOUGLAS

I am very pleased to welcome Professor Lawrence Lessig to speak to us tonight on the subject *Does Copyright Have Limits: Eldred v Ashcroft and its Aftermath?*

As I am sure most of you know Professor Lessig is now a professor at Stanford Law School and founder of the School's Centre for Internet and Society. Previously he was the Berkman Professor at Harvard Law School. My American friends tell me that Stanford is now the best American university for intellectual property law. Perhaps there is some connection.

Before his academic career Larry Lessig clerked for Justice Scalia of the US Supreme Court and Justice Posner of the US Federal Court's 7th Circuit Court of Appeals. Judge Posner is a leading judge, scholar and theorist who has written much about economics and the law. Appropriately Professor Lessig has degrees in economics, management, philosophy and law from several of the world's best universities, the Wharton School of Business at the University of Pennsylvania, Trinity College, Cambridge (the original Cambridge), and Yale Law School. He is the author of several influential books, including *The Future of Ideas: The Fate of the Commons in a Connected World*,[5] and *Code and Other Laws of Cyberspace*,[6] and numerous articles. He writes not just for lawyers but for intelligent members of the public and has a talent for making the complex lucid.

His interests lie in ideas and their future in a wired world. His work as a legal scholar concentrates on constitutional law, contracts, comparative constitutional law and the law of cyberspace. His rapid rise to fame comes from the force and timeliness of his ideas and the skill and energy with which he propounds them. His book, *The Future of Ideas*[7], should be required reading for anybody with a serious interest in the proper and free dissemination of ideas and information and the structure of the Internet as affecting those issues.

---

[5] (2001) Random House, New York.
[6] (1999) Basic Books, New York.
[7] (2001) Random House, New York.

His arguments are well illustrated. The freedom he espouses is that of free speech, not free beer. Resources are 'free' he argues if they can be used without the permission of others or the permission one needs is granted neutrally. In that context he argues that the question for our generation will be not whether the market or the state should control a resource but whether that resource should remain 'free'.

Three organizations with which he is associated, the Creative Commons Project which he chairs, the Electronic Frontier Foundation and the Centre for the Public Domain, are leaders in the attempt to diminish the extent of the monopolies created by intellectual property law. But he is not opposed to private property or the need to reward the creative. To paraphrase him in a recent response to Bill Gates of Microsoft, he is not a creative communist but a creative 'commonist'. His concern is that the monopolisation of intellectual property has gone too far and that it is infringing on our ability to draw on what most of us see as the commonly owned resources of society in the formation and expression of ideas.

What does he mean by the 'commons'? Let me use my own analogy with a local flavour, particularly appropriate in the middle of a hot Queensland summer and dear to the heart of Professor Brian Fitzgerald, the organiser of this conference. Australian beaches are publicly owned and freely accessible to all. How different would our coastal society be if that resource were locked up in private hands, only accessible to the proprietors of the land bordering our oceans or to those whom they licensed? It is not an idle comparison. Many European countries and American States do just that – lock up much of what we perceive as a free, public resource.

When the decision is made to place such a resource in private rather than public hands the consequences are difficult to reverse. Those who have lived in Brisbane as long as I have will recognise how public access to our river banks has slowly increased over the last few decades and how much the city has benefited. The river's development as a public resource has required imagination and significant expense because its banks were traditionally held in private hands. The floating walkway at New Farm is one example both of the imagination and the expense. It shows why it is important to make the correct decisions now needed to keep 'free' access to the still relatively new resource created by the Internet.

Professor Lessig first attracted broad public attention when he was engaged as an expert to assist Judge Thomas Penfield Jackson of the US Federal Court with the monopolization issues in what has been described as "the mother of all tech litigation: *Department of Justice v Microsoft*[8] in 1997. His contribution will deal with the decision in the US Supreme Court, *Eldred v Ashcroft*,[9] where he was one of the counsel who unsuccessfully argued that the US Congress' *Sonny Bono Copyright Extension Act 1998*, extending the copyright period for most existing works to 95 years after the author's death and for new works to 70 years, was unconstitutional. For his efforts he was named one of *Scientific American's* 'Top 50 Visionaries', for arguing "against interpretations of copyright that could stifle innovation and discourse online".

The constitutional arguments were that the Act infringed the free speech guarantee in the first amendment and the copyright clause. The copyright clause gives Congress the power to promote the progress of science by securing to authors for limited times the exclusive right to their writings. When I first read of the impending case about two and a half years ago the argument that interested me was that the retrospective extension of copyright was not for a 'limited time' when added to the earlier statutory limitation and understood in the context of the power's focus on the progress of science.

The argument did not succeed but, if we had a similar provision in our Constitution, it may have had a rather better run in our High Court. It is not as deferential to Parliament as the US Supreme Court is to Congress in respect of what we would think of as jurisdictional facts. I suspect we have not heard the last of the argument, given the demanding appetites of American copyright holders and the powerful dissenting judgments. With the Free Trade Agreement between Australia and the USA the issue will remain important for us as well.

Congratulations to QUT, Professor Peter Coaldrake its Vice-Chancellor, and Professor Brian Fitzgerald, the Head of the Law School, for organising this conference and for securing such an outstanding speaker as Professor Lawrence Lessig. The Chief Justice, Paul de Jersey, is on leave but it was with his encouragement and cooperation that the Court's facilities have been made available. I would like to thank him also.

It is appropriate that the Court provide its facilities to allow the public free access to this speech and we embrace the chance to be associated with QUT in advancing the progress of science.

---

[8] 87 F. Supp. 2d 30 (D.D.C. 2000).
[9] 537 U.S. 186 (2003).

Does Copyright Have Limits? Eldred v Ashcroft and its Aftermath

Professor Lawrence Lessig

The last time I had the chance to stand in a Supreme Court and asked, "does copyright have limits?", I was standing on that side of the Bench and several of the Justices got the answer wrong. I am very eager to be standing on this side of the Bench and asking the very same question, and even more encouraged to learn that in Australia the question may get a serious answer.

Let me put this in context. Copyright law begins in the Anglo-American tradition in 1662. The *Licensing Act* of 1662 established monopolies for publishers in England in cooperation with the Crown, to guarantee that those who had the power to speak would use the press in a way that either benefited the Crown's political interest or the publisher's monetary interests. That statute expired in 1695 and what followed from the perspective of the publishers was chaos.

From the perspective of the public, what followed was freedom. There were no protected monopolies for publishing; there increasingly became competition in publishing and that competition was scary to these publishers so they increasingly lobbied in a frenetic way to re-establish monopoly controls. They were the inspiration for a scene from *Wizard of Oz* and by 1709 they had succeeded. In 1709, Parliament passed a statute to re-establish monopoly power in the context of copyrights. That was the *Statute of Anne*.

This Statute was originally proposed to establish monopoly for copyright for an unlimited term. It was to be perpetual copyright. But in the course of its passage through the Parliament the proceeding was amended in a way that terrified the publishers because the amendment stated that copyrights would extend for fourteen years for new works (renewable), and for existing works twenty-one years. The critical question for us, hundreds of years after this decision was made, is why would they limit copyrights? What was the purpose? From my perspective, our first intuition would be the idea of free speech; that it was important to limit copyright to promote speech. In fact, free speech had absolutely nothing to do with the ideas of limiting copyright terms.

The core motivating idea was the restriction of monopoly. The English, of course, had learned to hate monopolies; they had essentially fought a war over Crown granted monopolies. As the United States Supreme Court decided in one of its really good intellectual property decisions, the *Statute of Anne* was written against the backdrop of practices – eventually curtailed by the *Statute of Monopolies* – of the Crown in granting monopolies to Court favourites in goods or businesses which had long before been enjoyed by the public. For example, the printing of the Bible was a monopoly granted by the Crown. Writs of Courts of Common Pleas were a monopoly controlled by and rented by the Crown. Clay pipes were granted monopoly control, gold and silver thread and most famously, of course, playing cards. This tradition of granting monopolies over stuff that already existed created the ire in the British people that led to a revolution against these monopolies. These monopolies for existing things were the product of endless lobbying by those who produced those existing things, lobbying to protect their monopoly.

The key insight that economics has given us, about the dynamic that this public choice problem presents, is that the monopolist will be willing to stand the net present value of his monopoly to protect his monopoly against loss from the government no longer supporting it. To protect monopolies they will invest as much money as they expect to guarantee a continued control over that resource. The 1656 Parliament ended it with respect to ordinary products in the *Statute of Monopolies*. You could grant monopolies under this Statute only for new works in the sense of a patent as our current law gives. Because the British knew the corruption of permitting monopolies to be granted for existing works, they regulated around it. They forbade it in the context of real goods. The *Statue of Monopolies* excepted from its control publishers and in 1709 Parliament removed that exemption. Publishers were included within the scope of regulated Acts to ensure monopoly powers would not be too great.

There are many publishers today who have inspired the love of the public. We do not have a clear sense of who the publishers were for the British at this time. We should remember that publishers at this time were hated. John Milton describes them this way, "Publishers are all patentees and monopolisers and the trade of book selling . . . men who do not labour in an honest profession, to learning is indebted".[10] These were a class of

---

[10] Phillip Wittenberg, *The Protection and Marketing of Literary Property* (1937) 31 cited in Lawrence Lessig, *Free Culture* (2005) E-prints in Library and Information

monopolists, particularly hated at the time. The London Monopoly is referred to as the *Conger* which worked to keep prices to British culture high and to restrict access to new works. The *Statute of Monopolies* in 1709 granted them a twenty-one year monopoly over existing works as a way to buy them off. The idea was that for twenty-one more years their existing monopolies would continue, but in twenty-one years those monopolies would end. What we all expected, of course, was that in twenty-one years they would come back to fight again to extend their monopolies. When these initial monopolies did expire, the publishers did return to try to extend them.

In 1735 and 1737 they proposed extensions of existing terms. Parliament rebuffed these extensions. Here is one pamphlet response:

> I see no Reason for granting a further Term now, which will not hold as well for granting it again and again as often as the Old ones Expire so that should this Bill pass, it will in Effect be establishing a perpetual Monopoly, a Thing deservedly odious in the Eye of the Law; it will be a great Cramp to Trade, a Discouragement to Learning, no Benefit to the Authors, but a general Tax on the Publick; and all this only to increase the private Gain of the Booksellers.[11]

These extensions were rejected. In fact three times they were rejected, leaving the publishers to turn to the next forum for extending their monopoly power – the Courts.

In the Courts it would not be possible for the publishers to plead for their own interests, hated as they were. Instead they pleaded for the interests of the authors. It was the author's rights the publisher was trying to promote. These rights, they said, were natural and as natural rights they were protected by Common Law. Furthermore they should be perpetual. The publishers' concern for authors is an interesting type of concern. Lyman Ray Patterson described it as, "the publishers had as much concern for authors as cattle ranchers have for cattle".[12] They were using the authors to advance their interests.

Science <http://eprints.rclis.org/archive/00002988/01/freecult.pdf> at 28 August 2006 (hereinafter Lawrence Lessig, *Free Culture*).
[11] Lawrence Lessig, *Free Culture*.
[12] Lyman Ray Patterson, 'Free Speech, Copyright and Fair Use' (1987) *Vanderbilt Law Review* 40, 28, cited in Lawrence Lessig, *Free Culture*.

They would fight for their cattle in this context, and that particular battle eventually resolved this conflict in British history by a Scot, Alexander Donaldson. In 1750 he set up in Edinburgh a publishing house for public domain books, meaning books whose copyright under the *Statute of Anne* had expired. The Conger sent him a very clear note – stop publishing your books, our copyrights are perpetual. Donaldson responded in a particularly Scottish way. He decided to move his business to London and sell books in London that were sold at 30 to 50 percent less than the going price. He did not believe he had to pay any royalties because he believed these books were in the public domain.

The Conger organised a series of law suits against Donaldson, designed to stop him and others from exercising what they thought to be their right under the *Statute of Anne*, and they won a series of early victories in the Common Law Courts. The most famous of these victories was *Miller v Taylor*,[13] which in 1769 upheld the idea that these terms were perpetual. Miller was a merchant who had purchased the rights to James Thomson's *The Seasons*. He sued Taylor who was reproducing Thomson's poems without permission from Miller. Lord Mansfield upheld the continuation of the Common Law copyright, holding that while the Statute of Anne supplanted Common Law copyright, it did not replace it. Copyright, according to Lord Mansfield, was perpetual.

This was the first round. For those who have lost first rounds, there is always hope for a second round. There was one in this case. On Miller's death, his estate sold the rights he had to a guy named Thomas Beckett. Donaldson then decided to take Beckett on directly by selling these works in the market without permission of the copyright owner. Beckett sued Donaldson. The House of Lords got the case in 1774 and decided that the *Statute of Anne* was meant to displace the Common Law, and that copyrights were, in fact, limited. Donaldson won in the House of Lords, and the *Statute of Anne* was held to mean that copyrights end. For the first time in British history, the works of William Shakespeare, John Milton, Francis Bacon and Samuel Johnson and many others passed into the public domain. Once in the public domain, the prices for works fall and, more importantly, competition among publishers increases, meaning the opportunity for new authors to find ways to publish their work increases as well.

---

[13] (1769) 4 Burr. 2303 (KB).

The view of this result was of course different depending on where you came from. In Edinburgh there was general celebration. No private cause had so engrossed the attention of the public. One paper wrote:

And none has been tried before the House of Lords, in the decision of which so many individuals were interested, great rejoicing in Edinburgh upon the victory of her literary property, bonfires and illuminations.[14]

In London the view was a little bit different. "Disaster," wrote one major paper:

By the above decision nearly 200,000 pounds worth of works was honestly purchased at public sale in which was yesterday thought property, is now reduced to nothing. The booksellers of London and Westminster, many of whom sold estates and houses to purchase copyright, are, in a manner, ruined and those, who after many years' industry thought they had acquired a competency to provide for their families, now find themselves without a shilling to devise to their successors.[15]

In 1789, the United States copied Britain, and passed a Constitution. Article 1 Section 8 Clause 8 says that Congress shall have the power:

> To promote the Progress of Science and useful Arts, by securing for limited Times to Authors and Inventors the exclusive Right to their respective Writings and Discoveries.

'To promote the progress of science' – that is the power – by 'securing for limited Time' – that is the restriction – 'the exclusive Right'.

This clause has two parts. You get the power to do *A* through the means of *B* to promote the progress of science by securing the right for a limited time. The idea of promoting was drawn directly from the *Statute of Monopolies*. The idea of limited times comes from the *Statute of Anne*.

In 1790 the Congress enacted a statute that granted copyright owners a 14-year term renewable once at the end of the first term and for existing works the same term was granted. Again, the motivation for these limitations was not free speech. The motivation for these restrictions was to limit monopoly. This birth of copyright often creates a misunderstanding

---

[14] Reported in the *Edinburgh Advertiser* and cited in Lawrence Lessig, *Free Culture*.
[15] Reported in the *Morning Chronicle* and cited in Lawrence Lessig, *Free Culture*.

because we do not really recognise the copyright to which the framers of the US Constitution were speaking. The copyright they were speaking of was tiny in respect to the copyright we have today.

The difference can be seen across a number of dimensions. Let us think of four: the term, the scope, the reach, and the force. Originally, the copyright term was relatively short – 14 years – renewable once. The scope of the copyright was limited to particular kinds of works: maps, charts and books. To get a copyright within that scope you had to go through a series of formalities. You had to register the work, you had to mark the work, you had to deposit the work and, after an initial term, you had to renew the copyright. The reach of the copyright pertained only to publishing. It explicitly said 'publishing' not 'copying' which meant that it was essentially regulating commercial actors, and the force of copyright was always mitigated by the courts. Its application was only as far as courts said it should apply.

These narrow contours around the regulation called copyright have seen significant change. First in term: the copyright term changed, both in its length and its structure in the United States. In its length it went from 14 years in 1790 which could then be multiplied if the term was continued to a maximum of 28. In 1831 the maximum term went to 42 years. In 1909 the maximum term went to 56 years. Beginning in 1962 the copyright term for existing works automatically increased, in fact eleven times, until in 1998 it was extended to 95 years for existing works. That is the difference in term. But the term changes in its structure too. Before 1976 to get the maximum term of copyright protection, you had to go through two grants of copyright. The initial term could be renewed and required an affirmative act. Between 80 and 90 percent of copyists, depending on the work or the particular period of history, never took that affirmative step. They did not renew their copyright because, presumably, the burden of renewing was not worth the benefit from the additional term.

In 1976 that changed. We adopted the international standard of one term, one grant of copyright, meaning that to get the initial copyright was to get the full term of protection, meaning in the United States the copyright term effectively tripled in 30 years. In 1973 the average term of copyright was 32.2 years, because 85 percent of copyrights never renewed after the initial term. Today the average term is the maximum term, which is 95 years. That is the change in term.

Think about the change in scope. Originally I said the scope was maps, charts and books. It has now been extended essentially to all creative work reduced to a tangible form, and appropriately so, because it should cover the widest range of creativity where there is a need for incentives to create. But the significant difference not remarked in our history so far is the change in the formalities and the consequence of that change. Between 1790 and 1800, no more than 10 percent of published work ever registered initially for copyright protection, meaning immediately 90 percent of that work was in the public domain. After the initial term of 14 years, over 90 percent did not renew the copyright, meaning after 14 years, 99 percent of work published had entered the public domain.

Between 1800 and 1976 the data is not as conclusive, not as certain. Probably 25 percent of all work published was actually registered for copyright after the initial term. Less than 3 percent of that work remained under copyright protection, meaning almost 97 percent was in the public domain. Copyright was a tiny regulation of a tiny part of the creative process – that part relating to commercial creativity. This changed in 1976 in the United States as formalities were abolished, which meant that copyright went from regulating a sub-set of published work to regulating all published work automatically, all creative work automatically, and after 28 years continued to regulate all creative work automatically. There is no filter to separate out work which needs the benefit of continued protection; protection is automatic and for the full term.

Think about the change in reach. Copyright law was born to regulate commercial publishers. It regulated the copying of the same book, meaning it did not regulate derivative works; those were free. And it did not regulate in the non-commercial space, which I am defining as those published works that did not register for the original copyright. In the first 100 years of copyright law this changed in just one way: transformative works, derivative works, are included within the scope of the original monopoly. Again, this extended only to commercial publication. Then in 1909, accidentally, because under copyright law this was an inappropriate way to refer to what they were trying to do, the word 'publish' was changed to 'copy'. The law regulated as far as existing technology for existing copying. It did not matter in 1909, because in 1909 the technologies for copying were machines like printing presses. But it created a potential that has produced the most dramatic change in copyright law in our history because the law now was regulating for men with machines and as 'men with machines' turned into 'women with machines' and then 'many more people with machines' the scope of the regulation changed. In 1970, as

Xerox machines become more and more common, the scope of the law changed.

Something quite dramatic happened as the Internet entered our space. We can see that drama by thinking about copyright's regulation of the copies in the context of an ordinary book. Review all the possible uses of a book. A bunch of these uses are unregulated by copyright law, for example:

- reading a book does not produce a copy. It is therefore unregulated by copyright law.
- Giving a book does not produce a copy. It is therefore unregulated by copyright law.
- Selling a book does not produce a copy. It does not get regulated by copyright law.
- Sleeping on a book does not produce a copy. It is not regulated by copyright law.

At the core of these unregulated uses is a set of uses that are properly regulated by copyright law. For example publishing a book requires the permission of the copyright owner. In the American tradition, there is also a thin slither of exceptions called fair uses which otherwise would have been regulated by copyright law because they produced a copy but which the law says should not be regulated by copyright law because it is essential these uses remain free. You can quote my book, meaning copy my words, in a totally idiomatic review – I tell you many people have done that so far. I cannot control you, nor should I be able to control you because the law says these uses of my words are fair uses even if I, the copyright owner, do not authorise them.

That is the story balanced as it was before the entrance of the internet. The internet, which by its design, by its architecture, produces this single fact: every act is a copy. You cannot do anything on a digital network without producing a copy. To read a book produces a copy. Every act with a digital object is an act which produces a copy, meaning automatically that the scope of this regulation is extended. That which before was presumptively unregulated now is presumptively within the scope of the law. There may be exceptions – fair use is one – but the base line has changed because of this technical feature of the way in which copyright law interacts with digital networks. Ordinary uses are presumptively controlled.

Originally copyright laws regulated through law, but increasingly that is no longer the case. It is technology that regulates copyrighted works. A good example of this is my favourite version of my Adobe e-book reader, *Middlemarch*,[16] a book in the public domain. When you click on the permissions behind *Middlemarch* you may print 10 pages every 10 days and you may use the read aloud button to listen to this book. These are the restrictions on public domain books. With Aristotle's *Politics*,[17] which did not have much of a copyright life in the United States, you may not copy any text selections to the clipboard, you may not print any pages but you may use the read aloud button to listen to this book. To my great embarrassment, for my book, *The Future of Ideas*, you may not copy any text selections; you may not print any pages; and don't you dare use the read aloud button to listen to my book. Now the point is, where do these controls come from?

They certainly do not come from the law. You cannot exercise these controls on public domain books and you certainly can not restrict any person's ability to read a book aloud, even if it is copyrighted. The point is, these controls come through the technology which the content is embedded in, and as this technology develops to include Digital Rights Management (DRM) technologies, the scope of this control will increase, and increasingly, this control is backed up by the law. My favourite example is Sony's Aibo dog. This is a little creature that you can buy for about US$1500, and you can teach it to do all sorts of tricks. Some fans decided they wanted to set up a little fan site that gave information to others about how to teach their dog to do tricks.

They taught people how to hack their Aibo dog, not with a machete but with code, to teach the dog to dance jazz. When they did this, they received a letter from Sony that said, "your site contains information providing the means to circumvent Aibo wares copy protocol, constituting a violation of the anti-circumvention provisions of the DMCA".[18] To circumvent the code's restriction on your ability to do stuff with your dog is a crime, even if the underlying act is not a crime. Let me assure you I know foreign audiences are often confused about it – it is not a crime in the United States to dance jazz. Outside of Georgia, even your dog can dance jazz without legal regulation. Here code 'controls' and the law says you cannot circumvent the code even for a legitimate purpose.

---

[16] George Eliot (1872).
[17] Aristotle (350 BC).
[18] Letter sent to aibopet.com and cited in Lawrence Lessig, *Free Culture*.

Add these changes together – term, scope, reach and force. Then add into the mix a topic which I know you are all familiar with, increasing media concentration. If you put all these forces together you reach a conclusion which is very hard for us to accept about who we have become, because never in the history of our tradition have fewer exercised more legal control over the development and spread of our culture than now. Not even when copyrights were perpetual, because they only regulated the single copying of a book. Never has the scope of regulation been as powerful and never before has it extended as widely. This is the change that copyright has undergone – radically transforming the nature of its regulation in just a couple of hundred years.

In 1998 Eric Eldred decided he wanted to become a civil disobedient. Eldred was running an online website, which was publishing public domain materials and in 1998 he expected to publish the work of Robert Frost, because a series of Frost poems were to enter the public domain then. Congress decided in 1998 to extend the term of copyrights by 20 years, including existing copyrights, and Eric Eldred announced he was going to fight this change by just violating the law. A naïve law professor (namely me) called up Eric Eldred and told him this was a really bad idea, that copyright law was an extraordinarily punitive law to break in the United States, and this mode of testing it was likely to land him in prison, rather than achieving his ultimate objective of publishing this work freely. We said we would help him sue – to declare the *Sonny Bono Copyright Extension Act* unconstitutional, the Act otherwise known in the public press as the 'Mickey Mouse Protection Act'.

Our claim was that this violated the progress clause. The core idea behind the progress clause is a *quid pro quo* – 'this for that'. We grant you a copyright in exchange for your creative work. In 1923 the Government said to Frost, "we'll give you a 56 year monopoly, if you create something new" and Frost said, "fine" and he did create amazing poems and literature which earned the benefit of that 56 year monopoly. But when that monopoly was extended for works that already exist, the *quid pro quo* of this for that was breached. This was for nothing because the work existed that the copyright was being extended for, and no matter what Congress did it would not get Robert Frost to produce any new work in 1923. This was a monopoly in exchange for nothing. It is like a contract with the State to build a bridge for a million dollars and then at the end of your completion, you say to the State, "I want two million dollars before I deliver the bridge to you".

This extension of course was part of a pattern. There were eleven extensions of existing terms in the last forty years. Always these extensions occurred as famous copyrights were about to expire. That dynamic is totally predictable in a world where it is permitted to extend monopolies for existing works, because those who have the benefit of the monopoly for the existing work are willing to spend the net present value to guarantee that monopoly is extended. In a Supreme Court, seven, eight thousand miles away, the question was asked, "Are there limits on this copyright?" and the Supreme Court answered, "No". What Congress was doing was OK. "There was no reason to believe", the Supreme Court wrote, "that these copyright terms would be perpetual". They may be perpetual along the instalment plan, but all the Supreme Court believed the Constitution required was that Congress should give the perpetual terms in particular chunks. Congress was free to do this, the limited times clause notwithstanding. At least, and here is the silver lining, so long as it does not change the 'traditional contours of copyright'.

There were two dissents in that case: Justice Breyer and Justice Stevens. Justice Breyer's was the more ambitious dissent. He asserted that the existing copyright term was already a perpetual term. He asserted this because he could do some math, and what he calculated with his math was that a 95 year term, was the equivalent of 99.9998 percent of the value of a perpetual term. If you have the value of a perpetual term, and you put on the top of it the 95 year term, it already was 99.9998 percent of the value of the perpetual term. And Justice Breyer calculated that 98 percent of the work whose copyright was being extended was no longer commercially available anyway. This was an extension for a very small proportion of work, ignoring the burden on the balance of work.

Justice Breyer's dissent inspired follow-on litigation. This is what we call Eldred Version 2, the case of *Kahle v Ashcroft*,[19] which the Ninth Circuit is scheduled to hear arguments some time in 2005. The insight motivating Kahle is that 98 percent of authors are not benefiting from the copyright term extension. This case focused on the 98 percent and its focus is to use the First Amendment to assert limitations on Congress' power to restrict access to that work. How do we have the right to use the First Amendment? The silver lining gives us that right, because what the Court said in *Eldred* is that so long as Congress does not change the traditional contours of

---

[19] Decision of the Ninth Circuit was handed down 22 January 2007, and is available at <http://www.ca9.uscourts.gov/ca9/newopinions.nsf/1FABEA163F4C714A8825726B00 5A12F0/$file/0417434.pdf?openelement> (accessed 7 February 2007).

copyright further First Amendment reviews are not required. By implication, if Congress changes the traditional contours of copyright further First Amendment review is required. As I have demonstrated to you, Congress has changed, in as fundamental a way as possible, the traditional contours of copyright by changing the system of formalities.

For 186 years of our history, formalities defined the scope of copyright's regulation and that scope, of course, was tiny compared to its scope today, guaranteeing that its force would be felt by a narrow, filtered class of works and the balance of works would enter the public domain. That changed from a system that filtered out works not needing copyright's protection from works that did. This change is as traditional a contour of copyright as any could be and the claim is that that change in 1976 of a traditional contour of copyright gets us First Amendment review, and if we get First Amendment review, then the presumption of deference that led the Eldred Court goes out and ordinary First Amendment review means we win. Or at least we get Congress inspired enough to re-create a filter, to attempt to take the full range of works burdened by the extension of copyright and separate out those that need or could benefit from the continued extension from those that would not. This opens a way for those works that would not normally to pass to the public domain, so that the burden of copyright is narrowly tailored to those which would actually benefit from an extended term.

I do not predict the Court will go our way. I remember when I was explaining Eldred to one of the most cynical members of the American Legal Academy, he said to me, "while you have convinced me that you are right, that under the Supreme Court's jurisprudence you should win, according to the rules the Supreme Court has enunciated for limiting Congress' powers, and that this is precisely the kind of case where Congress' power has gone too far, when is the last time that the Supreme Court ever ruled against all the money in the world?" And I said to him, "that is an extremely cynical, boring way to think about the way courts function. I do not think that is the way courts function at all". But I had to stop and think, when is the last time the Court ruled against all the money in the world? Even when they struck down segregation, it was only a bunch of poor, southern racists they were actually acting against. The major actions have never been, in this context, where all the money in the world is against a bunch of crazy academics. This reminds us perhaps of the limits of what courts will do.

I offer these stories not to predict anything about the court, but to remind us of this question: "Does copyright have limits?" I think properly phrased, the answer to that question, right now in the United States, is: "no, it doesn't". But it is our objective I think to imagine: what if there were limits? What would they be for? Why would we have them?

For example, let me tell you a couple of stories about copyright's affect in the United States right now. In 2002, Robert Greenwald produced the movie, *Uncovered*. *Uncovered* is the story about America's involvement in the Iraq war and the decisions leading to our engagement in that war. In 2004, Robert Greenwald wanted to produce an updated version of that movie, including a one minute clip from an interview the President of the United States gave on NBC's *Meet the Press*. He requested permission from *Meet the Press* to include the one minute clip in the film. They denied him permission. What they said to him initially was, "it's not very flattering to the President". Now, what is going on in this dynamic? In a world where Presidents have fewer press conferences, in a context of increasing concentration and therefore vicious competition to get access to people like the President, there is a strong incentive for the press to be nice to the President, to create a protective space where he knows he can enter and speak without these words being used in ways that might embarrass him. It privatises the presidency and this is a predictable consequence of copyright extending its power and the concentration of the media interacting with that extension.

Here is a more dramatic example in this story. In 2004, Robert made another film, *Outfoxed*, about the Fox News Channel. The Fox News Channel sells itself as a 'Fair and balanced news channel' and you would think, if you know anything about the way truth is to function, 'fair and balanced' would produce 'truth'. People would understand the truth in such a context. There was a careful study done of what people who watched Fox News believe about the world. The survey found that the more likely you were to watch Fox News Channel, the more likely you were to have completely incorrect assumptions about what was happening.

Whatever your view of Fox News or Fox News commentators like Bill O'Reilly, this is a significant issue of political import in the United States right now. The charge of 'fair and balanced' is an issue which has been litigated and continues to be a defining feature of how the network thinks of itself. To make this film, it was important that Robert Greenwald have the right to use clips from this Network. The Network was not going to give permission for Greenwald to use these clips, so he needed to rely on a doctrine called 'fair use'. If these uses were fair he was safe; if they were not fair, then he is personally liable – not his corporation – for millions of dollars in damages. And here is the trick: you can only know whether the uses are 'fair' after you have been sued. You face this choice – whether to produce the work and risk millions of dollars in personal damage, or not to produce the work and stay safe and sound.

Fox's response to the movie was significant in indicating what it thought about the copyright system. Fox called this 'piracy'. Roger Ales, the President of Fox, said, "any news organisation that does not support our position on copyright is crazy. Everybody should stand up and say these people don't have the right to take our product any more; it puts journalism at risk". The idea that pointing out that someone is inconsistent puts journalism at risk shows just how far the concept of journalism has moved from what its ideals should be.

The risk here, the real risk, is a system that creates huge legal exposure for someone who wants to make political commentary about one of the most important forces in American political life. That is the free speech issue copyright risks. But it is not just that issue which is important, for of course, Fox presents the other side of the copyright question quite well. It was hugely successful as a film in the United States. DVD sales were No. 1 in Amazon for months. That drove penetration into theatres that otherwise was never expected. It was not a big success here in Australia. One reason we might speculate about that has to do with the decision made by certain companies about whether advertisements would be permitted. For when the film was advertised or advertising was sought for the film, certain organisations owned by this corporation refused to run the ad. You could not advertise this film that was critical of Fox because the owner of the advertiser sought not to have that message displayed. This is the monopoly issue that copyright raises – free speech and the monopoly issue rolled into one.

On 17 January 2005, the *Australian* ran a story about Sir Cliff Richard, the most successful singles' artist in British history who launched a campaign to complain about copyright. His fifty year-old recordings are about to enter the public domain, and to cost the record companies a great deal of money – close to $1 billion estimated by this article appearing in the *Australian*. They claim that it is unfair, fundamentally unfair, that these copyrights expire. Why is it unfair? Because when his songs were recorded Sir Cliff Richard was promised fifty years of protection. He got it – 50 years of protection. His response is, yes, but the United States gives us 95 years of protection. But when he recorded his material, the United States gave him 56 years of protection. It then dollopped on another forty-some years to 95 years of protection. What does this unfairness boil down to? The unfairness is: it is unfair for you not to pay us twice, when the United States has paid us twice for the work which we have copyrighted.

It is not surprising that particular famous artists would be keen to extend the copyright term. We can predict that will always happen. We can predict that if any of us were as lucky as Sir Cliff Richard was to be successful in this world, we would be arguing to extend the term of our copyrights. What is surprising, is not Sir Cliff Richard, but that the other side of this debate is essentially invisible.

The *US Free Trade Agreement Implementation Act 2004* (Cth) which was passed recently (increasing the term of existing works) is probably thought of as a piracy of the public domain. Yet it too did not produce politically – as opposed to some particular activists – even a whimper. Not even to consider the modest suggestion that a means was adopted to separate out those works that need the benefit of an extended term, like Sir Cliff Richard, from those works that do not need any benefit from an extended term because they are commercially unavailable and just locked up under the existing copyright regime. Not even that idea was considered, and that is a reflection of how blind we, as cultures, have become to the balance which defines this debate. We need to recognise that because of this extraordinary explosion in technology we are at a critical time and have the opportunity to realise the potential innovation of this network, so long as this extraordinary and potential innovation is not zapped by monopolies.

Copyright, designed to benefit authors, if allowed to become too powerful becomes the tool of monopolies, and again we ask the question, "Does copyright have limits?" It does have limits. These limits are for us, forgotten. The powerful have used their power to buy the power to silence those who would question this explosion in power. And we stand silent. We have restored the Conger, precisely the entity we originally in our tradition designed copyright to dissolve; indeed worse than the Conger, for the power exercised is greater by the monopolists. Never in our history have fewer exercised more power over our culture than now. Nobody noticed this happening; nobody acts effectively to stop it. Yet the question which opens this lecture is an invitation for us to remember how we as a culture discovered those limits and how we could recreate them again.

Conference Keynote

The Vision for the Creative Commons: What are we and where are we headed? Free Culture

> THE HON JUSTICE RONALD SACKVILLE, PROFESSOR
> LAWRENCE LESSIG

Welcome *[as delivered at the conference]*
The Hon Justice Ron Sackville, Professor Lawrence Lessig, ladies and gentlemen; on behalf of the Faculty of Law and the Faculty of Creative Industries, it is my very great pleasure to welcome you here today.

In a lot of ways it is said that the working year does not really start until Australia Day. I do thank you for coming to join us in January and it is obviously the first major event which the two faculties – Law and Creative Industries – are involved in this year. And it is a very important event.

We have brought together an exciting range of speakers and we will be hearing today from representatives from the judiciary, government, industry and of course, from academia, to expand our understanding and debate about the concept about Creative Commons. And it is an important debate. It is really very much at the cutting edge of what the 21st century is about: the capacity to take information, content, material which may be copyrighted, and get that material disseminated through a means which has minimum transaction impediments, which benefits not only the copyright owner, but the broader community and particularly the creative process. Over the next two days you are in for quite a treat. Our first speaker this morning is **The Hon Justice Ron Sackville** *from the Federal Court.*

Ron Sackville's career is in three parts. He started as an academic at the University of NSW, a Professor of Law and for a period of time Dean of the Law Faculty. In 1985 Ron went to the private Bar in NSW, where he remained until appointed to the Federal Court in 1994. Probably Ron is best known for those periods prior to his appointment to the Federal Court: for his work in a number major Australian Enquiries and Commissions. Between 1973 and 1975 he was Commissioner for Law & Poverty in the Australian Government's Commission of Enquiry into Poverty. In the late 1970s he assisted the South Australian Government in a Royal Commission into the non-medical use of drugs.

It was my good fortune in 1994 to work closely with Ron when he undertook a major enquiry for the Commonwealth Government into the issue of access to justice. It is from that particular work, which lead to a blue-print for the reform of the Australian Civil Justice System and various elements of it, that much of the ongoing reform that we see even now, a decade later, can be traced.

During his period as a Federal Court Judge, Ron has maintained an extremely active role, not only as a Judge but also in broader public debate. In particular, in various areas of law reform. Obviously it is in the issue of intellectual property and the underlying issue of Creative Commons which we now invite Ron Sackville to address you. Please join with me in welcoming The Hon Justice Ronald Sackville.

Professor The Hon Michael Lavarch
(Dean, QUT Faculty of Law)

The Vision for the Creative Commons: What are we and where are we headed? Free Culture

*This was the second visit by **Professor Lawrence Lessig** that I hosted. In 1999 he came to Australia to teach in the Byron Bay Summer School at a time when I was Head of the School of Law and Justice Studies at Southern Cross University. In those days he was less of a superstar; he was on his way up. Today he is very well-known internationally, very much at the leading edge of Creative Commons, law and technology, and law and the digital environment.*

Professor Lessig has taken his degrees from the University of Pennsylvania, Yale Law School, and also Cambridge University in the UK. He has been for many people, including myself, an inspiration. Larry is very much a poet for the generation that has had to come to grips with the whole idea of the digital environment. His books, Code and Other Laws of Cyber Space, The Future of Ideas *and* Free Culture *have certainly stimulated discussion throughout the world.*

In this presentation Professor Lessig outlines his vision for a remix culture and his thoughts on the future of the Creative Commons Movement.

Professor Brian Fitzgerald
(Head, QUT Law School)

Welcome

THE HON JUSTICE RONALD SACKVILLE

Michael Lavarch, Brian Fitzgerald, Professor Lessig, ladies and gentlemen, it is a great delight to be introduced by Michael, who made the serious mistake of appointing me to the Federal Court during his time as Attorney General of the Commonwealth. My own career, such as it is, is a bit odd as far as the order of events is concerned, but Michael's is even weirder. He is the only person I know who has used the position as the First Law Officer of the Commonwealth as work experience for a real job, that is, being Dean of the Faculty of Law. If you think the Caucus is difficult, wait until you deal with a group of legal academics.

A conference on cultivating the Creative Commons, particularly one that I understand is sponsored by the modestly, if not tautologically, named Creative Industries Faculty, is not a place where you would expect to find old-fashioned people. But for those of us who are old-fashioned, like Richard Neville and myself, even Luddite, there is a special benefit in the opportunity to engage in face to face discussions on the proper role of, and boundaries to, intellectual property rights. In particular, notwithstanding the virtues of blogging, which my associates have attempted unsuccessfully to explain to me, the presence of Professor Lessig gives us all an opportunity to put a real, as opposed to a virtual, face on someone whose work on the Creative Commons and the future of ideas has been enormously influential.

As I am sure Professor Lessig knows, there is a long history of fruitful interchange between Australian and the United States' legal academics, even if the traffic has tended to be rather heavily in one direction. There are many Australians who have taught and studied at great Law Schools like Yale, Harvard, Stanford and Chicago, all of which Professor Lessig has been associated with at some stage. Given that I am a graduate of one of those institutions, the order in which I mentioned them is not entirely random. While academic exchange is nearly always mutually beneficial, this has not always been the experience of interaction between the leadership of our two countries, even though we seem to be in a phase of extended mutual admiration.

In 1919, the then Australian Prime Minister, Billy Hughes, was making a nuisance of himself at the Versailles Peace Conference. To the intense aggravation of Woodrow Wilson, Hughes insisted on ever more punitive sanctions against a defeated Germany. Hughes' strident views prompted President Wilson to describe him as a 'pestiferous varmint' and I do not think he meant the phrase as a compliment. Having read a number of Professor Lessig's works, I suspect that there might be quite a few holders of copyright who would regard him as a 'pestiferous varmint', but I am sure that they would use that phrase in the nicest possible way.

For better or for worse, I bring to this area of discourse the perspective of a judge who is occasionally, and more or less randomly, exposed to the complexities and challenges of intellectual property law. Even from this limited and sporadic perspective, it is impossible to avoid being struck by how rapidly, to use the words of Peter Drahos and John Braithwaite in their book, *Information Feudalism*[20], there has been a transfer of knowledge assets from the intellectual commons into private interest, private hands. This point, of course, was driven home recently, and forcefully, in Australia, by the debate concerning ratification of the *Australia-United States Free Trade Agreement* (FTA).

For a brief time patent and copyright law was actually at the forefront of public debate in this country. Intellectual property lawyers, or at least a smattering of them, enjoyed a fleeting moment of public exposure, if not fame. The word 'evergreening' temporarily entered the Australian vernacular as commentators debated the extent to which the holders of drug patents used dubious claims to extend their monopoly at the expense of generic drug manufacturers and, ultimately, the public. One of the most fascinating sections of Professor Lessig's recent book, which is catchily entitled *Free Culture: How Big Media Uses Technology and the Law to Lock Down Culture and Control Creativity*[21] (I have known some published articles as long as that) is his account in Chapter 13 of *Eldred v Ashcroft*[22], in which he acted as Counsel for Mr Eldred. Despite Professor Lessig's best efforts, for which he modestly offers a *mea culpa* – and I must discuss with Professor Lessig how far counsel's arguments really do influence judges when they decide cases – the Supreme Court of the United States upheld the validity of the so-called *Sonny Bono Copyright Extension Act*.[23] This Act retrospectively extended the term of copyright by twenty years in the usual case to a period of the life of the author plus seventy years.

---

[20] Peter Drahos and John Braithwaite, *Information Feudalism*, (2003) W. W. Norton & Company
[21] Lawrence Lessig, *Free Culture*.
[22] *Eldred v. Ashcroft*, 537 U.S. 186 (2003)
[23] *Copyright Term Extension Act* 1998

It is no coincidence that the FTA obliges Australia to enact precisely equivalent legislation. The Commonwealth has now done so in the implementing legislation. The *US Free Trade Agreement Implementation Act 2004* (Cth) has amended s33 of the *Copyright Act 1968* (Cth) to provide for a non-retrospective extension of copyright in exactly the terms upheld by the Supreme Court. Despite the Supreme Court's ruling, and the willingness of Australian negotiators to accept the position of the United States, it is extremely difficult to understand the policy justification for a further extension for the term of copyright, let alone the application of the extension to existing copyright.

Interestingly enough, one of the dissenters in *Eldred v Ashcroft* was Justice Breyer. Thirty years earlier as a young law professor he had written a famous article in the *Harvard Law Review* arguing that the supposed non-economic benefits of copyright did not justify the grant of monopoly rights to authors, and that the economic benefits of copyright, particularly with specific categories of published works, had been greatly over-stated.[24] In his opinion in *Eldred v Ashcroft*, Justice Breyer ridiculed the suggestion that a 20 year extension of copyright would act as an economic spur to authors to create new works. "What monetarily motivated Melville," he asked alliteratively, "will not realise that he could do better for his grandchildren by putting a few dollars in an interest bearing account?"[25]

In his dissenting opinion in *Eldred*, Justice Stevens, in words that echoed the famous speech given by Lord Macaulay in 1841 in the House of Commons, pointed out that "*ex post facto* extensions of copyright result in a gratuitous transfer of wealth from the public to authors, publishers and their successors and interests".[26] The real sting in the tail of this comment is, of course, that for the most part the beneficiaries of the extension will not be authors, or even their original publishers, but commercial entities which have acquired the rights long before the statutory extension of copyright.

Another significant feature of the FTA, which has not attracted a great deal of comment, is its insistence that the parties provide for criminal penalties to be applied where a person is found to have engaged "wilfully and for the

---

[24] Stephen Breyer (1970). "The Uneasy Case for Copyright: A Study of Copyright in Books, Photocopies, and Computer Programs". *Harvard Law Review* 84 (2): 281–355.
[25] *Eldred v. Ashcroft*, 537 U.S. 186 (2003) 14
[26] *Eldred v. Ashcroft*, 537 U.S. 186 (2003) 6

purpose of commercial advantage" in certain conduct infringing intellectual property rights.[27] These provisions in fact reflect a fairly well-established policy of criminalising deliberate commercial conduct which infringes intellectual property rights, particularly copyright.

There is probably nothing remarkable about this policy until you look at how it has actually been implemented in Australia. The *Copyright Act* provides that the person who distributes an article for commercial purposes, which that person knows is an infringing copy, is guilty of an offence punishable on summary conviction by a term of imprisonment of up to five years.[28] An offence punishable on summary conviction is one that can be dealt with by a magistrate sitting alone. This means, for example, that a local court in New South Wales, acting under Federal law – and of course in Australia State courts can be invested with Federal jurisdiction – can impose a sentence of imprisonment of up to five years for a deliberate infringement of copyright. The same court, under State law, can impose a sentence of no more than two years imprisonment for any summary offence in respect of which it has jurisdiction. The most plausible explanation for these extremely unusual arrangements about which I have had occasion to comment judicially in a case called *Ly v Jenkins*[29], is that they are designed to accommodate the contention of copyright owners that not only severe criminal penalties but special summary procedures are needed to curtail the activities of copyright pirates. There are many commentators who have appreciated, in the words of James Boyle, an American academic, that we are in the middle of "the second enclosure movement". [30] He sees that movement as exemplified by the recognition of patent rights in human genes.

Peter Drahos and John Braithwaite draw a parallel in their book between medieval feudalism and what they describe as 'information feudalism'. Under the earlier variety, a lord of the manor exercised not only private power by virtue of his ownership of land, but public power through a system of manorial taxes, courts and prisons. In the modern form of feudalism, as Drahos and Braithwaite see it, the transfer of intellectual commons has been to media conglomerates and integrated life sciences corporations, rather than to individual scientists and authors. The effect,

---

[27] *Australia-United States Free Trade Agreement* 17.11.26(a)(ii), 17.4.7(a)(ii) and 17.4.8(a)(iii)
[28] *Copyright Act 1968* (Cth) s132(6AA)-(6A) as at 1 January 2005
[29] *Ly v Jenkins* [2001] FCA 1640
[30] James Boyle 'The Second Enclosure Movement and the Construction of the Public Domain' 66 *Law & Contemp. Probs.* 33 (Winter/Spring 2003) 33

they argue, is to raise levels of private monopolistic power to dangerous global heights, at a time when states, which have been weakened by the forces of globalisation, have less capacity to protect their citizens from the consequences of the exercise of this power. William Cornish, a well-known intellectual property scholar, entitled his 2002 Clarendon Law Lectures *Intellectual Property: Omnipresent, Distracting, Irrelevant?*[31] in order to highlight the major dilemmas which enmesh intellectual property: *omnipresent* – to capture the case where intellectual property rights appear to be "spreading like a rash"; *distracting* – to describe rights which serve few of their intended purposes but which cause persisting itching; *irrelevant* – to refer to technology which in practice seems to render some forms of intellectual property nugatory.

Why have these developments occurred? From an Australian perspective, three major factors have combined to generate the pressures to which the Creative Commons movement is a response.

The first, obviously enough, is the power of interest groups whose economic well-being depends upon the privatisation of intellectual property resources. In general, the interest groups favouring the extension of intellectual rights are very well resourced, effectively organised and politically powerful, both at a national and an international level. Often they can enlist the support of national governments in multilateral and bilateral negotiations. The United States, in particular, has used trade negotiations to ensure, in the words of § 301 of the *Trade Act 1984* "adequate and effective protection" for the intellectual property of United States corporations in other countries. Trade benefits may be (and often are) withdrawn from countries which fail to grant such protection. The United States has played a leading role in the negotiation of multilateral arrangements, such as the *Trade Related Aspects of Intellectual Property Rights* (TRIPS) Agreement, which have done much to advance the interests of the holders of patents, copyright and other forms of intellectual property.

I do not mean to suggest that there are never powerful interest groups opposing the expansion of intellectual property rights. The history of copyright law, for example, is replete with battles between opposing interest groups, such as music publishers and the manufacturers of tape recorders and other electronic equipment. Even so, the struggle is often unequal.

---

[31] William Cornish, *Intellectual Property: Omnipresent, Distracting, Irrelevant?* (2006) Oxford University Press

A second force for extending the boundaries of intellectual property is bilateral and multilateral international arrangements. Like the FTA, these agreements often require the parties to create new species of intellectual property or to enforce existing rights more effectively. The shape of much of Australia's intellectual property law has been determined by international agreement. Since the Commonwealth Parliament, pursuant to the external affairs power, can legislate to implement international agreements, the effect is that there is virtually no limit on Parliament's power to privatise intellectual resources.

Technological change is a third powerful force, since technological developments can quickly render obsolete or ineffective existing laws and enforcement mechanisms. As copyright holders, for example, realise that they cannot protect their interest by purely technological means there emerges, in the words of Professor Cornish:

> a whole set of distinct demands for higher legal fences as part of the digital agenda, which politicians press at the behest of industry lobbyists and their star writers and performers.

When the new technology and international treaty obligations coincide the pressures for the extension of intellectual property rights become almost irresistible. An illustration is s116A of the *Copyright Act*, a provision designed to prevent a person from making so-called 'circumvention devices' which are capable of circumventing 'technological protection measures'. The origins of s116A, the construction of which was in issue in the recent case of *Sony v Stevens*[32] (now before the High Court)[33], lies in two World Intellectual Property Organisation treaties which address the problems for copyright owners by changing technology.

The privatisation of intellectual property resources raises issues that transcend the particular concerns of intellectual property lawyers and their clients. They go to the nature of freedom in a society which, in equal measure, creates opportunities for astonishing innovations and severe restrictions on creativity.

---

[32] *Kabushiki Kaisha Sony Computer Entertainment v Stevens* [2002] FCA 906
[33] Note: since this paper was presented, the High Court has handed down its decision and this matter - see *Stevens v Kabushiki Kaisha Sony Computer Entertainment* [2005] HCA 58

The Vision for the Creative Commons: What are We and Where are We Headed? Free Culture

PROFESSOR LAWRENCE LESSIG

It is a great pleasure to be here and especially to be greeted this morning by Justice Sackville's extraordinary presentation, which reminds me that I spend most of my time living in the flat earth society with people who continue to insist the world is flat. To come out to a place where the obvious is obvious, especially to people with extraordinary influence and power, is a great relief. I am extremely happy to be here and share something of the vision of what Creative Commons is supposed to be about.

Here is the purpose of what my talk this morning is supposed to be: it is to place this movement in some context. I have struggled in the last couple of years to find a way to show what is really at stake here. To move the discussion beyond the really boring tired debate that seems to dominate most of the discussion about these issues, especially in the United States – whether you are in favour of intellectual property or against it. That is not the question. No one is asking that question, and until we can begin to recognise what's at stake for our culture, we will lose this extraordinary opportunity that technology offers us. That is my objective here, and I want to begin by introducing an idea that should be familiar: the concept of remix.

The idea, first, is that you take creative work, mix it together and then other people take it and they remix it; they re-express it. In this sense, culture is remix; knowledge is remix; politics is remix. Remix in this sense is the essence of what it is to be human. Companies do it. Apple Corporation says it took its iPod and remixed it. Politicians do it. Bill Clinton took the Republican Party's platform, remixed it, called it 'Democrat' and became President. Liberals do it. Here is a wonderful propaganda site that exists on the net for Liberal propaganda – 'daddy why didn't you or any of your friends from Enron have to go to war'?

We all do it, every day of our life. We go watch a movie by somebody, we whine to our friends about how either it is the dumbest movie we have ever seen or the most profound political insight America has produced in fifty years. Whatever, we are remixing our culture by experiencing it and re-expressing it. In our choices every day, we decide what our culture will be by deciding what we consume and what we comment about. The choice whether to watch Disney or read H.C. Anderson is a choice about what our culture will become. We are remixing by consuming and we, by consuming, are constructing every single act. Creating and recreating culture is an act produced by reading, by choosing, by criticising, by praising. This is how cultures get made.

The critical framing point about this active remixing that we have to remember in the context of this debate about free culture is: remix is free. It is free. In our tradition it has always been free, free in the sense of unregulated by the law. You need no permission to engage in this act of recreating your culture by commenting or transforming or criticising or praising. You need no permission: it is free. It needs to be free. There need to be limits on the power of entities, whether government or corporate, to control us. It needs to be free if we are to avoid infantilising our culture. It needs to be free as an expression of a basic human right: the right to engage in this act of producing who we are. It needs to be free in all the ordinary ways in which we engage in this practice of remixing our culture, the ordinary ways in which we write. This is the idea. We 'write' our culture by what we say or praise or criticise; this act of writing needs to be free.

What are the ordinary ways in which we remix our culture today? What is the technology of remix today? By 'today' I do not mean literally today for those people who are really doing the most remixing out there, namely our kids using technology. I mean 'today' the way most of us over the age of 35 think about culture and how it is remixed. What is the technology for us today? And the answer to this is: it is a technology grounded in texts, in words, in the act of writing, in the act of remixing texts. We see a movie; we talk about it; we criticise it; we might write a letter to the editor criticising the free trade agreement – in fact I encourage you to do that regularly. We express these acts of remaking, using words and it's that technology which today is free. It is the technology of text, which 400 years of culture and politics has produced as free.

We take it for granted that writing is free – not totally free; you can say things which are libellous and face consequences. Not totally free; you cannot lie about certain things. Not totally free; you cannot take my words and pretend that they are yours. But free, not in the sense of anarchy; free in the sense of the well-regulated society. Four hundred years of culture has produced a legal tradition that embraces this idea that writing is free.

Writing is allowed in our culture where writing is understood to be the writing we engage in through texts. This is second nature to us, we do not even notice it. We forget that for hundreds of years people had to fight for the right to write and publish what they thought. They had to fight for that right against monopolist publishers, controlled by the Crown. They had to fight for the freedom which we take for granted to use words and express and change our culture.

It is second nature to us to compare texts as a way to find contradictions, to contrast texts as way to understand differences. It is at the core of what education is, to imagine literacy in the sense of teaching children to remix texts as a way to understand what they, the children, mean. We think creative writing is to go in and take the words of Hemingway and mix them with the words of Shakespeare as a way to express something, both about the child that does that mixing and about the cultures he or she is remixing, to understand and to know. Knowledge requires this freedom to engage in this practice of remixing and this practice of remixing we know so far is text. This is the world we have inherited. It is a world filled with a tradition of freedom that we must pass down to our children, because here is the critical point: this technology, by which we remix our culture, is changing. The means by which we express ideas differently is changing. The ordinary ways in which we engage in this practice of re-expressing and understanding our culture is changing. There is a radical change in technology which will radically change what it means to remix our culture.

Again, those of us over the age of 35 cannot begin to recognise what this means. We need to see it to get a glimpse of some of what this might be so let me take some examples here. In the context of music, the Beatles created this amazing album *The White Album*, which of course inspired Jay-Z to create this album, *The Black Album*, which then in the expression of what remix is today, inspired this guy, DJ Danger Mouse, to create *The Grey Album*, which synthesises tracks from *The White Album* and *The Black Album* together to produce something different. Or in the context of film, in 2004 at Cannes *Tarnation* by Jonathan Caouette, an extraordinary film, was said to be one of the best in its category, a film made for US$218. The most expensive item in this film was a set of wings that the kid had to buy for a particular scene. He made this film by taking video from his life and remixing it together at a level that could be qualified as one of the best films at Cannes. Most importantly for us in the future is going to be mixing in the context of politics. It is here where these techniques become the core of how a wider range of people communicate.

This is digital creativity; this is digital remix; this is what it can be. Changing the ordinary ways in which we express our ideas and criticise and praise the ideas of others. Changing what it means to write. This is how writing will happen. It is how writing happens for our children right now. This is what the technology of ordinary ways will be, changing the way we remix culture, changing the creative potential of that culture, changing the democratic potential of that culture, changing the freedom to speak, by transforming the power to speak – making it different. Not any more just broadcast democracy but increasingly a bottom-up democracy, not just *The New York Times* democracy but increasingly blog democracy, not just the few speaking to the many but increasingly peer to peer. This is what this architecture invites. It is in its nature to open up the opportunity to speak and criticise and transform to anybody connected to this digital network. This is the potential of this network, the potential.

We have got to begin to imagine that potential in the same way we understand text today. We need to imagine what a world would be like where people could engage with these objects in as freely a way as we engage with text today. Imagine it spread; imagine it as second nature. See it in the way our kids experience technology today.

There is a wonderful program that is going on in *Dog Kennel Hill School* in Britain, a school for children, not for dogs. They have a project called *The Living Image Project* in which these artists are participating. Their objective is to understand how the youngest of our children understand the act of creativity, by giving them the tools of creativity – all the way from crayons to the most powerful computers – and watching what they do with these tools. Ellen, age 5, drew two pictures. She did not like the colours on her first picture, so she remixed the colours on the second picture, and then she took the two together and began to produce what she understood creativity to be – the remixing of these different media into one form of expression. Or in this example, Tom, age 7, took a photograph of his bedroom, then drew a picture of a 'happy story'. He then added to the photo every child he knew and then changed the colours to make it a happy picture. Or Lewis, age 10, who comes from a kind of dark place where his picture of his neighbourhood is pretty dark. They were a little bit worried when he first produced this really dark expression of life, but then he finished it with a more positive final expression. The point is, for them, remixing images and sounds through technology is as natural as it is for us using words, where we take a clever spin on someone else's phrasing; that's what creativity is for us. For them, it is taking the culture that is around them and re-expressing it through these technologies. This is the difference between us and them.

We have just ended 80 years of a kind of Soviet culture, where culture is broadcast to us and this is our experience of it. We consume it. Made somewhere else, and we passively consume it. For them, culture is something different. For us the good in culture is – more channels. For them it is an active process of remaking and remixing culture, that is what they do with technology. The potential here for them is enormous. The potential for them to be able to argue and understand using this technology is enormous.

The potential progress for our culture is enormous as this power is exploded and given to them and they learn to use it. We need to begin to extrapolate from what we have seen to what could be. Imagine a graph of progress where we start at the very bottom corner with the embarrassingly crude technologies of power point. That is the beginning of the cut and paste culture. Business people are so excited, they go to the net, they download pictures and they put them up with thousands of words on their screen and that is what creativity is for them. It is just the beginning.

We can then imagine the next stage, kind of the iMovie picture, where people take images of their kids and they make them into movies and synchronise them with *Star Wars* episodes. I have a wonderful friend doing a project where he is doing little home movies and he is putting *Spiderman* clips into them, or clips from major movie studios, and he is writing to the studios and asking permission for these clips and saying, "I am just going to show it in my own home, just to my family, that's what I want to do and can I have permission to do this" and, of course, he is getting these brilliant letters back from the studios, "no, I am sorry we cannot give you permission to take 3 seconds of *Spiderman* and mix it in. It would be impossible for us, consistent with intellectual property law, to give you that permission".

Imagine a wider range of people engaged in the ability to make what *Read My Lips*[34] does all the time. This is the point. We cannot begin to see what our world would look like if this literacy were to explode beyond the tiny,

---

[34] *Read My Lips* is a series of independent films lip-synced by Johan Söderberg and featuring some of the most hated and loved people in history to some of the most hated and loved songs of all times, including the Bush-Blair love duet. Available at <http://www.atmo.se> at 28 August 2006.

little ineffective corner of literacy that text is today. To the literate that is what we understand culture to be. We academics think text is the king, but it is irrelevant. Text is irrelevant. For 95 percent of the world, they cannot begin to understand what text is supposed to do. We engage in careful, elaborate arguments using text, however, it goes completely over some people's heads, because people experience culture differently. It is not that they are inferior in the way they experience culture, it is that the culture they know is a culture through these other forms of expression. We speak Latin, they speak a language that is embedded in their culture and we ought to build a world where they are free to use it. Imagine this cut and paste culture, imagine this world where that power is spread broadly, where that is ordinary, where the ability to engage in this form of speech is widespread and our culture is facile with it – not in the sense that some of these examples are facile, but in the sense that people are really good at it. Imagine that future.

Here is the problem with imagining that future. Right now, those activities, those forms of expression, those kinds of creativity, are all basically illegal. It is illegal to engage in that kind of creativity. These new uses of technology are illegal under the laws as they exist right now. The *Read My Lips* remix is illegal because of an explosion in the scope of law and in the reach of law, which together entail a simple rule. To engage in this act of creativity you need permission first. Permission is not coming. For example, DJ Danger Mouse knew the Beatles never give permission to do anything with their music. Jonathan Caouette makes a film for $218; Cannes says it is a brilliant film; he then wants to distribute it internationally; he calls the lawyers; the lawyers tell him it will cost $400,000 to clear the background music in the video clips that he made as a kid - $400,000!

A favourite example of mine is the Bush-Blair Love Duet remix from *Read My Lips*. I want you to understand just how weird lawyers can be. I do not care what you think of Tony Blair or George Bush. I do not care what you think about the war – I have a good idea but I do not care – the one thing you cannot say about that remix is what the lawyers said when they sought permission to synchronise that music of Lionel Ritchie with those images. You need permission to do the synchronisation and distribute it. When they sought permission, the lawyers said "no, we will not give you permission". Why? "It is not funny".

The question we have to ask is: why are we in this world where on the one hand technology is giving us all this amazing power and on the other hand, the law is taking it away. We need – we, meaning those of us on the free culture side of this debate – to be a little bit more honest about why we are here. We are here in this awful place because the very same technology that enables this powerful remix is a technology that enables something called piracy. The same technology does both. And, surprise, surprise, technology does good and it also does bad. This piracy has induced the only response that we in America seem to have to social or political problems – a war. A war which my friend Jack Valenti calls 'his own terrorist war' where apparently the terrorists are our children. This is the war that we are waging and we are developing. As we always do in the United States, amazing new weapons to fight this war – powerful law, which we then enforce in the United States and force other nations to adopt, not through international bodies alone but through bi-lateral trade negotiations. You want to get access to our country's markets? You have to adopt our extraordinarily extreme intellectual property protections. In fact, we force developing nations, like China, to adopt intellectual property regimes that are more restrictive than the ones we live under today.

We have these amazing new laws and technology to fight this war. We aim to protect copyrighted work, but the consequence is that we kill this potential for remix; for with the very same weapons that will wipe out the pirates, we will wipe out the opportunity to engage in this cultural practice of speaking.

I want to be clear about something, intellectual property is good. I am in favour of it. Why are we pro-IP? Copyright is essential to the creative process. I am wildly on the side of pro-IP, and piracy is bad. Is that clear? IP is good; piracy is bad. But here is that really innovative suggestion: so too is war bad. Right? War is awful because war has consequences both unintended and intended, and the consequences of this war are extraordinarily profound. They will destroy the potential for this type of literacy to spread through our culture. They are doing it today by rendering this activity illegal and by doing this we say to our kids, "you are criminals when you engage in this behaviour". We raise a generation who thinks their activity is criminal. But what do kids do when they are told they are criminals? They think, "Oh cool. I'm a criminal". This is a deeply corrosive consequence from this war. Of course, the industry thinks the way to solve this problem is just to wage an ever more effective war against our children. "We will pacify the enemy", they say. We have heard this before, right? Literally those words we have heard before 'pacify the enemy'. We take time (we in the United States), to learn that war is a prohibition and wars such as the wars we waged in SE Asia are not wars that will be won through pacifying the enemy. These children, these criminals, these quote 'terrorists', will learn something different about democracy if they think that activities that seem to them to be totally obvious and totally creative and totally productive, are called, by the great Soviet, 'criminal'.

That is the first consequence, and the second, more profound consequence is: we cannot begin to teach this type of literacy within our schools. It is totally obvious that a teacher of English literature is allowed to take the children and say, "take the texts, mix them together and write an essay from them". That is what we learned 'freedom of text' to mean. But you cannot take a film class and invite the children to take the work of George Lucas and mix it together with Hitchcock and produce a demonstration of how the work of these two film makers worked and interacted. You cannot do that because that is called piracy under the regime of understanding that exists in intellectual property law today. We cannot begin to teach this literacy in our schools, so the capacity, the potential, is destroyed because we call it illegal. That is the critical point.

People say, "well people will always be breaking the law". Sure they will be breaking the law; they will be thinking of themselves as criminals, but we will never incorporate this practice into our ordinary school. But the consequence today is tiny compared to the consequence tomorrow. For right now it is possible to break the law. You can take these images, mix them together. You can do it because the technology allows you to do it. Tomorrow that possibility will be taken away. It will be impossible. There are always kids from MIT, or maybe from this University too, who will be able to crack the code and do whatever they want to circumvent the protection measures. But for ordinary people, it will be impossible because digital rights management technology will have been mandated by the law to be incorporated in every feature of this network, so that the permission to engage in these acts of creative remixing needs to be sought from the content owner, and guess what? Their permission will not be granted. We will build into this architecture a technology – digital rights management technology – that will take away the ability to engage in this kind of expression. It will remove it and there will be no capacity for the ordinary people to circumvent that. We will return, using these technologies, to this couch potato culture. They will feed us stuff; we will consume it; criminals will remix it, but the rest of us will be happy in our passive relationship to this culture.

When they started this digital rights management technology this idea that remix would be impossible was not part of the debate. Digital rights management technology was first suggested and people started fighting for something called 'fair use', and what they thought fair use meant was the right to make an extra free copy of the CD. That was the critical right, that you got an extra bite at the apple. You buy the CD but you can copy it and put it on your computer. That is freedom for that part of the debate, and there is now a very important settlement that I think is going to become dominant. The settlement is we have strong digital rights management through all of our content, but a liberal quote 'fair use policy', where by fair use we mean we get to make 3 or 4 free copies.

If you buy this content, you get to make whatever number of free copies but those copies live only within the home. That is the settlement. But notice what this settlement does: it solves the architectural revenue problem for the current content industry; the twentieth century content industry gets it problem solved. They get to sell copies. They are going to adjust the price because to sell one copy is to sell really two and a half copies, but, they still get to sell copies. We solve their problem. But the weapons, both legal and technical, that have solved their problem have simultaneously destroyed the potential for this remix culture to occur because what remix culture needs is not the freedom to remix within your home; that is not what you need; you need the freedom to remix and to express it to others – the freedom which our tradition guaranteed to us when it came to text, but which we are not giving our children when it comes to anything beyond plain text.

What is the problem here? I do not think the problem is technology. I do not think the problem is something called 'copyright'. The problem here is a regime of copyright that does not fit to this technology. It is a regime of copyright which is, for this technology, too cumbersome, too bloated, too expensive, too lawyer-centric, which is just begging for reform. The costs of doing right under this regime of copyright are just too high and the scope of control under this regime of copyright is just too great.

Historically, in response to new technologies that challenge existing copyright regimes, we have had a fairly traditional response. The historical response has been balance. But perhaps because my country leads this response today, our present response is not balance but a kind of extremism, and it is an extremism that exists on both sides of the debate – 'they' refer to the 'terrorist war' that they are fighting; 'we' (I do not mean me, but people think this is me) – the other side – respond to this by basically rejecting intellectual property. Both responses are mistakes.

After Napster collapsed, Apple released a new advertisement to launch their new iTunes music store. They thought they would put together a hip new vision of what freedom would be in the digital age. You can imagine the advertising executives pride in the way they had captured the spirit of the age, which is the right to download music so long as you were drinking a Pepsi. You would think the health authorities would have been worried about that, because one in seven Pepsis gets you one song. Imagine the health consequences of people drinking all those Pepsis just to be able to download their song. Apple spread that advertisement out there on the Web, like that was their cool image of how they understood what the generation was about. It immediately produced a counter advertisement.

The point is that extremism on one side begets extremism on the other side, and both extremisms are wrong. It is sort of IP McCarthyism that lives in the United States right now, where if you question IP, you are called a 'communist', literally. It destroys the opportunity for any of the traditional historical balance in the legislative process to occur. This potential for what this technology could be is lost.

What do we do in response? We need to find a way to wage peace. That is what we need in the middle of any war, a way to wage peace. We need a way to use intellectual property to enable remix, to enable it to occur without threatening intellectual property. We need to make this system of creativity co-exist with the system of intellectual property regulation. The solution is found in an insight, which Richard Stallman had twenty-one years ago this year – a way to use IP to enable free software. We want to use IP to enable free culture. That is the aim of creative commons – to find a simple way to mark content with the freedoms that the author intends the content to carry, so that when you encounter such free content, you know what you are allowed to do consistent with the law.

You go to the Creative Commons website (http://creativecomms.org); you pick the opportunity to select a licence: do you want to permit commercial uses or not? Do you want to allow modifications or not? If you allow modifications, do you want to require a kind of copyleft idea that other people release the modifications under a similarly free licence? That is the core, and that produces a licence. That licence comes in three separate layers.

The first, most important layer perhaps, is a commons deed, which expresses in a human readable way what the freedoms are that go with this content. Second, is a lawyer-readable licence – which actually guarantees the freedoms that are associated with this content. Third, critically, a machine-readable expression of the freedoms, that makes it so computers around the world can begin to gather content on the basis of the freedoms. We have a search engine that is now fantastically great at collecting content on the basis of the freedoms that are associated with that content. These three layers together are crucial. We need to find a way to make the freedoms understandable, unchallengeable and usable in a digital age – understandable by ordinary people, unchallengeable by lawyers, and usable by computers. That is the objective.

My favourite example of how this is works is a guitar track composed by Col Mutchler, called 'My Life', who donated it to Opsound (www.opsound.org), a sound resource that makes all of their content available under creative commons licence. That inspired Cora Beth, a 17-year old violinist to add a violin track. She then released that back to the Internet, calling it 'My Life Changed'. This hauntingly beautiful song now lives freely out there, free for other people to remix. Just last week, I came across a further remix, this time by Triad, a group that is dedicated to the public domain. They added an extraordinary vocal track and called it 'Our Lives Changed'. I like what they have done with it.

Of course, everything is not amazing. There is no guarantee of quality. Anyway the critical point about this is that these remixes are all legal. And here is the part that it is hard for my colleagues, my lawyer friends, to recognise: these remixes are legal, and yet there was no lawyer required to make them possible. No lawyer stood between these creators. People who had never met each other were allowed to create, legally, consistent with the intellectual property regime and release their content because the freedom had been built into the content first. This is what remix culture could be, and we want to build the tools the make it possible, both the legal and the technical tools, to make it possible, to make it flourish.

What next in this process? Let us recognise what is the general principle, or we should say, the general principles; there are two that Creative Commons stands for. The first is that we want to find a way to lower the cost of the law, not eliminate the law, but lower the costs associated with the law in making creativity possible. Second, we want to enable 'commonses' wherever they might help innovation, not in contrast to property, but complementing property, recognising that the complement of commons and property is what makes the greatest creativity possible. For example, the iCommons project is the most important part of this project right now, as 70 countries around the world port the licences to their local jurisdictions to establish a common standard for expressing freedom internationally. In addition we have projects within the culture space to increasingly open the content that is out there to creative re-use. We have a project which we are about to announce called 'Save a Book' project, where authors whose books are out of print, but still under copyright, can release the content under our creative commons licence. We will guarantee that they are digitised and made available. The licence is non-commercial so that if the book becomes a hit again, they can re-release it in a commercial form. The aim of this project is to make the content available digitally, just the way libraries were intended to make the content available originally.

We are also talking about a project called the 'Remark the Public Domain' project. The problem with the public domain right now is that nobody knows what it is. Who knows what is in the public domain? In the United States we have an insanely complicated system for figuring out what is in the public domain and what is not. You have to pay hundreds of dollars to figure out whether a particular thing is in the public domain. It is the sort of project, a database-like driven project, which we could do collaboratively to begin to understand what is and what is not in the public domain.

The most important next project is the launch of something we did in early January 2005: the Science Commons. This project aims to take the same two principles and extend them to science, lower the cost of the law and build commons where commons might encourage innovation. We are looking at open access publishing, which of course has taken off internationally, and to support that with the licences that are necessary. We are looking at the problem of databases, which increasingly are bound up by restrictive covenants that make it impossible for that data to be used in the way data must be used today – meaning massive parallel processing on data to find insights about the underlying material. And also in the context of patents, to find ways to building patent commonses, as IBM has just announced with respect to 500 software patents, so that innovation can occur without confronting the extraordinarily high cost of dealing with patents.

Those are ideas that we have launched already. Increasingly we are beginning to toy with the idea of something called the Business Commons, which is to recognise that even business, commercial enterprise, depends upon certain features being un-owned as a way for them to build their commercial proprietary stuff. The point in all of these contexts is to find this common standard for expressing 'free'. As Richard Stallman has struggled to explain, not 'free' in the sense of 'free beer' but 'free' in the sense of 'freedom', express freedom associated with content, to encourage this extraordinary range of creativity that could be realised.

Is there hope for this project? Last Christmas there was this wonderful article published in *Billboard* magazine, which is a kind of apologist for Hollywood, about our project. Here is what the article said: "A copyright theory [a theory] called Creative Commons promoted by an organisation of copyright practitioners and academics, has emerged as a serious threat to the entertainment industry" says Michael Suskind, member of the International Association of Entertainment Lawyers (IAEL). A serious threat, right, by the non-profit organisation, also known as Creative Commons.

We are not even creative enough to have a distinction between our theory and our name. We urge creators to give up their copyright protection (you might wonder where you would have seen that in anything we have been talking about but that is what *Billboard* reports it as). This position has "spread like a virus onto the international stage", Suskind explained, with anti-copyright forces adopting these arguments against the music industry. If that theory is accepted by legislators, copyright laws could change; copyright owners could lose protections and US [that is the important word] copyright income "could be at risk" he says.

The International Association worried about US copyright income, but of course they are not going to worry about US copyright income. They are worried about US lawyers' income. You might think is this the empire striking back? No, do not worry – it is the imps-for-hire striking back. That is the fear– that we are going to threaten lawyers in some sense. But it is not just them. Bill Gates, gave an interview, where he was asked about this intellectual property war. This is what he said:

There is some new modern-day sort of communists, who want to get rid of the incentives for musicians and movie makers and software makers under various guises, they don't think that incentives should exist.

Communists: is that who we are? I mean remember communism, whatever Marx said, was the world where all property was owned by the State. We are not for that. You might remember corporate fascism was the world where all property was owned by monopoly corporations. You might think we live in a world very much like that, but we are not for state ownership or monopoly capitalist ownership; we are for what this has always been about: authors expressing freedom associated with their content. We might be called 'commonists' perhaps. I like to use the word 'commoners'; that is who we are. The commoners' movement here is Creative Commons. Are we a serious threat? Let us be a serious threat to lawyers in common. Not a big problem in the world. Are we a virus? Let us be a virus that enables artists to spread culture, to understand culture, to free culture; let that be what this virus does. Are we out to change law? No, that is not our purpose. That is the whole insight. We do not have to change one law to enable people, to enable this project to succeed, because we are using existing law.

It might be that this project, if it succeeds, does change the law. But the critical point to remember and emphasise over and over again, especially in the world where the earth is thought to be flat, is if we change the law, it is not to kill IP. We are not against IP. It is instead to bring IP into the 21st century, to make writing legal in the 21st century. Technologists have given us a way to write. The lawyers have told us that way is illegal today. We owe it to our children to give them the freedom to write that we knew, and that our forefathers spent hundreds of years creating.

Creative Commons Worldwide

The iCommons Project

> DVC TOM COCHRANE, NEERU PAHARIA AND IAN OI

A critical part of the Creative Commons strategy has been the 'porting' of the Creative Commons licences to national jurisdictions.

*In this presentation leaders of the Australian iCommons movement (QUT's **Deputy Vice Chancellor Tom Cochrane** and **Ian Oi**) along with the Assistant Director of Creative Commons, San Francisco (**Neeru Paharia**) talk about their experiences internationalising the Creative Commons..*

Professor Brian Fitzgerald
(Head, QUT Law School)

The iCommons Project

DVC Tom Cochrane, Neeru Paharia and Ian Oi

Tom Cochrane, DVC QUT TILS

My name is Tom Cochrane, Deputy Vice Chancellor here at QUT and on behalf of QUT I would like to add a note of welcome to this relatively temperate January day in Brisbane.

Brian Fitzgerald, whom I am sure, just about everyone here knows, first approached me over a year ago with a speculative question about the University's attitude towards becoming formally connected with the Creative Commons initiative. Part of this involved the concept of an institutional affiliation. We did not hesitate. The reason for this was simply that our recognition of the universality of issues involved in this area meant that responses needed to be done rapidly.

In an atmosphere of increasingly polarised views, innovative and creative approaches to intellectual property law, particularly those which constitute interest in compromises, are increasingly attractive to a wider and wider range of concerned people. It is my view that the licensing issues that we are discussing here are themselves one of the best forms of response to some of the tensions that we have heard described earlier today.

I did have a few remarks that I was going to make about the free-trade agreement, but a fair few of those have been made already by Justice Sackville, and I would only add to those querulous observations. One is to ask, looking back, which sugar producer, which beef lobbyist in Australia, could possibly have entertained a view of the future in which they would understand, if they would care to, that half of the bill – physically the text of the bill – to implement the FTA in Australia (which is a 140 page document), 70 pages of those were concerned with the required amendments to the Australian Copyright Legislation.

My second querulous observation is to ask that, if one accepted that the United States may have a strategic international interest in effectively extending its own precedent setting copyright legislation – the well-known DMCA – to other jurisdictions by the most efficient means possible – this would be through bilateral trade negotiations. And with what more willing partner on the globe with which to have an experimental first step at almost complete compliance? Perhaps content with those two questions we should pass to the main session. I merely make those comments to add to a view about the huge importance of the issues about which this conference is concerned at all levels. In building a different kind of future, it is my belief that a progressive and constructive approach is the iCommons Project.

Our first speaker is Neeru Paharia. Neeru is an Assistant Director of Creative Commons. She graduated from the University of California at Davis in 1997 and received a Master of Science in Public Policy and Management, concentrating on information systems from Carnegie Melon University in 2000. Prior to Graduate School Neeru spent a year in the Kyro Fellowship program, a leadership program in public affairs. Neeru comes to Creative Commons from McKinsey & Co where she worked as an associate consultant. She is also a film-maker, illustrator and blues guitar player and she has shown her work in various film festivals and publications. This is her first time in Australia.

Ian Oi is Special Counsel in the Canberra office of Blake Dawson Waldron. He practices primarily in the area of information technology, communications, intellectual property and cyberlaw. For a number of years, he has particularly focussed on the development of licensing, distribution and management of Open Content and Open Source Software. Among other things, Ian is Co-Project Lead and Leader of the Drafting Team for the iCommons Australia Project, which promotes Creative Commons licences in Australia. Ian has also drafted contractual frameworks for the development and deployment of Open Source Software and Open Source Software Licences in an Australian environment.

NEERU PAHARIA

Good morning, thanks for having me. I am filling in for Christiane Asschenfeldt who is our iCommons Coordinator. She could not be here today so I am here to talk about iCommons and to also tell you about a few of the other projects we are working on in Creative Commons.

First, congratulations on the Australian launch. It is fabulous.

To review very quickly: we offer copyright licences which are between a full copyright and the public domain. These are the attributes you can choose:

- Attribution
- No Commercial Use
- No Derivative Works
- Share Alike

You can choose a licence from our website. You will get a piece of code which you can paste into your webpage and it will display the 'Some Rights Reserved' logo next to the work you are licensing. That links to the Commons deed of the relevant legal code, which incorporate the chosen layers of the licence. The Creative Commons licence makes it clear to other people who wish to either download the work or re-use it in some capacity, that they can do that in the conditions specified under the licence.

iCommons

We started the project with licences that were based on US law. We found that it is necessary to translate these licences, at least the legal layer of the licences, not necessarily the Commons deed or the digital code into different languages and into different legal jurisdictions. We have done this by developing a porting process where we identify a project lead, they produce a draft, we go through a public discussion, we do another draft, a review and then finally adoption.

Here is a little bit of the Creative Commons timeline. In 2001-02 work began on the original Creative Commons licences. In December 2002, we launched the first versions of the licences. In April 2003, Christiane Asschenfeldt joined us to begin iCommons, working with institutions around the world to port the legal level of the licences into different legal jurisdictions. In March 2004 we launched our first country – Japan. Over the year, eleven more countries have launched licences. In January 2005 Croatia launched their Creative Commons and today we are here in Australia.

Here is an overview of some of the countries we have been launching. Australia has now moved into porting licences to join fourteen countries with licences. We are in discussions with over seventy countries, and hopefully we will have 84 soon. As iCommons evolves we are moving in a few different directions. We have been working on building the number of countries that have licences, talking to as many countries as possible. We also are hoping to build some infrastructure to increase the number of licence-adoptors, to build some community building efforts in countries to work with institutions, artists, any kind of content-creators to licence their work. Hopefully the total amount of licensed content will grow by following these two different axes.

There have been some porting challenges, because laws are different all over the world. The most significant challenges that actually may impact on the Commons deed are to do with: attribution and moral rights, which have some impact upon derivative rights; and agreements with collecting societies where authors may not be able to waive either their Commercial or Non-Commercial rights.

So what else do we do?

Christiane Asschenfeldt runs the whole iCommons Project, so what do the rest of us do? We pretty much just hang out in San Francisco. There are other a lot of other things that we do at Creative Commons and I hope to share some of those things with you today, because I believe they are very exciting and they can also hopefully inspire you to do some of the same.

We think of what we do in three main buckets:
1. get as much content licensed as possible
2. make that stuff all searchable
3. get people to re-use that content

One of the aspects of the licences is this piece of machine-readable code. It is RDF Code, it actually goes into the html code of your webpage, and you never see it. However, computers can read this Code and can do really interesting things with it. One of the main things that we use the RDF for is to build a semantics search engine. What the search engine can do, is that it can go onto the web, it can find the subset of the web, that is under a Creative Commons licence, it can discern what kinds of items those are and what kinds of licences they are under. The semantic web is a vision of the World Wide Web consortium and Tim Berners-Lee as well.

We have built a first-instance of a semantic search engine using Creative Commons. If you have heard of Mozilla the Open Source Browser Software, they actually have a search box in the corner where you can find our search engine. You can, for example, do a search such as 'find me all images of sunsets that I can modify and build upon'. You can download the chosen photo, alter it and republish it under the Attribution Non-Commercial Share-Alike licence. That is Creative Commons in action.

Also, Mozilla has a plug in, where if you visit a webpage that has a Creative Commons licence on it, the icons will show up in the bottom corner of the webpage, and that is also facilitated by the RDF Code that goes into the webpage.

Another project that we are working on, that we are really excited about, is called ccPublisher. This is the Internet Archive. They want to host everything they can. They have a bunch of different projects, but their main goal is to archive the whole Internet. They have this thing called the 'Way Back Machine' and you can type in a URL like Yahoo 1995 and get a page of what Yahoo looked like in 1995. It is very cool, especially if you have disputes with people about information which Professor Lessig can also tell you about. It is a very good tool to know about.

The other great thing about the Internet Archive is that they will host Creative Commons licensed works for free. We have capitalised off this by building a desktop tool called ccPublisher. What does it do? You can download ccPublisher, drag and drop your files and choose a Creative Commons licence. It will then imbed the licence information into the MP3 file itself, it will upload it onto the Internet Archive for you and return to you a URL where you can download your song (which can be converted into various formats for streaming and download). Now your song has been published to the Internet for free to the Internet Archive and it will be there forever. This tool also works with video and audio, and we hope it is a way that people can actually more easily publish their content to the web.

We recently did a project with *Wired Magazine* where they released sixteen songs under a Creative Commons Sampling Licence. What the licence allows you to do is to fileshare all of the songs and to sample them. In some cases you can sample the songs commercially and in some cases non-commercially, but you are allowed to fileshare all the songs. Among the artists are David Byrne, Gilberto Gil, the Beastie Boys and others.

It was really great that the CD came out, but we thought we really want people to start interacting with the CD – they have the rights to do it – let us find a way to get people excited about remixing this stuff. We have just launched a contest called 'The Fine Art of Sampling Contest' which you can find at CC Mixter (http://ccmixter.org/). If any of you are interested in music mixing or not interested in music mixing you should try it anyway and enter the contest. Basically you download the songs, throw them into a music editing software, mix them up and then upload them back into the system. There are two different categories. In one category the winner will be in the next Chuck D *Fine Arts Militia* album. In the other category, we will be releasing the CD with *Wired* CD with the best remixes and just promote it as much as we can.

This is a good segue into talking about Mixter, the new content management system, another software project we have been working on. It is like Fenster and Orchid, which are social networking software programs which show how people are connected to each. Mixter Software is a content management system that basically does the same thing; however, it also shows how content is related to other content. For example, if I am on someone's homepage and he or she likes, for example, Sound Forge, I can click on a link and see who else likes Sound Forge. This is exactly how Fenster and Orchid work. The more significant feature about Mixter is you can see how music is related to other music. You can listen to samples and you can visit other homepages as well. You can see how this content is related to other content and how people are remixing each other's stuff. This is one of the most exciting things about Creative Commons, the whole concept of remixes, that Professor Lessig talked about. But we thought why not facilitate this, why not make this explicit in these kinds of communities, so people can really see how content is built and changed when different people interact with it.

We will be releasing this content management system under an Open Source GPL Licence, and anybody can start their own Mixter communities – blues guitar mixter, video mixter, mystery mixter, education mixter – which I think is one of the most compelling cases for it. With this particular case of Mixter we are going to start a web-stream, like a remix radio-stream. You can imagine you are listening to a stream of radio, you like a song, you click on, you download it, remix it and put it back into the queue.

These are some of the technology projects we are working on. There are a few more in the areas of:

- Business development
- Community development
- Content recruitment

Here are some examples of projects using Creative Commons licences.

The Corporation

I do not know if any of you have or heard of *The Corporation*. It is a documentary film that came out of Canada. About 75 percent of their B rolls came from the Prelinger Archives which is hosted on the Internet Archive, it is all public domain footage. There is a very compelling case for a pretty astounding film that made a significant use out of public domain material. It was all free.

Magnatune

Thinking a little about some of the commercial value of Creative Commons – what Magnatune (music label) does, is to release MP3 files for free under Creative Commons licences. They make their money by selling wave files and by licensing the music to video-game producers and for commercials. If you are a non-profit filmmaker, you can use it under the Creative Commons licence. They have a very innovative way of price-discriminating between different uses, and they use Creative Commons as one piece of that.

Public Library of Science

This is an Open Access journal that recently started in the San Francisco bay area. It has received a lot of attention. All their publications are under the Creative Commons Attribution Licence.

MIT OpenCourseware Repository

This is an open repository full of lesson plans, all under Creative Commons licences. They put all these lessons up and people from Vietnam and Spain and from all over the world are downloading these lesson plans, translating them and using them in their classes, all without any kind of transaction cost.

ACRO Repository

Australian Creative Resources Online (ACRO) is the concept of a digital junkyard where some of the footage you take is valuable and you use it, but then 90 percent of it you throw away. This is placed in the repository and people can use it for different things. I was in discussions with Phil Graham for about a year about this. I was glad to hear that it is coming along.

Youth Media Projects

Another very compelling case for Creative Commons, where young people want to make news and share content with each other, they can rip stuff off each other, edit it and make new stories in this collaborative way. We talk a lot to different organisations about integrating the licences into their systems. On a popular music community – garageband.com – you can upload your song and as you are uploading your song, you can choose a Creative Commons licence.

Morpheus

Another project we have been working on is with Morpheus in the peer-to-peer (P2P) basin. A lot of this is with embedding licence information into MP3s, which the ccPublisher and a few other applications do for you. What you can do is to embed your Creative Commons licence into the MP3 and then if you are on Morpheus and are searching for CC sampling it will show you a group of tracks that are under various Creative Commons licences and then you can download them. This is a very good tool to find non-infringing content on the P2P networks.

Flickr

Flickr image site is another positive Creative Commons project which already has over half a million images under the licences.

Sound Click
Sound Click music community has about 90,000 songs under Creative Commons licences.

That brings us to the question of how we curate this. We think there is an opportunity there for anybody who wants to go through the Creative Commons pool and find the good stuff and pull the good stuff out. iCommons is really about the community-building phase, about how to go out in partner with institutions, broadcasting services and artists' associations to get people thinking about Creative Commons and interested in adopting the licences.

We have also been working on some legal innovations, such as: the Developing Nations Licence; the Sampling Licence; the CC GPL which is not a licence, but it is wrapping our metadata and commons deed model around the GPL; the shared music licence; and the Science Commons, which Professor Lessig also mentioned.

Here are a few statistics to give you a sense of how we have been doing. As I mentioned before, we launched the original suite of licences in December 2002. At the current point in time, around 5 million webpages link back to our licences, and according to Yahoo's index, one out of 1200 pages has a CC licence on it. This is pretty astounding considering the size of the Web. Our growth rate has been positive – around a 47-50 percent quarterly growth rate in terms of traffic. If you Google a search under Creative Commons there is a huge spike in the last couple of months – a very high growth rate.

I mentioned a little about the different attributes and we have also been able to see what people are choosing. Before, when you could choose Attribution, which you can no longer do, 97 percent of people chose to require attribution. In the case of Derivative Works about 67 percent of the people chose to allow people to make Derivative uses of their work. About 67 percent also, disallowed commercial use – some interesting statistics about how people think about their content. Most people are very happy that people take their work and do different things with it. They don't want them to make money off it and they want credit for it.

To close, we also ran a moving-image contest last year where we asked people to make a video that explained our mission better than we could. We received a lot of different entries and the best one made use of public domain footage. He took a lot of public domain footage, he took Creative Commons licensed music and he mixed it up.

IAN OI

My presentation is decidedly low-tech. In fact it is the most mundane of the presentations here. What I am going to cover is a bit of the background on the iCommons Australia team in terms of where we came from, how we got our act together and how we got to this point, and some of the developments that we will be looking to develop in the near future.

I will preface it by saying that a lot of my material is in an article that Brian Fitzgerald, Tom Cochrane, myself and Vicki Tsamitas drafted for the book

International Commons in the Digital Age.[35] The book is put together by our good colleagues at iCommons in France and collates together an excellent collection of materials from Germany, Netherlands, Taiwan, Sweden, Finland and Australia regarding the International Commons project. It is of course licensed under a CC Licence, and you can download it all off the Internet.

The process of iCommons coming together is in a sense crystallised in this book. But, in relation to the Australian aspect, I have to say that my personal involvement in iCommons really crystallised at a symposium of copyright lawyers in November 2001 when I met Brian and Tom. We were talking about Creative Commons and realised that no one to our knowledge was doing anything about implementing this into Australia. It took a while to get our act together, but in the course of doing so we developed a team of interested people, primarily lawyers from around Australia, from Brisbane, Sydney and even some expatriates over in the US. We started by looking at the US generic licence forms and following through the principles of the porting process. There were two kinds of considerations that we had to bear in mind. First, in the porting process, it was very important for us not to lose sight of the overall objective of providing and implementing a coherent, consistent international licensing regime for the Creative Commons licences, so that the same licensing elements (and the same things that we thought we were licensing in Australia) would be licensed in the same way anywhere else in the world. Of course, our US colleagues would say the objective was the other way around. Our perspective was that if you are an Australian licensor and you are using Australian licences you should have the same certainty around the world as you would in Australia, and the same effect.

Secondly, we also needed to ensure that particular aspects of Australian law that might not be present in the US or other jurisdictions were properly reflected so that you did get that same effect in general in those other jurisdictions. Even if the letter of the licence was not exactly the same, you would have the same effect, and you would not necessarily need a lawyer to interpret the licence to tell you that it had the same effect. You could simply look up the human readable code for that licence and be pretty certain that the same effect was carried out.

---

[35] International Commons at the Digital Age, ed Danièle Bourcier and Mélanie Dulong de Rosnay (2004) Rommilat, 33
<http://fr.creativecommons.org/iCommonsAtTheDigitalAge.pdf> at 1 February 2007

Arising from that, there were a couple of drafting things that we went through – three or four different things that were unique to Australia that we had to take into account. Sometimes the Australian law made itself into the drafting. At other times, we took the Australian law into account but said 'no, we do not need to do anything with the licence, but we may need to follow this up'. One of those things was GST (Goods and Sales Tax) law, which has a very broad statutory definition of what is a supply and what the tax might possibly apply to. We had to consider whether we had deal with this in the licences. At the end of the day, we decided we do not have to deal with this in the licence, but what we will do as a follow-up activity is to provide some commentary to ensure that people who are using Creative Commons licences do not inadvertently fall into a situation where they will be subject to an Australian law regarding a particular tax that they did not realise would be imposed in that situation.

Another category of things we considered was liability provisions. The generic Creative Commons licences have a provision, drafted based on US law, that says 'OK, no responsibility is taken, these materials are provided as is' and if you want any more assurance, you need to obtain that assurance outside the licence. To make that effective in Australian law, we have to accommodate particular laws such as the Trade Practices Act, which make it very difficult to have a disclaimer of liability in certain kinds of transactions unless it is in a particular form. We drafted some wording in there, some legalese to deal with that. Consequently the net effect is the same as under US law, but the wording is slightly different because it accommodates Australian legal peculiarities.

There are two other areas which are a little bit more interesting. One of them is to do with commercial royalties in Australia, particularly as those royalties are collected by collecting societies. The second issue is moral rights. We have in Australia a statutory regime that is comprehensive regarding the moral rights of creators and authors and it has implications for the licences which we had to decide how to deal with.

Dealing with the commercial royalties issue, the generic form of the licence reserves to the licensor the exclusive right to collect royalties for any public performance of the licensed work or any cover version that may be created from that licensed work, if the performance or subsequent distribution of a cover version is intended for commercial purposes, effectively commercial advantage or monetary compensation.

There are a couple of things about the Australian environment that, we noted, make it a little bit different to the US. The first is, in relation to musical works and music that is going to be performed and communicated, that under Australian law, the performance rights collecting society (that is Australasian Performing Right Association (APRA)) cannot legally collect royalties for the exercise of the performance right of musical works – to perform a music work – unless APRA has first been assigned the rights.

All APRA's 33,000 members have to assign to APRA all their public performance rights, before APRA can collect the royalties on their behalf. Those 33,000 members include all Australian song writers and composers whose works are applied commercially. That affects a significant proportion of the creators that are already out there and working, and who may wish to participate in the Creative Commons. This is something that APRA members and anyone who potentially wants to become an APRA member will have to be aware of. They will not be in a position to use a Creative Commons licence to license their works, unless they have reached some alternative arrangement.

The wording of the Australian licence accommodates this up to a point, but there is still a danger and a risk for potential APRA members who do not realise what they are doing to potentially get themselves into trouble by trying to license out something that they may have effectively signed away to someone else. This is a follow-up area of work, and the people at APRA have been very good at giving feedback and comments on the effect and the potential interaction with Creative Commons. I look forward to working with them to develop some further commentary and to get some guidance out, and to find easier ways for creators to both work with Creative Commons and to also collect royalties via APRA. That is one area of work that needs to be done: collaboration with collecting societies in Australia and other organisations that are relevant.

The last thing I am going to talk about from a legal point of view is the moral rights side. The Creative Commons licence has already recognised a right of attribution, that is to say, the right to have your name put on a work if you are the creator. In Australia, we have a statutory regime that recognises that particular attribution right. There is no inconsistency in principle of policy between the Creative Commons licence and our Australian statutory scheme, but we needed to tweak the licence wording a little bit in that area.

There is however another moral right which caused a bit more of an issue for us to think about, and that is the right of integrity. This is the right of the creator not to have their work used, altered or changed in a way that would be damaging to their reputation. This is something that is not directly dealt with in a Creative Commons licence. The Creative Commons licence rights are very broad. They would allow you to do anything that comprises the rights in copyright, except to the extent that the rights are reserved. This is where there is a little bit of ambiguity. The wording says that if there are rights that are not expressly granted, they are reserved. This wording in the licence potentially could be interpreted ambiguously, as to whether the moral right regarding integrity was being asserted under licence so that a user could do anything except alter it to damage someone's reputation, or whether the silence means that the user can do anything regardless of the moral right of integrity.

We thought about this, and started correspondence with our international colleagues in Canada and UK and there was a lot of tooing and froing of positions. One of the things that weighed on us in Australia at the end of the day was that, the person who is in a position to waive moral rights to consent to uses that would damage their reputation is the author and only the author, not the copyright owner, who may or may not be the author. In other words, the person who is in position to grant the licence of a Creative Commons' work may or may not be in a position to grant that moral rights consent. Because of this potential gap, the interim position that we have adopted for this licence is to affirm that moral right of integrity. The licence provides that you can do anything you like except that you cannot damage the author's reputation. I stress that this is an interim step. One of the things we and the Canadians (who are also in the same position - they have a similar statutory scheme), want to work towards is developing an option within one of the licence attributes for Creative Commons for this very issue. Do you want to go in and allow people to do anything they like? Or, do you want them to do whatever they like except if it damages your reputation? We see the best solution as being to give people this choice.

In terms of legal issues, those are basically the main features of what we considered and did. We changed the spelling of licence from LICENSE (the US usage) all the way through the documents to LICENCE (the Australian usage). I have to say that I did not care so much about this spelling change, but other people on the drafting team did care about it, so they won. We are at the stage now where the Australian licences have gone live. We have some work to do regarding: providing more guidance to make these licences more usable; cutting out the middle man of lawyers, by way of working with other organisations such as collecting societies to make arrangements smoother; and putting out more information out there to make the Creative Commons Australia licences more practical.

Government and Creative Commons

The Government's Role in Supporting Creative Innovation

Why Government and Public Institutions need to understand Open Content Licensing

> LINDA LAVARCH MLA, PROFESSOR STUART CUNNINGHAM, DR TERRY CUTLER, DR ANNE FITZGERALD, NEALE HOOPER AND TOM COCHRANE

The Government's Role in Supporting Creative Innovation

We move from the micro back out to the macro in our next section, which will feature the Queensland environment more broadly in the area of innovation, where the operation of a Creative Commons licensing regime will have real meaning in terms of the operation of the Queensland economy and society. The conference programme indicated that the speaker on this topic would be the Minister for State Development and Innovation, Tony McGrady. Unfortunately, the Minister was called away on short notice. His Parliamentary Secretary, **Assistant Minister Linda Lavarch MLA**, *therefore spoke on the Minister's behalf. [After the conference, Linda Lavarch was appointed Attorney General for Queensland.]*

Professor The Hon Michael Lavarch
(Dean, QUT Faculty of Law)

Why Government and Private Institutions need to understand Open Content Licensing

This presentation focuses on the role Creative Commons and Open Content Licensing can play in copyright management within government or the public sector more broadly. The Chair was **Professor Stuart Cunningham***, then Acting Dean of the Creative Industries Faculty. Since the conference Stuart has become Director of the ARC Centre of Excellence for Creative Industries and Innovation, which funds a number of projects aimed at furthering research and education on open content licensing in Australia, including the Creative Commons Clinic, Creative Commons and Open Content Licensing and Digital Liberty projects.*

The members of the panel who provide papers here include **Dr Terry Cutler,** *who looks at the public policy issues surrounding open content licensing;* **Dr Anne Fitzgerald***, who discusses the Copyright Law Review Committee's review of Crown Copyright under Australian law;* **Neale Hooper***, who discusses open content licensing options for governments; and* **Tom Cochrane***, who closes with a discussion of the importance of open content licensing to public institutions and universities.*

Professor Brian Fitzgerald
(Head, QUT Law School)

The Government's Role in Supporting Creative Innovation

LINDA LAVARCH MP

I received a phone call about an hour ago to say that Minister McGrady had an urgent family matter to attend to and asked if I could stand in his stead today, and this, I quite welcome. I did not welcome the circumstances in which I was asked to do this, but I was going to come to the Conference anyway.

I would be remiss in not recognising Professor Lawrence Lessig. Welcome to Queensland. I have met you before via the video-conferencing screen. I would also like to recognise Deputy Vice-Chancellor Tom Cochrane and Professor Brian Fitzgerald and congratulate you on organising this Conference. It is very timely for what is happening here in Queensland and very apt that the Conference is here in Queensland, so congratulations on organising it.

The comments I wanted to make refer back to the launch of Creative Commons in Australia in April 2004, with Professor Lessig via the video conferencing screen at Queensland University of Technology (QUT). I came down in no official role, just out of interest because it sounded interesting. But I was like a blank page, knew nothing about the project itself. I walked into that room and my knowledge grew as the project was launched. After a very short amount of time, I was on the edge of my seat and the neurons were firing and doing brain gymnastics because in a role as a legislator or a parliamentarian it is very rare that you get, or you are presented with a new way of thinking. And that is how I felt that day. And the words of Professor Lessig's address here this morning were remarkable, stimulating, exciting. To complete the picture for you, two officers from the Office of Spatial Information who went to the launch introduced themselves to me and we were like a babbling brook walking down George Street, talking of what the Creative Commons Project was all about and how it did turn your thinking on its head.

As a legislator I call it, or have dubbed it, the Speed Bump Rule. We all live basically by the Speed Bump Rule — whoever was that first person that drove at a very fast speed through a car park has imposed upon the rest of us for the rest of life speed bumps. We have a very pessimistic view of people and human nature and when we are dealing with issues at a legislative level, it is at a level where you try to imagine the most evil and dastardly deed a human could do. Then in our tool box we only have one tool, the big stick. And this is why I noticed the speakers spoke with optimism and I found that after the Creative Commons launch, being the eternal optimist that I am and a great believer in the best of human nature, it did turn my thinking around as a legislator.

But now I will turn to the Minister's speech. Just one last word before I do. I know that here in Queensland this will broaden the audience that will be talking in the terms and the premise of the Creative Commons Project. The title of the Minister's speech today is *The Government's Role in Supporting Creative Innovation*. Now the speech is not about what should the government do; what we will speak about is what is happening here and now, right here in Queensland. In my sort of moment of jest I call it the Queensland Boast, but of course it is much more than that and I just want to set the scene for you.

In 1998 when the Beattie Labor Government was elected to parliament and to government here in Queensland, we came in on a policy called 'The Smart State Strategy'. The thinking behind that strategy was that Queensland has always been a mine and a farm, and in our mining and farming the technologies that were being used were still, in many quarters, a hundred or more years old. And whilst we could rely on our economic base, based on the world prices of what was mined and what was farmed, we knew that that was not sustainable. In contrast the Smart State Strategy looked at ways of investing in emerging industries, investing in new technologies to bolster our traditional industries and to ensure that we have sustainable jobs for the future and a healthy economy here in Queensland.

In the early days of the Smart State Strategy it was changing the way of thinking here in Queensland; it was turning people, turning industry, on its ear and saying, "You can do better; you can embrace new technology; you can embrace new thinking". We put our money where our mouth was, investing in science and technology and innovation, and making innovation an essential plank to that strategy, and to the quality of life and the future of the Queensland community. To get the message across, the Premier decided that our number plates should read: 'Queensland. The Smart State'. Well, our daily newspaper, of august record, decided that we were, 'The Sunshine State', and we were going to remain 'The Sunshine State', and started a very negative campaign. But it is interesting what happens out there in the community, despite this overwhelming negative campaign about being a smart state and having a smart state strategy. It still remained and could be built upon in the community. It did not get scuttled in other words. Nearly seven years, on, it is now becoming a much more widespread notion and something that all Queenslanders are very proud of. Even when you go into primary schools you get little seven and eight-year olds going, "we're Queenslanders, we're from the Smart State", and you know the message has got through then.

We are up to the stage now where last year a paper went out for full consultation in relation to 'The Smart State – Where to From Here?' I understand quite a lot of submissions were made and they are being considered at the moment. I have no doubt that the premise of the Creative Commons Project was embodied in a submission and is probably at this moment being considered. It is not part of government policy at the moment. But what I just wanted to give you was some examples on that broader basis of innovation and supporting the creative industries here in Queensland, along with science and technology, and just to give you the colour and the feel of what practical things the government is doing.

One of the interesting debates and one of the areas where there is still a lot of work being done is how to commercialise the innovation that is happening. We are now becoming world known in relation to our mining software and product which is being developed here and now. Another area where Queensland is forging ahead is electronic games development. Our local companies, Krone and Auran, are leading the way for the games industry in Australia. Their products are sold internationally, particularly in the United States and Europe, and have expanded to Asia.

The other area where Queensland is leading the way is in relation to the e-health Network. You may have seen in the news about the medical teams over in Indonesia that are now using the e-health technology to assist the tsunami victims. And this e-health technology is recognised internationally as the largest and most utilised video conferencing network of any single health network in the world. And in e-security we have the largest research community in the southern hemisphere. QUT has had a lot to do with that coming to fruition. Indeed, in the very near future this will be boosted further with the opening of a dedicated e-Security Research Centre at the proposed Boggo Road Development. It was our old prison, so instead of securing people, we are now securing information there. This is a very exciting project here for Queensland and for Australia indeed.

Our bio-technology industry is also growing rapidly, receiving world-wide attention. We recently had the Australian Oz Bio Tech Conference here in Brisbane. It was the first time it was in Brisbane and there were 1300 delegates, the biggest ever, and can I say it was a very exciting conference. The other area where we are forging ahead is in relation to therapeutic drugs and other products. Queensland is recognised as having some of the most unique plant, marine and animal life in the world and again leading the way forward, and this time in legislation. The Queensland Parliament enacted the *Bio Discovery Act* last year. A lot of the marine and animal and plant life will come from the national parks and state lands here in Queensland. Under that Act, for the first time in the world, the State will benefit financially from the commercialisation of the use of that product into therapeutic drugs and goods. You were talking about traditional knowledge before. Whilst it does not cover the IP area, traditional knowledge is recognised under that Act. A requirement is that those pharmaceutical companies, or the bio-prospectors, have to reach agreement with the traditional owners of that traditional knowledge if they are to use that knowledge in the production of drugs and other goods. And that is the first time that this has been recognised in legislation as well.

The other area that we are putting a lot of effort into is the business side of the innovation and technologies. We have been a strong supporter of innovation because we understand that it creates the opportunities. We have helped by hosting conferences, like Oz Bio-Tech, assisting companies that take part in trade delegations through direct grants to help companies develop and commercialise technology, by assisting industry to set up clusters in areas where we have potential to create niche markets, and we have invested 2.4 billion dollars in science research and innovation in the past six years or so.

What we are also doing in relation to creative industries is investing. Here in Queensland we have a creative industries strategy and we have provided $15M towards QUT's impressive $60M Creative Industries Precinct at Kelvin Grove. We have also developed in conjunction with industry a $4.4M creative industries strategy, as I have said, which focus on the business end of the creative process. We realise that creative industries have enormous potential to create more jobs and wealth for Queensland and we are also working to enhance and spread our Smart State reputation globally.

I hope you take that away back to your home after today because I know that as I go around the country we are the envy of all other states, through the recognition, the strategies and the dollars, the investment. We have also found that the creative industries have already contributed 1 billion dollars to the value of Queensland's goods and services each year and that there are 65,000 Queenslanders employed directly or indirectly in creative industries. It is no small employer for the State. That probably measures up with the manufacturing industry which employs somewhere just up to about 180-190,000 people, just to give you some idea.

The only other thing I wanted to mention to you today is that last year we supported a successful writers' foray into Los Angeles, which showcased the work of 14 Queensland writers to film development executives and top-named agents. And we are very proud of the fact that that has already had a great success with our local author Nick Earl picking up a deal to option his novel, *48 Shades of Brown*,[36] for film development, and we understand that there will be some further good news to follow there. That was a government initiative to take the writers into Los Angeles.

If the Minister was here today, the message that he would want to get across to you, and the message that I want to give on behalf of the Queensland Government, is that we are committed to helping our creative people sell their products and we are committed to the creative industries here in Queensland. I wish you all the best for the remainder of the Conference and look forward to meeting a few of you over lunch.

---

[36] (1999) Penguin Books, Victoria.

Why Governments and Public Institutions Need to Understand Open Content Licensing

PROFESSOR STUART CUNNINGHAM, DR TERRY CUTLER, DR ANNE FITZGERALD, NEALE HOOPE, AND TOM COCHRANE

PROFESSOR STUART CUNNINGHAM

Creative Industries is a relatively new way of describing the sectors from architecture and design, through visual and performing arts, through media, to the emergent new media forms. It is really a grab-bag of a whole range of sectors. The big challenge is: what is connecting all those sectors? Our Faculty has eleven disciplines, and that does not exhaust the range of creative industries sectors that have been grouped under this terminology. The terms were invented by a creative industries task force in 1997 in the UK and they defined Creative Industries in this way:

> Those activities which have their origin in individual creativity, skill and talent and which have the potential for wealth and job creation through the generation and exploitation of intellectual property.[37]

As you can see from that definition, it is not sectorally specific; it is functionally specific, and it raises issues of intellectual property to centre stage in terms of the future coherence and growth of this sector. The Creative Industries Faculty here at QUT is the first. There has been one further naming of a faculty as a Creative Industries Faculty at Edith Cowan in Perth, but we were the first, and really we have, if you like, to use a business terminology, brand leadership in this term in Australia. We were very interested, and it shows through that definition why we were interested, in working closely with law and with the Law Faculty and really this is one of the reasons why we have been very pleased to co-host this event with the Faculty of Law here at QUT.

Where does this panel sit in relation to the architecture of this Conference? Professor Lessig's case for the development of the Creative Commons

---

[37] "Creative Industries Mapping Document" (1998) *Department for Culture, Media and Sport* <http://www.culture.gov.uk/Reference_library/Publications/archive_1998/Creative_Industries_Mapping_Document_1998.htm> at 13 February 2007

yesterday laid out a compelling vision of a remix, or what I might call a DIY– Do It Yourself – culture where formerly passive consumers become active, engaged and sassy, talking back to the dominant hegemons or controllers of cultural production, appropriating and re-forming communities of practice outside the vectors of media ownership and control. In this vision, where do the state, government and public institutions fit?

Traditions of left progressive thought and activism in the US typically are far more sceptical of the potentially useful role that the state or government might play in forwarding progressive change than otherwise is the case in social democratic traditions, out of Western Europe, Canada or places like Australia and New Zealand. Professor Lessig's case, at least in the bald outline in which he presented it yesterday, steps around these questions. Governments in this vision are challenged to reform their antiquated IP regimes and stop falling into line with corporate interests, but rarely are they seen as having the potential to be much more pro-active and promoting open content licensing as a way of forwarding of their public service and good governance responsibilities and charters. This is what this panel will consider.

DR TERRY CUTLER

The job that I was given was to start to look at some of the public policy issues that might be involved and I took that brief broadly to frame some of the broader issues that are quite interesting. I am focusing on three points.

We can see a systemic failure of public policy across the whole domain of innovation and investment in creative capital and intellectual property. The symptom of this systemic failure as I see it has been an abnegation of public policy leadership basically to non-government organisations, not-for-profit organisations and, increasingly and interestingly, to the private sector – stepping into this vacuum. This failure has been compounded and continues to be compounded by what I see as failure in the government's own administration of public assets.

Let me briefly elaborate on three areas. First, the systemic failure of public policy with respect to the whole area of knowledge and creative assets. In this, I see the fabulous Creative Commons initiatives as being a necessary but far from a sufficient response to the intellectual property and technology challenges of this century. That is an important point to keep coming back to. What we are doing with Creative Commons is terrific, but as Tom Cochrane said, it is a sort of artful compromise around some of these issues, necessary but not sufficient.

What are some of the symptoms of this systemic failure that I point to? First, the carve-out of intellectual property law from the whole framework of free trade and the notion of free markets. If dear old Adam Smith were to come back today he would be absolutely staggered that we have this whole area where the economic framework is still in the mercantilist model that the wealth of nations was attacking and undermining and replacing, because it is a model that relies on Letters Patent and charters of privilege, which of course was the whole foundation of the mercantilist system that Adam Smith drew the line under in a compelling way. It is ironic that Free Trade Agreements are the vehicle for the capitulation of anything but free markets in intellectual property and ideas.

The second area of carve-out, and this is really the important one, is from competition policy and competition law. One of the things we often neglect with the direct importing of legal regimes and trade agreements and international treaties, is that we do not look at what we are not importing in terms of the offsetting regimes that accompany some of these legal frameworks.

If we look at intellectual property law and copyright, while we have holus bolus with a stroke of the pen adopted the US regime under the Free Trade Agreement, what we have not imported are some of the offsetting protections. If you look at Europe there is a strong tradition there, particularly in the patent and drug area, around the legislative promotion of generic drugs – sort of a framework concept that we are far from here. But more importantly in the US and in Europe, the whole framework of anti-trust legislation has been crucial in providing balance to a lot of the abuses around intellectual protection, and of course we have none of that here. That has been a really neglected part of the whole Free Trade debate.

The other thing that strikes me when I look at the systemic failure is the lack of focus and attention in public policy discourse in the US, where you are not seeing the addressing of issues, you are seeing in what we can describe as parallel areas, or issue areas. One of the things I like to do when I work with my technology companies is, when they come up with some bright ideas as draughtsmen, ask them what does this sort of problem, or product, or potential service, most look like in action. You learn what it might mean to implement and employ something, and it is interesting to ask yourself the question, 'what do these copyright and IP issues often most look like in other areas of public sector debate and public policy concern?' I thought when I was looking at the Conference programme, would it not be great to get some people from other fields, like interesting thinkers around economics, particularly around development economics. This took me back to one of my heroes, Amartya Sen, who of course, won the Nobel Prize in 1998 for his work in development economics, and his science is really around social choice theory.

What does that imply for intellectual property? It is how we make choices around the balance of priorities within a community, and one of Sen's famous observations from his work was that famines have never occurred in a country with a democratic political framework. That got me thinking, because when you look at his work, it is all about the causes of famine in un-democratic – in unopen societies – where there is a failure of equitable distribution. We are saying that in these key areas, failure of distribution does not occur in the democratic society where people sort of vote against anyone who disregards basic needs. He defines poverty, which I find really interesting, as a serious deprivation of certain basic capabilities, often through expropriation. You have these areas of public policy investigation that are posing seriously interestingly questions, which in my view apply directly to the discussion of intellectual property and copyright issues. It is interesting in my mind to ask the question of why does intellectual or knowledge deprivation (you know freedom is the lack of capability) occur in this class of sustenance we call intellectual capital, which is so crucial to feeding the mind and creative spirit? Why do we have to accept potential poverty in this area, when we do not accept that in the physical world? And failure within a democratic society is a failure of the greatest magnitude.

The second area of systemic failure I see is caused by positive policy distortions, and here governments are at fault. The problem here is the total lack of balance in current government policies with respect to the generation and exploitation of knowledge and intellectual capital. I was reading yet another Federal desk report on commercialisation of IP in the public sector and the only matrices they looked at when they looked at public sector research institutions and universities were twofold – one patents and secondly the number of spin-off companies – and this sort of mindless obsession with the notion that success is getting intellectual property out into a spin-off company as quickly as possible is distorting the public discourse and behaviour in this whole domain hugely.

The problem there is the lack of balance it causes against the offsetting public policy imperative (and we can see the lack of public policy discourse around the whole notion of technology diffusion and take-up across the whole economy and within the community). It is again this lack of balance, and the lack of attention to the issues of distributional efficiency or equity, that this matters. If we look at what is happening in the digital and technology world, what we are seeing is the impact of network effects at the macro-economic level. The more rapid the technology diffusion, the more rapid the take-up, the greater the externalities that arise from the wide-ranging penetration of new ideas and know-how. But that notion of realising the community benefits of the externalities is completely at odds with the notion of expropriating public sector funded knowledge into the micro-economic level of the firm and start-ups and so forth. This is a lack of balance which is starting to become a serious problem, not only in Australia but more widely.

The second point I noted was the abnegation of public policy leadership and what is interesting is that all the exciting initiatives, like the Creative Commons and so forth, are not coming from government, but from non-government organisations, special interest groups and so forth. If we look more broadly across the intellectual property domain, and not just at copyright but also at the whole patent domain and what is happening around technology innovation generally, we are seeing a fundamental ground shift in the way the private sector is thinking about intellectual property and its exploitation, which is very reassuring.

There is a fabulous book that just came out by a Californian practitioner called Hank Chesbrough called *Open Innovation: The New Imperative for Creating and Profiting from Technology*.[38] It really brings together the sort of radical shifts in the way that major technology companies, like Intel, IBM and CISCO, are thinking about how they exploit IP assets and recognises that you cannot develop intellectual capital on a vertically integrated, closed model in the way that we did in the past, and that the open diffusion and transfer exchange of innovation across firms within markets, is now working to the benefit of all.

We pull out the great anti-heroes of copyrighting – Microsoft or the Motion Picture Association or whoever – but in doing so we often ignore the fact that there are profoundly important developments happening and a shift of the ground in the corporate scene which reinforces a re-balancing of the

---

[38] (2003) Harvard Business School Press, Cambridge.

public policy agenda despite the lack of attention of government. One of the signals of this is also the greater focus and push by industry around standards, formation and so forth. You will see in the online world the role of groups like The World Wide Web Consortium in very much pushing an open innovation model, where in fact sort of proprietary IP is positively frowned on. That gives me some encouragement, but it is a great pity that its developments have not been paralleled in government thinking in the public policy debate.

The third point I just wanted to end on was the obvious one of the failure of government's administration of its own public assets – our assets. There are a number of areas here that are interesting and a number of them were highlighted for us from work that I did with Stuart Cunningham and CIRAC here at QUT on the role of innovation and research and development in the whole digital content sector. There has been a serious lack of attention to the impact of IP regimes on collaborative practice and inter-disciplinary research, and that is going to be one of the big issues into the future, but more directly the lack of explicit recognition of the role of, particularly, public cultural institutions in the innovations system. What you see when you look at it, when we looked around this whole digital content arena was in fact that a lot of really important break-through innovation was coming out of museums, places like The Centre for the Moving Image, which I chair, around meta-data standard development and so forth. It was totally not recognised in the charters of these organisations, not legitimised in terms of how governments see the role of these cultural institutions, and, not surprisingly, not funded. It has been a really important, default, but largely underground role, and the challenge for government is to see the positive role of public institutions within a whole innovation system.

A related point is the role for public cultural institutions, in particular, as open content repositories. We have seen the initiatives like the BBC Archive in the UK, but the role of the ABC, museums, galleries, places like The Centre for Moving Image, open content repositories, in a country like Australia is crucially important because in a small country economy like Australia it is only in the public sector that you find the scale that potentially can make a difference. Here public cultural institutions can play a disproportionate role in creating critical mass around open content repositories and it would be great to see more attention given to that.

Finally, the failure of government to address the issue of Crown copyright is extraordinary. We have been so slow in reforming this area in Australia compared to the intelligent discussion and debate you see in countries like the UK. We are so far behind, but it is one of the areas where the more you talk to industry players, a change in policy so that governments put the IP assets they develop or control – our assets – back into the public domain is one of the crucial things that could make an enormous difference to not only access to content but also industry development in Australia. If Queensland is going to be such a Smart State, and thinking about the question of how Queensland might respond to being the birthplace of the Creative Commons in Australia, then it would be fabulous if we could see an announcement that Queensland is going to adopt a Creative Commons framework for its crown IP. Let me end with a note that comes back to that parallel of content, knowledge and the reservoir of creative expression that makes up our civilisation, and say in no democratic society would we let people go hungry and starve to death for lack of food, but we do not put the same passion and attention into making sure that the intellect and the creative spirit does not starve to death because of a poverty of ideas and creativity.

That is really a perfect segue into the next presentations, which will be as a group. Dr Anne Fitzgerald and Neale Hooper will be presenting on certain projects within the Queensland Government, in particular a project called Information Queensland, on applying Creative Commons philosophies to Crown information.

Dr Anne Fitzgerald

I should preface this by saying that what we are saying here today is not an official statement. Although a lot of what we do say is already included in published documents, submissions made by the Queensland Government, in particular, to the Copyright Law Review Committee's (CLRC's) present enquiry into Crown copyright which is available on the CLRC website. Neale Hooper and I had a hand in drafting those along with people from other departments, so I should also put a rider here. It is very difficult to come and talk about something you have been so closely involved with for such a long time and to try and encapsulate it in a few minutes. Apart from yesterday, for the previous six working days, I have taught intellectual property law for 5 hours per day, five days straight at Macquarie University, and then Monday here in the Internet Law course at QUT.

The topic, and particularly the way Dr Cutler has led into it, does raise a lot of issues. A simple solution is to say you would have more freedom, more competition, more ready access to material, if you removed copyright. If we remove that set of proprietary rights, if we say that no one has rights in information, apart from the person who can get their hands on that information and then make something of it, that will allow that person to inevitably turn it into another proprietary product, which will probably be locked up and made less accessible.

The answer to the question is not so simple as to say abolish Crown Copyright. Unfortunately licensing as a concept and practice was not particularly addressed in the Crown Copyright Issues Paper and Discussion Paper (July 2004). It has been approached much more from the point of view of the academic, or ex-academic, doctrinal lawyers, rather than the way that copyright is used in practice, which is essentially from a licensing perspective. What we have seen, in looking at freedom and access and the remix of material, which is essential to culture, the fabric of society, the running of our communities, knowledge about law, judgements, government information and so forth, is that it is not necessarily the case that that information is going to be made more freely available and accessible by the removal of copyright. It may be made more accessible by retaining copyright. It is very strange in this era to think about removing copyright. The approach that has been developed through Professor Lessig's group – which is really now expanding internationally – is to assume the existence of intellectual property rights but to more creatively make material available. Whether we call it free licensing in a software sense, open content licensing has a lot of attraction.

I would like to go through very briefly what we are talking about with the CLRC Inquiry. For those of you who are not really familiar with it, there are special provisions in Part VII of the *Copyright Act* which set out special rules relating to Government ownership and Government use of copyright material. Special rules apply to the kinds of materials in which governments attain copyright. These rules can be seen to operate somewhat more broadly than those that would otherwise apply under the general provisions of the Act. For example, sections 176-178 of the Act say to us that government obtains copyright in materials that are produced by or under the Director or control of the Crown. If we deconstruct that we can see what we have got here is, as well as harking back to our general provisions of the *Copyright Act* and how copyright comes into existence in works 'made by authors', we have this add-on, this particular phrase, 'Made by or under the direction or control of the Crown'. It has not been subject to any significant interpretation. There is one case which has dealt with it in passing, but when you look at the kinds of materials in which copyright would exist from a government perspective, and the kinds of materials which governments need to be able to control, you can see that you can categorise them into really essentially three broad groups.

What we have is the usual situation that any employer is going to be in of materials that are made by the employees. In a government context we could interpret that statutory formula as also including material that has been commissioned by government from outside contractors or suppliers. It is as if a default rule is read into that – it is arguable as to whether this is the correct interpretation of the law but it has been accepted by academic commentators as being the way that the law operates – to say that where government commissioned material, where something is made under the direction or control of the Crown including under a commissioning contract, that copyright would by default, unless there is some agreement to the contrary, vest in the Crown.

There is a whole other group of materials which in fact the CLRC did not address at all in its initial report on Crown copyright. It was pointed out to them in the submissions that went in from Queensland Government that there is a massive amount of material that government holds and collects and that is essential to the performance of the State's constitutional function, which would also arguably come within the statutory formula of 'made under the Director or control of the State'. And that is where you have got provisions set out in legislation, regulation and often hugely detailed administrative guidelines, requiring people to lodge materials of a whole range, so that some kind of document, which may be a report, which in itself would be the kind of material that would attract copyright protection, you are required to do this under a statutory obligation to produce that material and lodge it with the State.

Those kinds of materials are usually required for carrying out public administration – the kind of thing that, when you are in Government, it is pretty obvious that you need that material embodied in those documents. Essentially you need the information and it just happens to be embodied in documents which also attract copyright protection. It is material that is quite essential to the functioning of the State. It could be detached from those particular documents and reorganised so that you do not have to worry about the copyright in the document in which it was submitted. But those are really the three broad types of groups which we could say you could identify in terms of the kind of material that Government deals with.

The present CLRC Inquiry kicked off from a two-line comment that was made by a previous Committee, the Intellectual Property and Competition Review Committee, in its 2000 report, which was an overview to ascertain whether the intellectual property legislation was satisfactory under the competition principles. It essentially addressed the second of those two categories that I have referred to. Where you have got it being interpreted as there being a default rule that goes into operation where governments commission material to be produced by contractors, essentially people are saying, 'well this puts the Government in an unfair bargaining position'. A lot of people do not understand the operation of this rule.

Without getting into the arguments of whether that is correctly the case, or whether that is in fact government practice in this day and age, the CLRC Inquiry, as it states at the beginning of the first discussion paper that it put out, the Issues Paper (February 2004) essentially starts from this. There are some competition concerns about the operation of these provisions of the *Copyright Act* which invest copyright in the State. We can identify the concerns about competition on the one hand. But our concern really in this context is what has tended to be the concern of the State, which is not so much the competition concern of enabling other people to get hands on that government material so they can make downstream products from it, but enabling members of the public to obtain ready access to that material so that they have ready access to information which is relevant to them.

The CLRC put forward a range of suggestions as to how what it perceived as the unfairness in the system could be addressed. Interestingly, it did not seriously propose any extension of the existing set of exceptions in copyright. Copyright, as we know, is really a balance of interests: the balancing of the rights of the creators of the material on the one hand and the interests of dissemination of information, the interest of the general public on the other. The CLRC in its 2002 report *Copyright and Contract*[39] had stated that the rights of copyright are in fact defined by the exceptions and limits.

Interestingly, the CLRC in this enquiry is not really interested in access to copyright material by general members of the public; what they are interested in is not so much there being a greater set of exceptions or limitations, which would enable people to use parts of those materials;

---

[39] Copyright Law Review Committee, *Copyright and Contract* (2002) <http://www.clrc.gov.au/agd/WWW/clrHome.nsf/Page/Overview_Reports_Copyright_and_Contract>

what they are more interested in is those materials being copyright free and essentially being collected and created into new copyright products. Probably it would have been better if they had addressed this more openly in the report. Because the other thing is that when we start looking at that spectrum in Australia we start looking at the inevitable differences between our law and that of essentially all of Europe and the United States.

Our low level of originality means that copyright is easy to attain, whereas in the United States you will not really obtain copyright in a factual compilation or in a collection of material in which there is no pre-existing copyright. The same would really have applied throughout much of Europe. In Europe they have introduced specific database legislation to protect those kinds of collections of materials. The problem that we have is that unfortunately, the CLRC did not significantly address the interests of increased access to Government material, the underlying theme seemed to be, 'let us see how we can remove copyright in whole from various categories of documents so that those entire categories can be freed up', obviously for some implied further downstream use. If that further downstream actually use results in production of copyright materials that, in turn, will have a deleterious effect on access to the materials which we were trying to free up. My point about it not really being an issue of access is that CLRC in this enquiry did not raise in any way the issue of fair use. It had been recommended in the CLRC's report of 1998 that I participated in as a member of the Expert Advisory Group. The CLRC recommended the introduction of a broader style US fair use provision. That recommendation was supported by the Joint Standing Committee on Treaties, which reviewed the implementation of the Australia-US Free Trade Agreement, acting late last year, so lots of interesting issues are raised by the idea of removal of copyright from government materials, but essentially what we can say is that that step in itself is not necessarily one that is going to result, in the not too distant future, in improved access to those materials.

NEALE HOOPER

I found myself in violent agreement with many of the comments and observations of Dr Terry Cutler. I was almost wondering whether that was what I should be doing and then to balance things up a little there was a bit of a sting in the tail of his address when he came along to the concept of Crown copyright. I understand and respect those views. It is a point of contention. There is obviously a public policy balance here and that is what we are really discussing and debating, that the whole idea of balance is what it is about. Open content licensing, let us be clear about this, is not the silver bullet. It is not the panacea. It is not the only solution to all these problems. But we are operating in a creative industries environment as a matter of intellect and as a matter of looking at the options that are available for the management and licensing and use and access of the products of intellectual endeavour – the open licence model is a very fine model, which is worthy of very close consideration.

I am expressing my personal views here. But I bring a wealth of experience from the public sector. My understanding and my experience has been that government is bringing quite an open mind to the degree to which it might utilise and implement these open licensing models. The reality is that government is, as Dr Cutler said, a very significant repository and custodian of major data sets. The citizenry have a right very often to access those databases. They are strategically important from a Government perspective. In fact they often arise – and this is what Anne Fitzgerald was alluding to – they often arise incidentally to the operation and provision of government services on a day-to-day basis. But they are strategically, fundamentally important to the efficient operation of government. The citizens of the State have paid, indirectly and directly, for the creation of those data sets.

Terry Cutler will take issue with me now about how that contribution by the public might be best recognised. I do not wish to put words in his mouth, but I suspect he would say, 'let us just dispense with Crown copyright. It has already been paid for by the public once. Why should it be paid for again?' Of course, the private sector and commercial enterprise and undertakings equally would have free access to that, so it becomes a question of balance. It is not a question of all or nothing, and I suspect Dr Cutler does not think that either. But the irritant, or the point on which we are refocusing in the public policy arena, is what balance we strike about accessing public sector intellectual property and, indeed, intellectual capital. I hope you will forgive me for that, but I just wanted to set it in perspective and it is not a question of all or nothing.

With respect to the CLRC, they are somewhat naïve to think that you either do have Crown copyright or you do not. Their view seems to be basically there is no good reason for it, so let us do away with it. I agree also with Terry Cutler about the importance of rational and considered debate on these topics. The UK has gone through that process. Significantly, and very often, critics and those in favour of the abolition of Crown copyright do not mention that under those other initiatives of reform, etc. a lot of the fundamental rights of government (if I can use that term) in fact are preserved under licensing regimes or whatever.

It is not as if the UK has just abandoned Crown copyright; it has not. It has achieved an objective with a better balance, enabling government to still conduct itself in, hopefully, an effective and efficient manner, but at the same time freeing up – and if I may say this as a practitioner in this space, I am all for that – the utilisation of very valuable public sector intellectual property assets. The moving, if you like, or the promotion – I like the word promotion – of those public sector assets, in a sense out into the private sector, all under collaborative arrangements, is a highly desirable outcome. We want further commercial movement and activity in this State and in Australia as a whole.

I agree very strongly on a personal level with Terry Cutler's comments. Australia has dropped the ball in many respects. We can be doing so much better and we have such respect from around the world, if only we realised how highly regarded our software writers are, our creative people. We can do as good a job as anyone. With the light touch – and I am getting a bit political here – that government has displayed to date, primarily at the federal level, we might have done a better job had we been a little more pro-active and perhaps worked a little more closely in liaison between the private and public sectors.

Government is obviously a recipient of information as well as the creator and custodian of information. It is vitally important in my view that government does understand the open content licensing regimes because, as a recipient, for argument's sake, of open source software, which government will undoubtedly increasingly take up, if for no other purpose other than the increased security which the technical experts assure me is available through open source, the government needs to be aware of the terms and conditions, the obligations that it is under when it receives that open source or open content material. In other words, Government needs to be acting in a responsible, lawful manner in accordance with its contractual obligations.

On that purely pragmatic basis of being a recipient of information – a simple example is the open source software – it needs to be mindful and aware of those conditions. On the other side of the coin is that it also needs to be aware of the possibilities offered by the Creative Commons, the open content licensing arrangements, which all had significant part in the open source software initiative, that is where the genesis was, because the open licensing arrangements afford governments significant opportunities to increase the accessibility to these data sets or its other intellectual property; yet, at the same time, not simply relinquish unthinkingly its intellectual property rights.

As I said at the beginning, it is not all or nothing. It is not copyright or public domain. That is not the issue. The open licensing arrangements provide, as I see it, a very useful tool under which Government can rationally make available, more readily perhaps and I am not opposed to that at all, access to its information and data sets. For instance, without once again being political, the Queensland Government does have things called Information Standards. They have got an Information Standard No. 13, which deals with access to Government information. I am not saying that is a panacea. I am trying to say Government to some extent is starting to address these issues.

We also have Information Standards in relation to intellectual property more generally, so I am trying to say that Government is starting to think about these issues. They have been doing it for some time. A Smart State initiative has at its core a very significant emphasis on the collaboration between the private and public sectors, the promotion of public sector intellectual property out into the private sector in appropriate circumstances. Which is most instances, unless there is a good reason why the ownership should not be retained by Government. There is a whole debate about the intellectual property ownership in legal judgements and Acts, which I will not get into. That is a separate issue. But in these creative endeavours the multi-media world, etc. open licensing affords government a very real opportunity, through initiatives such as the spatial information industry, which deals with mapping information – say in a Department such as Natural Resources and Mining. And, if you think about it, the repositories of the data sets, say for mining, for land title information, etc. these are all extraordinarily valuable, important data sets. They need to be managed properly.

The open content licensing regime enables Government, for instance, to give free access where appropriate to the citizenry, if there is a non-commercial use. We have heard all these issues before about who is the information to be made available to? Is it a commercial entity? If that commercial entity is going to make a profit, the public policy issue is, if the Crown can still retain the copyright in it, but enables that private sector entity to value add to that, to create further products, you know the jargon, derivative products, enhanced products, well that does not mean that the

Crown's intellectual property should just be abolished. It should be respected. It should be acknowledged under the open content licensing model. It does not mean an abolition of Crown copyright, but what it does do, it frees it up. It enables people to use it more readily on clearly understood terms and conditions.

In summary, government needs to understand the issues around open licensing regimes. Creative Commons provides a very exciting and useful model under the licensing and management regimes that government needs to seriously think about and there will be use made of it in appropriate circumstances. Let the debate begin as to where that should apply in relation to what material and how we best implement that in an effective and efficient way.

DVC TOM COCHRANE

Before the age of 17 one of the questions with which my childhood was most frequently visited was, 'what are you going to do when you grow up?' I had a variety of answers to that, and not one of them contained the word 'copyright'. Not one of them expressed the sentiment that I was going to spend a lot of time thinking about and talking about and writing about copyright. I suspect that everyone in this room is the same – that this is not necessarily a vocational aspiration that you identified at a tender age. But we are all here and we do, I know, represent a full gamut of views on these issues.

What I want to do with my part of the presentation today is to step outside this room. And although the perspective is informed by some of the jobs that Stuart Cunningham just outlined, and in particular a background as a Library professional for some years, and involvement with some of our cultural institutions, in particular in an advisory capacity with the National Library in the 1980s and 1990s; and although it is informed by the experience of being on the two references that I enjoyed being on with the CLRC, the second of which was extremely engaging and on the question which is to prevail in the sense of contract overriding copyright law – my remarks are based on experience as an administrator responsible for seeing that, in a very large institution, we do the right things.

Universities and large cultural institutions are quite rightly seen by most people as places of enlightenment. They are places where expertise is developed and where you expect to find experts. They are places where, usually, you expect people to be very confident about their opinion in their discipline, and particularly in their opinion about how the place should be run, and to be proud of their way of dealing with complexity, except in one area. Raise a copyright issue or query, issue a copyright notice, make a statement about the matter, and the most familiar responses are that passing look of bewilderment, followed by the moment of relief at realising that someone else is going to think about this. More recently, I might add, and in the context of the word 'music', more responses are better described by the words 'indignation' 'disbelief'' and outright contradiction, as happens in cases where we send a network broadcast to the university community reminding them of what they can and cannot do in terms of the deployment of music, including music for private consumption in the work place.

The essential issue in our institutions is that they are places where people use, deploy, repeat, manipulate, generate, modify, share and publish information and knowledge. If I extend the writing metaphor that was used so usefully in Professor Lessig's keynote address, the issues that face us in the next few years are not to be resolved by a process of virtual infinite sub-division of the components of that knowledge and information into building blocks that have price tags. If I extend the metaphor, it is not that each letter of the alphabet as redeployed in each new word is to generate itself new revenue. Now that statement is in direct contradiction to what is a generally expressed, but not necessarily in that form, view about what the next few years might be about.

I want to talk about a couple of things in a couple of arenas that have developed by way of copyright activity and response in our institutions and then engage at the end in the issue of what open content licensing, and, in particular the now-approved Australian version of the Creative Commons licence might, on the ground, mean for QUT and for other institutions.

We have intense activity in our institution under the general banner of on-line teaching. It provides every day a stream of questions about what is to happen with the deployment of copyright material. For some years we had an online teaching environment in which our main constraint was that material which was copyright, material which the University should be expected to recognise as copyright, could not be deployed in that environment.

The break through came in the passage of the agreement between CAL and the AVCC in 2001, which mirrored really the way that the Australian legislation at that stage was being reformed. And without going into some of the deeper questions of the legal precepts and some of the assumptions about IP on which our statutory licensing is based, I must say that when we exchanged views with our colleagues in other jurisdictions, in particular in Europe and, for other reasons, in the US, the statutory licensing scheme in its current form – and generally speaking at its current pricing – is the envy of many people who are responsible for administering learning and teaching environments and research environments in other institutions. Having said that, there are many issues involved in considering the future of that, and those who are concerned with that will be spending a lot of effort on that in the next few years.

What is interesting about the most recent developments in relation to copyright law in Australia, and which I have seen from my particular portfolio perspective in the last few years, is the extent to which those who are responsible for network administration, those whose background is professional IT work, need suddenly to engage with issues that frequently surprise them. Of course, one of the things that has happened with the most recent amendments to the Act is that it has become necessary for Universities and other institutions to clarify the extent to which they need to respond to safe harbour provisions and other provisions that really need to be administered by those people in our institutions who are not, in their normal vocation, involved with content issues.

It is well known that one of the great paradoxes in the economics of what we do in Universities is in the area of research and research output. I am sure most people now in this room are familiar with the proposition that one of the most extraordinary things that happens is that a very large amount of the formal research output of our institutions is developed by people who do not expect direct remuneration for what they do. They are doing it for recognition, certification, engagement with their discipline communities worldwide. Their discipline communities are their most important points of engagement and unless they have specific commercialisation intent, or unless they are publishing in an area which normally returns royalty, what they expect is that recognition.

The process of quality certifying it is also one which is provided gratis. The great majority of refereeing activity is provided for nothing. This is an old issue. For years people have been pointing out that when that material is re-purchased by the sector seen internationally as one entity, at the most inflated prices that exist in the world of publishing, something is seriously amiss. In the last few years we have seen a lot of discussion, a lot of theorising about what might happen, but more recently more practical steps being taken to try to ensure the freeing up of the on-line research literature. What is interesting to me is that, having monitored this from virtually the beginnings of the argument, which are over ten years old, the real momentum has been gained, being led by disciplines and researchers, not by institutional fiat, not by any kind of more heavy-handed approach. Having said that, the reality in which information is provided day to day in our institutions is that we are increasingly finding high-bred models for provision so that in some cases an information request might be satisfied by having recourse to finding quality information on the net, other times it is satisfied by having recourse to the increasingly impressive array of material that can be licensed in libraries in both universities and elsewhere.

Into this mix of issues about learning and teaching and about research and research output arrives the artful compromise (I did not say artful compromise yesterday, but artful is a great adjective) and one of the things that we will do here following the decision last Monday is that we will look at the way this can be deployed in a way that is useful for our students and for our staff. I know the way we do that will be quite constrained in some of things that we look at, but let me just share with you a couple of things that people have said in the last few months, once they have got the hang of what this Creative Commons stuff is about. Someone in our Business Faculty – a Head of School in our Business Faculty – listened and then said, "Tom, that is going to be very useful in resolving ambiguity in cases where we want students to work collaboratively to prepare material which then gets assessed.

In particular, case study work, which is quite often a feature of higher undergraduate or postgraduate study in business, was in his eyes an ideal case to assert Creative Commons licensing over.

In some cases all this will do is clarify and codify for people things that they now have great uncertainty about. And the problem with uncertainty is that it generates not only confusion and inefficiency, but it also, in the long term, can be seen to generate inhibition in what people are willing to do.

Another issue arising for us is the frequency with which student work either as exemplar or simply for the purpose of generating greater community in class groups is to be shared online. In the area of research there is a more public discussion about the applicability of Creative Commons licensing to some of the repository developments that we have. We already know, we were reminded yesterday, that the Public Library of Science is using this kind of model but there are many others that might and will be considered in the future. Indeed we have our own institutional repository for refereed research output and other research output at QUT.

One of the first things we will do is review whether there might be some way that we should be looking at the terms of this licence applying to all or some part of that repository. On both research and teaching and learning fronts there is a set of things for us to do. In the Creative Industries area, in particular, it is also going to be looked at with great interest in terms of its practical implication and implementation over the next few months.

Creative Commons and the Creative Industries

Perspectives from the Creative Industries

> RICHARD NEVILLE, PROFESSOR RICHARD JONES, PROFESSOR BARRY CONYNGHAM AM AND PROFESSOR GREG HEARN

__Richard Neville__ is one person that I am sure does not need an introduction, but we must give him one.

He is very well-known throughout the world as a social commentator and a futurist. We all know Richard from various initiatives he has been involved in from the Oz trials, right through to his social and political commentary in Australian television and media. I met Richard at a conference in Brisbane in 2004 and he said that he had been in India and had listened to Richard Stallman, who is the free software guru, talk about free and open source software. He said how fascinated he was with the concept. I asked him, 'Have you heard about the Creative Commons?' and he said, 'Sort of.' I said, 'Would you come and speak at a conference we're planning?' and he said, 'Yes, I'd like to. I really think these initiatives are very good'.

As well as the paper by Richard Neville, a number of other experts also provide us with their experiences and thoughts regarding the adoption of Creative Commons in the Creative Industries. __Professor Richard Jones__ presents reactions to open content licensing from the Australian independent film sector; __Professor Barry Conyngham AM__ discusses his personal experiences as composer, educator and academic manager; and __Professor Greg Hearn__ considers the implications of Creative Commons for the business side of the creative industries.

Professor Brian Fitzgerald
(Head, QUT Law School)

Perspectives from the Creative Industries[40]

RICHARD NEVILLE, PROFESSOR RICHARD JONES, PROFESSOR GREG HEARN AND PROFESSOR BARRY CONYNGHAM AM

RICHARD NEVILLE

In the Botanical Gardens, where I walked a few minutes ago to clear my head, there was a line of poetry on a plaque near a tree. The poet is incredibly out of fashion at the moment – and this line of poetry says something like, "all pines are gossip pines the whole world through". It is under a Bunya Pine. It takes 4 seconds to recite that poem, or that line, that fragment if you like, and it is on a bronze plaque. No permission, I imagine was sought to use it. And no permission was required to go back into the archives of your library or on the Internet and dig up some of James Elroy Flecker's other poems, one of which is called 'A Message to a Poet a Thousand Years Hence'. It is a brilliant poem. I will not recite it now, but he actually sends a message to a poet in the future, and that is a poem that was probably written in about the 1920s.

There is an anecdote from Professor Lessig's book *Free Culture: How Big Media Uses Technology and the Law to Lock Down Culture and Control Creativity*, dealing with a group of filmmakers in Italy doing a documentary on opera. In a scene they filmed, the stage hands in the opera house were watching an episode from 'The Simpsons'. They wanted to use this and, of course, asked one of the creators, Matt Groening for permission to use four (4) seconds of footage. Groening said sure. Next step however was the lawyers who worked for Fox, and they replied US$10,000 please. That four (4) seconds was never used. We are living in a culture when four (4) seconds from a distinguished poet has always been free, even forty (40) minutes worth, but four (4) seconds from a very satirical and kind of interesting show, The Simpsons, even though the creators would be happy to allow it to be used for the furtherance of creativity and discussion, is blocked.

There is a resurgence of creativity in our society today and not just in the West. It is happening globally, and it certainly excites people at universities and in the corporate world. I ask myself, what is it about the ages of

---

[40] We acknowledge the assistance of Suzanne Lewis and Vicki Efthivoulou in editing this paper.

creativity that are in common with each other? When you look back you can count them on less than two hands: Ancient Greece, the Greece of Socrates – what was it about incredible turbulence that produced so many ideas? Not just Socrates, the pre-Socratics, and going right on to Plato and Aristotle. Sure there were slaves and they did a lot of housework, so the men had more time. If you are my age you are supposed to be so dominated by text. According to some today's trendy, exciting, new generation is visual and musical. I do not accept that, because in the end we come back to something even more basic, which is conversation.

Socrates invented democracy, but he never wrote a book. As far as I know he never wrote a line – he had dinner parties. But what if Rupert Murdoch's Fox was there and he bought the rights to those dinner parties? Would we be in touch with the ideas of Socrates today and would other philosophers have been able to come along and build on Socrates' ideas? This idea of sharing and collaboration is absolutely vital to what we are talking about. I am all for providing an incentive to creative artists and I do respect to a point, intellectual property. But surely there is an incentive to disseminate, to be creative and to disseminate what you think is important and to impart knowledge. I think that this incentive overrides the financial one.

What other ages can you think of? We will skip through Christianity and Islam, but if you think of Elizabethan England we have exactly the same. We do not know who wrote Shakespeare and if it was Shakespeare, he sure workshopped a lot. It is a very collaborative environment that nurtured all those brilliant poets, including the genius of Shakespeare and the Shakespearian era.

When next are you going to think of? Maybe the Renaissance, when people again started to talk to each other, collaborated. In fact, just to give Christianity its due, St Francis of Assisi started talking to the birds. He reconnected Christianity with nature, for the first time since the whole of the Dark Ages. Giotto painted images that helped to kick start the Renaissance, which was nothing more than a huge conversation. Half the works that are painted by so-called masters probably were not even painted by the masters, but no one seemed to be quite so uptight back then.

In my student days artists were the creative people – a very small elite group at university. They had to have duffle coats, long hair, smoke a bit of pot, smoke a lot of pot, and get government grants. I was really shocked when I found out that one of Leonardo de Vinci's best friends was an accountant. I thought, "gee, I got all that wrong", but actually it was the accountant, Pacioli I think was his name, who invented double entry book-keeping. There you are. Even the accountants were creative in the Renaissance.

Think of Paris at the turn of the century, think of the jazz era, New York and how could I not even mention the Sixties? Love it or hate it, these are creative periods, a lot of social and political change, and what is the core value in those periods – collaboration, sharing. The music of the Sixties is not just about the content. The Beatles were a bit more generous about sharing than has been indicated. In fact two of them wrote a song for the *Oz* trial and the music was much more collaborative. That is the whole idea of festivals.

Having music festivals was to try and, not very successfully, close a bit of gap between the musicians and their audience. The street took fashion back from the couturiers. No one went to Paris in the 1960s. Vogue was forgotten, it was Mary Quant and what people wore down at the Chelsea Antique Market. Politics of protest was much more about not having particular leaders but sharing ideas and thinking of very creative and inventive ways of protesting the war in Vietnam. If you saw a picture of, for example, the CIA/Vietnamese guy shooting the suspected Vietcong, that would be in the Sunday papers. A magazine like *Oz* could get that picture, put blood all over the face of that unfortunate victim and put on a headline which said something like, 'The great society blows another mind'. You could communicate. You could respond, as has been said here this morning, respond to the culture around.

One of the flowerings of the 1960s, apart from the music and the fashion and the sexuality and the drugs (the point about marijuana was that it gave people a sense of community and collaboration, we can argue about the long term implications of that, but that is what it was about) was cutting through this idea of the isolated genius in the garret, the huge ego. We are talking now about the late 60s and early 70s. What happened – technology changed. There was cheap printing, cities all over the world could consume incredibly cheap newspapers and magazines all through the United States and Europe, Australia, even South America. And that is not all. There was something called the UPS, which is not the United Parcel Service, but the Underground Press Syndicate.

In other words, any newspaper that thought of itself as being radical anywhere in the world could use articles from any other newspaper anywhere in the world for free. In fact *Oz* magazine went one step further:

we abolished copyright altogether. We just said that anyone who contributes to *Oz* – you have just got to let your copyright go. It did not stop anyone from contributing and it did not hurt the sales of *Oz*. If I had not done that, I would have been able to retire onto a gorgeous island somewhere in the Pacific. I am proud of that. I am not advocating the abolition of copyright at all, but I am saying it did not really bring the walls down.

Tariq Ali, another 60s radical who has not yet dropped off the perch, came out here and reminded me that he had a newspaper called *The Black Dwarf*, which also published all this stuff and, in a way, did not take intellectual property too seriously or copyright too seriously. One day he opened his mail and there were the songs written for us, a song called 'A Street Fighting Man' by Mick Jagger. They had printed it on the front page for anyone to use or record. I said, "what did you do with the lyrics?", and he said, "oh, I tossed it in the bin". There was a certain sense of disposability.

In this cauldron of late 60s was Rupert Murdoch. He had moved from Australia to London. A darker side of the 60s looking back at them now, was of course, sexism. Some of the images in *Oz* were of nude ladies. I was amazed to read in one of the histories of Murdoch recently published, that Murdoch flipped through *Oz* magazines, saw a topless girl and said, "we should have something like that", and he made it the 'Page 3 Girl' in *The Sun*, and it made his fortune. He did not pay us anything, any money for the ideas, and he is the one charging $10,000 for the four (4) seconds.

We have a situation today where the documentary *Outfoxed* uses internal memos by people at Fox Studios to outline how the news would be shaped that day. It was more or less a directive. Murdoch actually took legal action to try and stop those being used in the film. He failed. What is the slogan of Fox Media in the States, does anyone know? –'Fair and Balanced'. First of all that is a black comedy in itself, but are you aware that Rupert Murdoch tried to copyright 'Fair and Balanced'? By an inch, he failed. But the next time something like that will succeed, and there is a danger of entering an age where people will, and corporations and very rich people with an incredible retinue of lawyers, will end up owning words in English dictionary. That is not all that far fetched. On some of the art that we saw today that was screened in the presentation, the political art, in other words the remix, how many people in this room had seen some of that before – quite a lot. And you saw it on the Web presumably? And there is a ton of that stuff and even more amazing stuff called Flash Art, which uses a type of cartoon which is hard to copy and show.

What concerns me about that material being locked out of public discourse at the moment is that it is only available to people with a certain amount of Web curiosity and prowess. I think it is a completely fantastic way of communicating and I do think it supersedes text and cartoons in delivering a message of dissent in our day and age. But until we can construct a means where that material can be broadcast more easily, then what is going to happen is that the dissent will remain locked up in a rather small group. That is the danger of what is happening now.

I said earlier that creativity and collaboration was becoming a hugely admired thing within the corporate world right now. If you take a big company like Siemens, one of the sponsors of QUT in some areas, it is a great big, German organisation, but highly creative. Seventy-five percent of the revenues of Siemens comes from products and services only invented in the last five years. That is 75 percent and that percentage is rising. They do not let researchers work alone, they have innovation groups and they are very into the future. They use collaboration like a lot of corporations to encourage creativity and diversity. Yet, while it is used internally in corporations, in terms of the broader discourse, a lot of creativity is being locked out.

We had the statistic this morning that 67 percent of artists, or creators, feel absolutely happy about their work being modified. The point I am trying to make is that, to me, the bigger issue here is: what is this debate? What is this issue between intellectual property and the Creative Commons? What is the deeper meaning of it? In a strange sort of way, it is paralleling other kinds of bifurcations that are going on and it relates to the spirit of the age that we are inhabiting right now. Just as, whether or not Australia and America sign the Kyoto Protocol. That is an issue bigger than just the environmental politics of it. It is to do with sharing, and participating, being together on a journey.

One of the most remarkable things about the response to the tsunami disasters in our region in the Indian Ocean is that it was the citizens of the world who led the desire to contribute, the willingness to express their compassion financially. Never let it be forgotten that the first offer that Australia made was something like $35 million. That was the first offer John Howard made. The first offer made by George Bush was $15 million. That was about 3 or 4 days after it started. And then we got a lecture on US generosity. Blair did not come back from his holidays for quite a long time.

The point about all this is that, by the time their policy advisers had worked out what was happening, the citizens were already doing it, the citizens of the world. What did they know, what were their feelings, what were the conversations they were having with the rest of the world, either metaphorically or real, that enabled them to respond in a way that seemed to indicate a different kind of spirit of the age that we live in? That sometimes we have to sacrifice something to gain more. There is an old spiritual teaching: the more you give, the more that you get. And we are locked into situations now of personal interest and of national interest. But in a globalising world the national interest must ultimately be subservient to the world interest.

I am trying to say that the problem is not about stealing; it is about sharing, and it is about understanding that everybody profits by liberating creativity and letting collaboration stalk the planet. In short I think that it is a very vital and hopeful signal about the spirit of the age that this Conference is happening because we are really locked. We are all members of the human race and the future of the human race is a race between self-destruction and self-discovery. And for the self-discovery of the human race to be successful we must have a Creative Commons.

PROFESSOR RICHARD JONES

Although I haunt academic corridors these days, I am primarily a filmmaker and it is this perspective I bring to these discussions. What I have been thinking about is how Creative Commons might engage independent film makers in Australia. My particular focus is not on where I think Creative Commons flourishes, which is in its potential to help emerging film makers get their work out into the world. Instead, I have been looking at the independent film sector, which is governed by funding agreements, cast and crew awards, up front distribution contracts and, in general, more traditional approaches to IP. This talk is based on interviews with a small but productive group of Melbourne film makers, many of whom spent the time politely biting my head off, particularly when I outlined the more utopian, indeed evangelical, ideals and rhetorical strategies of Creative Commons. Filmmakers are, by nature and profession, a suspicious lot. To quote Dorothy Parker, when approached with 'an exciting new idea' the first thing we must ask ourselves is – "what fresh hell is this?"

In the light of the enthusiastic language used by leaders of the Creative Commons at this conference, in particular our North American colleagues, this talk is going to feel a bit like mentioning a pre-nuptial in the throes of passion. If you have almost hit the heights, please just hold on for a moment while I outline some difficult issues we need to grapple with first.

The people I interviewed have made over 30 publicly funded films each, with many national and international awards and wide distribution, mainly television. We are deeply involved in film making as a practice, as a passion and as a political action. We are the type of people who would ordinarily be quite engaged by the ideals of the Creative Commons. But film makers also tend to see trouble a mile away. We have a sort of professional radar. You have to anticipate problems all the time in making films, and we are often approached to participate in other people's grand schemes, many of which come to nothing. As nuts and bolts folk the rhetoric used to promote Creative Commons means little. What really means something is: what are the practical implications? What are the problems? What solutions? How do we take the next step? As they say in China: "talk doesn't cook rice".

I want to introduce a few key issues, some of which I am pleased to say have already been raised at the conference. The first question is: so what's new? We continually share our audio and images, and way before the so-called 'digital revolution'. To this extent, the promotional rhetoric sounds like 'spruiking'. There is little interest in configuring the Creative Commons movement as an incremental step in a long history of shared creativity – with all its attendant problems - instead proposing a radical, indeed revolutionary, break with the past, which is cast as progressively more problematic, as increasingly 'a barrier to creativity'. Thus, the Commons rides in to save the day, to bestow on us our freedoms, like Brecht's 'bourgeois mounted messenger', whether we need them or not. Perhaps it is just the language, but this signals a highly paternalistic approach and has disturbing echoes of the neo-conservative language used to support other US led global endeavours.

What I will argue is that the conditions and aspirations of independent film makers in this country are not usefully addressed by the founding arguments used to promote the Commons. There are significant and specific local industry conditions that make these arguments - for example, the high cost of lawyers and executives stomping on artists' creativity - a little hard to take. These rationales are off-kilter with how we produce our creative work in the Australian independent film sector. The more iCommons Australia avoids uncritically importing American assumptions and addresses the specific needs and aspirations of local film makers, the more likely the uptake of its licenses and its cause in the independent sector.

This may well be a problem related to the global reach of the Commons, but it may also be that leaders in Australia have not engaged sufficiently with the public institutions that support and fund independent films here. These organisations, for example the Australian Film Commission, Film Victoria, the unions and our professional bodies, such as the Australian Screen Directors Association and the Australian Writers Guild, have grappled with the delicate issues of making public funded work freely available for many years. They are worth engaging with, not the least because in funding our films they have substantial impact on what rights we can licence to the Commons.

A difficult and unspoken issue is clearly the amorphous border between 'amateur' - not as a measure of quality but as an issue of earning living - and 'professional' film makers. I can see iCommons working quite effectively for 'amateurs', although I don't find the work available to date particularly inspiring. The minute you make films for a living however, you step into another world, although not the one described by most promoters of Creative Commons. The costs of production and the variety of contracts with funding bodies, distributors, authors, cast and crew, musicians and so on, make it very difficult to licence our films to the Creative Commons at the moment. I expect that this won't be resolved unless and until public funding bodies, film unions, distributors and producers are able to incorporate Creative Commons licencing rights into our production agreements. It will take an enormous and protracted effort to accomplish this, and I am not sure at this stage whether the will is there.

Our general experience as film makers is of a sharing and caring environment similar to the Commons, which in itself is nothing new. What seems to be new, although largely rhetorical, is the digital 'revolution'. This so-called revolution has been with us for over twenty years now. It is actually only revolutionary if you fetishize the digital side of the equation in a binary that counter-poses the analogue to the digital. This opposition, often implied in the language of Creative Commons, isn't particularly helpful. We move seamlessly between analogue and digital processes, in both production and distribution. If you remove the digital references, what you find is the age-old issues of 'originality', authorship, copying and theft. In many ways, this is the same old wine, in a brand new (digital) bottle.

What is at stake, and what the Creative Commons still struggles with, and has yet to resolve, is the difficult issues relating to moral rights. These are critical concerns with widely divergent responses from different member countries, which makes it difficult to share films in a global digital environment. Should the licences remain silent on moral rights, require an explicit disavowal or facilitate authors in protecting them? I won't approach this question from a legal perspective except to say that the focus should be on how to best retain and enforce moral rights, and for reasons other than the legal issues pertaining to jurisdiction and interoperability. Instead, I hope to show that moral rights are not necessarily about an author's ego or artistic preciousness, or their unwillingness to share the products of their labour, as is commonly assumed. Rather, this is about responsibilities that extend well beyond our individual rights and aspirations, and for good reasons. You might say "well just don't sign up to the Creative Commons, don't share the work". That is a serious option, but I would reply that we will all be the poorer for not finding ways to resolve the issues, for just walking away. I don't suppose I need to remind you of the exceptional contribution made by Australian independent film makers to our history, culture and political debate over the last 70 years, or our tremendous desire to continue getting this work into the public arena.

Let me explain a little more about why I think the American experience can't easily be mapped onto the Australian independent film industry. The highly influential US version of Creative Commons is decidedly reactive. It plays to the 'autre', an individual genius who is hard done by in a crass encounter between 'Art' and money. This relies for its momentum on the assertion that executives, distributors and even producers are squashing our creative expression, our freedoms no less! Well, hang on a minute. In this country film production is not dependant on evil, money hungry moguls and grasping, conniving lawyers. This is most particularly true of documentary production, which is likely to form the substantive base for sharing work via iCommons. Independent Australian films (and film makers) are primarily developed and funded by public organisations. We work with a network of institutions, like the Australian Film Commission, Film Victoria, SBS, ABC and others. Their executives and commissioning editors are not stomping all over us poor creatives and ruining our great work. Thankfully, there is a significant flow between the independent film sector and these public institutions. Every commissioning editor and project officer I know is also a filmmaker in their own right. They frequently have exceptional track records, are seen as part of the team, and are not the sorts of executives who do not know what they are talking about, who say, "just cut it here", or, "just make it a love story" or whatever. If you have seen 'Swimming with the Sharks', you will know what I mean about this particularly US version of what it is like to work with 'the suits'.

We often thank our commissioning editors publicly for contributing the ideas, expertise and resources that make our films happen. The 'us vs. them' binary that drives much of the rhetoric of Creative Commons, as I have said, cannot be mapped very easily onto the industry we work in. This is not to say there isn't creative tension; it is simply to say the public funding system in Australia does not necessarily lead to the same issues that Creative Commons people from the US are talking about, although this seems to be an underlying dynamic in the Australian movement, at least to date.

In seeking to protect their moral rights, which is a high stakes issue in any form of distribution, film makers are not necessarily solely interested in attribution, their own reputations and the integrity of the work as it reflects on themselves. They are often more deeply engaged with the distribution issues embedded in the politics of the film. How is the work going to be placed? Where is it to be placed? What context is it going to be used in? Can someone else pick it up and pass it on to someone who won't respect the original agreements? For example, if we are licensing a film made with indigenous communities, are re-users going to understand and respect all the issues involved? What if there are images of deceased indigenous people in the film?

If we put our films into the Commons, it doesn't seem that we can qualify the context of use very well. For example, I have made a film about racism and against racism. If I put it into the Commons, could someone else pull it out – a little section of it – and actually use it as a racist clip, because it is de-contextualised and reconstructed? We all know it is one thing to have a license that protects your rights, and quite another to have an ability to enforce it, or even to know that these rights have been compromised. Prior written agreement per use seems for the moment at least to be the only viable option. It is interesting that while the CC logo represents the Commons and its ideals, it is not in the Commons. Any use of the logo, except for the purpose of indicating that the work is licensed under the CCPL, can only be made with prior written consent, presumably based on articulating the context. Thus leaders of the Commons have encountered the problems I am talking about, and seem to have fallen back on traditional IP processes to solve them.

An example of the type of moral rights issues that emerge: a colleague is making a film called 'My Father's Eyes', in which she has a profound and moving look at the way her father photographed her as a young girl (and seems to have sexualised her through his images). In the context of her voice-over in the film, you understand it, but this context could be ripped out and images could be used in all sorts of other ways. What I am arguing here is that the real and insistent position of many independent film makers is – "do not reuse my work in strange and unintended ways. I'm just not going to let you do that". Unfortunately at the moment this only seems possible by withholding the work from online distribution until a way is found to agree on context, not just use (and re-use). Of course, any published work can be pirated and re-used. This is not just an online issue. The potential for theft shouldn't mean that we don't vigorously seek protection, or at least try to minimise the risk.

Usually the first question we ask when approached about using our images is "well, what's the context?" We swap materials with each other often, at least when we can, but need to say, "well, show your final version to us, and we'll approve the end use of it, and not just give a generalised consent to any use whatsoever". These days the people in our films often have a similar requirement. This 'right' can and I think should be given to on screen subjects, particularly in work that is made by, for, about and with specific individuals and communities. For example, I am working with men in a maximum-security prison at the moment. We are doing photography as a way of engaging these men in education. This includes a series of fantastic portraits. These prisoners have signed consent forms, but they are only asked to consent to two specific contexts of use: an exhibition for family and friends at the prison, and non-public screenings to develop further funding for the project. I think this is a respectful way of working with the men, particularly because a generalised consent does not sufficiently protect them. It wouldn't enable them to specifically consent to uses in new or unforseen contexts, for example a book publication or web compilation of the images. My experience is that most of the prisoners would consent to unlimited use if I asked. However, I can't bring myself to do this, because I know from experience that in ten years their life circumstances may have changed dramatically, and that some may not want anybody to know that they had been in a maximum-security prison. I've photographed the men as well, and completely accept that even though I could potentially put these photos online, I shouldn't, much as I'd love to. I am responsible for how these images may move out of our control, and the impact this might have on the prisoners' lives. I don't think this example can be distinguished as extreme or highly unusual. Many independent film makers, particularly in documentary production, work in sensitive environments with similar consent issues.

While this 'protective' approach doesn't completely safeguard the subjects, it does limit the risk. This is a political decision; it is a social decision; it is an issue of control. But it is control sought for reasons other than ego or money. One challenge to the Creative Commons is – can you construct a licence to say – "yes perhaps you can use the work but specifically describe the context to me first and I will tell you for sure then". Another option, which I have used, is to require that we receive the material that a user wants to include our images in - with briefing notes – and that we select and cut the images into it. I am not seeking this just for myself, but for the subjects, actors, crew, funding bodies and everyone else involved in the films. This is where Creative Commons comes a little unstuck. It seems to be geared for a sole author, not for the complex network of creators that contribute their images, stories and creative work. I feel much more obliged to the film's subjects and contributors than I am to anonymous digital re-mixers in Europe. If this protection cannot happen, Creative Commons strips away the politics of context. I would like to see some serious work towards resolving the issue, particularly by moving on from the libertarian abstractions I read on www.creativecommons.org.

I guess we are still more comfortable sharing our work in a face-to-face environment via a network of obligations, friendships and professional standards that I don't find on-line. In a face-to-face relationship, creators are frequently quite generous about sharing their work. I remember a film colleague helping me to ask his mate Paul Kelly to let me use a song called 'Before Too Long' in a film for prisoners in Pentridge, and Paul wanted to support that. He asked me about how it would be used, why and so on, then said – "look I'll make sure you get the rights cleared. There you go. Let's play a game of pool". We are looking at an eyeball to eyeball negotiation, one that ultimately comes down to the sort of trust you get amongst a community of filmmakers who have long term friendships and professional relationships, and who know where each other lives!

Another thing that concerns me about the American experience, as reported by the US Creative Commons' folk, is the notion that lawyers are substantially depleting our budgets, creating 'barriers to our creativity'. But from the budgets most of us work on, lawyers get hardly a penny. Sorry about that. The reason is that we do not need lawyers all that often. When we are funded by Film Victoria, we have access to a Film Victoria lawyer.

ABC has lawyers. SBS has lawyers. Touch wood, I have never been sued, although I have done my own contracts for almost twenty years, including a substantial amount of licensing rights. We all know how to license third party content – we can license music with our eyes closed. This is generally a pro forma process, and there is considerable help available via free copyright advice services and industry bodies. It seems to me that we are in a quite different world to Professor Lessig's experience of the US film industry: another US rationale for the Creative Commons that does not make a lot of sense to independent filmmakers here.

There is an area where Creative Commons' ideals can really come to the fore, although it seems to get little attention. The real interest of independent filmmakers is in this notion of the release of Crown copyright via Creative Commons' style licences. We are generally not looking to re-use some individual artist's view of the world or for the kind of 'clip art' I have seen available in the Creative Commons. We all do political, cultural and historical documentaries that aim to have some sort of public impact. Hence, what we are looking for is better and cheaper access to our national sound and image archives, such as those held by the ABC and Film Australia. My experience is not that the ABC or Film Australia withhold access for political reasons (although there is one example of this that quickly turned around in the face of industry concerns), but rather that the legitimate costs of providing this service are often too high, and many of these costs are met by film-makers via license fees. I have no doubt that the ABC and Film Australia would provide better access with increased funding. Even the commercial networks in Australia don't have a serious reputation for 'blocking' independent film makers' access to their footage. In fact, 60 Minutes recently gave a colleague a great deal of assistance in finding the right footage for a very reasonable price. If the Creative Commons can provide a service here, by lobbying for the release of Crown Content, and arguing for increased public funding for access, this is likely to have a tremendous impact on independent film making and public debate in digital environments, and would go a long way to facilitating the sorts of freedoms Creative Commons espouses.

With the Creative Commons online archive, there is a bit of a wait and see attitude. How good is the reference engine, can we find the materials we need easily, and are they useable quality? Is the material we are looking for actually in the Commons? It is hard to think that the Creative Commons 'bank' will come anywhere near the depth and quality of, for example, the 70 year collection of films, photos and sound held by Film Australia. Why set up another archive when a tremendous public resource already exists, and can potentially be added to by users? Further, the archival librarians in public institutions are the unsung heroes of documentary film making, and I cannot see an online engine providing the service they offer to the independent community. I can ring them up and say, "Look, I remember there was a shot of Malcolm Fraser walking out of a court room", and they will say "1974 – Queanbeyan County Court'; and give me details of who shot it, how much footage, and sometimes even a shot list. A filmmaker's time spent searching for usable footage can be extremely costly, and can draw significant attention away from all the other work. If you replace these human wellsprings of knowledge with some sort of digital search engine, what have we lost?

Another issue to touch on briefly is that in our funding agreements we typically assign all rights to the funding body, distributors and broadcasters. Our films cost a lot of money. We do not fund them ourselves. We cannot afford to make these films in a way that would be professionally satisfying, most often because we believe in paying our crews decent wages. To acquire the funding the trade off is that we assign our rights. If the moral rights issues were resolved, most of us would put our films, or bits of them, into the Creative Commons. The thing is, we generally do not own them. To be more specific, one of our biggest problems in contributing to the Commons is that actors are paid residuals and, in order to maximise the money that goes onto the screen – the production values – we buy the most limited licences possible for the distribution required. Generally, the more rights and territories you license, the more it costs. Our licences are limited by medium, territory, duration and use. If we are making a film in Australia, we will generally only licence the relevant Australian rights, otherwise we are spending a lot of money that goes out of the production budget unnecessarily. We could afford another four days' shooting with that money. It is very hard to offer much into Creative Commons, with its worldwide reach, because what we can offer is so limited. Creative Commons therefore has to have a fairly significant engagement with funding institutions like the Australian Film Commission, and of course the Media Entertainment and Arts Alliance (who deal with actors wages and residuals[41] to enable funded film makers to contribute to the Commons. This, as I've said, is best achieved by

---

[41] 'Residuals is the term used to describe royalties paid to actors, directors, and writers for airing programs originally and in subsequent replays and re-runs, and for cassette sales and rentals': Robert G Finney, 'Unions/Guilds' *The Museum of Broadcast Communications*
<http://www.museum.tv/archives/etv/U/htmlU/unionsguilds/unionsguilds.htm> at 28 August 2006.

seeking to have Creative Commons style licensing opportunities incorporated into our production agreements.

These are difficult issues. They may ultimately prove prohibitive for 'professional' film makers. And yet I think there is a general sense of the Commons as a good thing, although it is nothing new. What is relatively new is machine readable licences, the digital exchange, the increased opportunity for sharing and caring, re-mixing and so on. These activities may contribute to opening up the limited number of distribution channels and facilitate public discourse, which, in the Australian independent sector at least, doesn't seem to be in decline. However, like the pre-nuptial, these issues have to be addressed specifically, pragmatically and in detail if the Creative Commons is going to move from a brief, passionate interlude to a sustained and no doubt difficult engagement with the needs and realities of funded film making in this country.

BARRY CONYNGHAM AM

My contribution to this discussion will be from a few perspectives based on my personal experiences as composer, educator and academic manager.

First as a creative professional. I have been an active composer of contemporary classical music for nearly forty years. I think that the changes that have come in music the last few decades are, in fact, paradigm shifts. I was fortunate enough as a musician to enter into the digital age very early in the 1970s at the University of California and at Princeton where I was first exposed to and studied computer-generated music. A few years before, the famous German composer, Karlheinz Stockhausen, said that all the orchestras and all the opera houses would disappear within 30 years and that all music would be electronic. I believed him and set out to see what the future was going to be made of. Well, the opera houses and concert halls are still there but I do not know how many people in this room have heard live non-electronic music recently, other than their own bathroom, singing. Today, virtually all music comes out of loudspeakers; even if we can see the 'live' performer or performers the sound comes to us indirectly, electronically. Even if music involves the voice, or instruments designed and constructed hundreds of years ago, we now mostly, overwhelmingly, hear music and see it being made via electronic means. We all know that this transformation started more than a century ago but the second half of the 20th century saw the completion of the process such that now we conceive, create and experience almost all music with great involvement of synthetic electronic production. Digitally based techniques have accelerated this. With this in mind, issues of reproduction and ownership attribution have all come under pressure. In this context it seems to me any innovation that seeks to create new ways of dealing with fundamental issues of ownership, use and sharing and that appears to be solving problems caused by the changes that have happened in this period, has to be thoroughly interrogated and — if useful and progressive — embraced. But I do think that even in the presentations this morning we run the risk of simplifying the discussion: we have got so used to a black and white world, dare I say a zero and one world, that the debate seems to be happening as if it were a bipolar argument. We must not let simple explications and arguments be the basis of the decision. The interrogation must encompass the complexities and the humanity of the modern world. So as a composer, while I am interested, even excited, by the possibilities of the Creative Commons, I still wish to maintain a sceptical perspective and look carefully at the detail and the implications.

I also react as an educator and teacher. Like many composers, artists and writers, I have been involved in teaching, in my case, creative music teaching, for many years. I think the Creative Commons idea has the power to impact positively on teaching — it assumes freedom to use other people's creative output, which is very valuable when you are learning. When you try to teach people how to make music, one of the things I encourage them to do is to discover all the possibilities — to imagine all the ways a work can go: where can this tune go next, where can this line go next, where can this harmony go next? And I am sure that writers, painters and all creative teachers try to get the developing artist, the student, to know as many of the potential ways of creating a particular piece of work as possible. It seems Creative Commons, by its very nature, is enhancing that. We now live in a market place that covers the world: everything is owned, everything is for sale, including ideas, music and art. Every time you use or sample or test someone else's idea you wonder if you need permission or if you have the right permissions. Maybe that will not always be so, but certainly for the moment the world we live in is essentially market driven on a global basis and therefore something that enables some creative material to be used, tried out, borrowed, extended without having to go through a commercial transaction is very worthwhile.

One of the outcomes of the Creative Commons idea is to facilitate and encourage the mixing of things. Within music, the notion of mixing has always been there. Seventeenth-century composers such as Monteverdi mixed songs of their time to create something new and vibrant. Japanese traditional music was vitalised by mixing different sources of musical material. Classic, pop, jazz — virtually all genres — have been affected by this process. Music is about mixing things. Music, until the last hundred years or so, was also social activity, a shared activity, an instant 'live' activity. Not recorded, not frozen, not made from pre-recorded material. Music was made by people, together. Now, of course, the twin processes of technological change and commercialisation mean most music is recorded and indeed made from the endless mixing of pre-recorded material. This evolution demands constant exploration of the mixing idea. And what is more beautiful than mixing lots of peoples' ideas? In a way it has been ever thus but the consciousness, the tracing of the sources of the mixture is now more explicit. And for a developing musician, it seems to me that to be able to mix things freely, from hopefully the very best of your fellow artists, to extend the range of the possibilities, is a powerful part of learning and finding your own personal expression. To be able to do that in the freest most comfortable way is very attractive.

Like most artists, composers aim to create their work on their own, creating their own world. But to get to that point they must also absorb and experience the art of others. It seems to me that for developing artists, being able to work with any material freely without fear of liability is a liberating force that I quite like. But I do have one major misgiving. It goes back to the nature of creativity. To me, being creative involves imagination and I guess one of the concerns about the nature of a lot of digital art, in all its forms, is that it concentrates more on judging what has come to you and then saying 'yes' or 'no' to it. Selecting, structuring and mixing can become the main activity — even the only activity. For me this is the second stage of being a creative person. The first part is the making of the content or at least the affecting of it in a substantial way. In other words, its not just taking material and deciding whether you like and think it is interesting, or you think someone else might get some pleasure or some intellectual impact from it if you present it in a different context or mix. It is also that you work the material in your own way before you use it.

The key is the use of imagination. For me it is essential that I imagine my worlds before I create them. I am concerned that the way we have taken on the power of digital electronics in music (recorded material) has been dominated by the model of collage. While collage has been very productive, in music, visual arts and all the arts, it is only part of the creative process. So while the Creative Commons may enable greater sharing and access to all the sounds and ideas in music it could have a tendency to reduce the creation of the basic stuff of music. Music will become one huge remix.

My last perspective is as a person responsible for an institution. As the Foundation Vice-Chancellor of Southern Cross University, I perhaps had a slightly different perspective than other CEOs or managers, perhaps a different motivation in my reactions to many things. I was keen to progress the institution and was interested in innovation, new ideas, and new ways of dealing with things. I was willing to take risks. So my first reaction to Creative Commons as an academic manager, the CEO of a new institution, was that I saw it as something that might add to the opportunities and the choices of the University. But my message here is that even in this receptive situation there were restraints. As the person responsible for a complex organization I had to exercise appropriate good sense and healthy scepticism. What looked good on the surface, sounded inspirational and liberating, might not ultimately deliver, or might carry an unseen cost. Also, within any large institution, even a relatively new one, many individuals are inherently conservative, resistant or at least suspicious of the new. There will be people who, if they are established enough, will not want to give up what they have or will be on the lookout for issues that reduce their influence or authority. So to all involved in Creative Commons dealing with institutions: have patience with your friends — they may be drawn to the idea but because of their institutional context they will need to be given strong, balanced and clear arguments.

Finally, a comment on the moral rights issue that was raised this morning. I was fortunate enough to be involved in the campaign for moral rights in Australia from what I think was close to its outset. The fact that the Creative Commons' legal framework has been created in such a short time is quite amazing, given that I remember the first campaign for moral rights in Australia that I was involved in was back in the late 1970's early 1980s. But, as I am sure most of you know, the Australian legislation was only passed very recently. The fact that the legal structures and processes have come together rather quickly here is very encouraging. One observation in relation to moral rights. It seems to me that of all the moral rights that creators desire, attribution seems the strongest. People value acknowledgement. The commercial impact may be far less important to most than the personal impact. I think for most creators, reward of a financial or material nature is secondary to the 'reward' of knowing that you have communicated with your fellow human beings, and they know who you are. If there is wide connection and communication of meaning and it is acknowledged, I think that is worth more than many thousands of dollars. I believe that artists are, foremost, people who are trying to do that — to communicate, to share something, and to say something that will make peoples' lives better. If the creative commons idea with its emphasis on improving the breadth and accessibility of content can do this while protecting the original creator it will have a greater chance of been embraced by those creators.

PROFESSOR GREG HEARN

My question is "why might the business side of the creative industries be interested in the idea of the Creative Commons"? I want to suggest that at least four trends that have some resonance with the idea of a Creative Commons and these are trends that business people are talking about. They are not radical ideas at all. Then I want to talk about what I see might be some of the resonances and some of the challenges as a result of these shifts.

These ideas come out of two or three studies that we have done in CIRAC with the music industry, with the creative industry sectors across Queensland, and now into the national mapping project that we are doing in CIRAC where we are looking at all the sectors of the creative industries. Without being empirically driven by those studies, they are reflections that I have had as a result of that work.

The first shift is from the idea of a consumer to a co-creator of value. You probably have all had the experience of going to IKEA and being co-opted into becoming their labourer and assembling the furniture when you brought it home, so the idea of a co-creation of value is not new or radical. More and more consumers are co-creators of value. In a sense the whole marketing process is about figuring out what is valuable and how to capture that value and produce it. We can talk about students buying a degree from the university. What is the value of that degree and how much do they actually contribute to the creation of the value of that degree through their own labour and their own effort? Think about eBay, an interesting example of co-creation of value, and in the creative industries, as Richard said, this idea is not such a radical idea at all. The best example in our research is in the computer games industry where fans often create the code and, in fact in some cases, own the code. Co-creation of value is an idea whose time has come. The creation of value is not the same as the appropriation of value – who gets to put the value in the bank accounts is a very separate issue – but co-creative activity is a trend that is on the rise.

Another trend is the shift from supply chain thinking to the idea of a value network. In the industrial age, the idea is of a tangible material product moving along a supply chain, from producer, perhaps a beef cattle baron in outback Queensland, to a consumer in a fancy restaurant, perhaps in Japan. In the creative industries, and in all sorts of other industries, that idea of a supply chain is giving way to the idea of a much more complicated set of relationships that could be described best as a value network. Everybody in that network has to create value and add value to be part of the network, otherwise the network will simply route around them. A network has the advantage that it is multi-directional and that there is more than one path that is possible.

Value networks are a trend that is more and more manifested in the creative industries as well. As a result the shift is from value residing in products, individual products, to the value actually residing in the network. Everybody has a Visa Card, the value of a Visa Card does not reside in the piece of plastic, but resides in the number of people and services that it connects you to. Operating systems are, of course, the classic example of network value. It just happens that our operating system has been appropriated by one company, but nevertheless the value is not really in the code, it is in the connection and in the cost of changing that network and including other examples that we could point to. I guess you could say movies, that typically rely a lot on word of mouth, are an example again of the value in the network, because word of mouth is simply a cultural network, and the value of all sorts of products in the creative industries, in particular, are driven by cultural networks.

From simple co-operation models or simple competition models, the idea of complex 'competition' is another trend to consider. A beautiful word coined by a couple of business academics but simply means that in any value ecology there are not just competitors and consumers; there are suppliers, competitors and there are complementors. There are companies that are not your direct competitor that are nevertheless very important in your particular ecology because without their product, your product has no value. Microsoft has no value without Intel. And more and more we need to understand the way our value has been created as being an ecosystem of both competitors and co-operators. That is not a radical idea; that is just the way that business works, and moreover, those roles change in quite a dynamic way. People who are your competitors one day may be collaborators the next day. We need to get away from simple ideas of cooperation or competition.

Finally, there is an important shift from thinking about the creation of value at the level of individual firms, to the need to think about whole innovation systems. Firms simply do not survive unless they are part of a labour market, where they need to have access to skills. They need to have appropriate legal infrastructure, and they exercise their corporate activity in the context of government policy and government interventions. In thinking about how value is created, it is not just created in firms; it is created in a total innovation system. I think a lot of those ideas characterise thinking in business generally these days and they also characterise and are exemplified in a number of cases in the creative industries as the canary down the mine of the innovative sector, that is, in some senses out in front of other industrial sectors.

How does the concept of Creative Commons then resonate with those kinds of ideas? Well I think there are some obvious ones, and I think there are also some obvious challenges. There is a resonance in the sense that Creative Commons is clearly inspired by the idea of networks. Also value creation in the Creative Commons is a network function and that is something that business processes are evolving towards anyway. Ideally it reduces transaction costs, which means that ecologies are more efficient. It builds skills and creates a labour market which, both Barry Conyngham and Richard Jones saw as also being a very valuable part for film and music sectors. It allows naturally competitive and/or cooperative relationships by the variety of licences that you can structure.

I am arguing that the world of Creative Commons and the world of the corporate are not that far apart if you are looking, perhaps, into the future over maybe a decade or so (perhaps even shorter than that). There are a number of evolutionary trends in the way that social life and business, as being part of that, is evolving, that come together around the idea of a Creative Commons. But I do not think it is all necessary light and no dark. Networks are often thought of as a good thing because everybody is involved with them, but networks are not necessarily, or inherently, equalitarian. Networks themselves evolve to quite large discrepancies in the number of nodes that are connected to particular players. I suspect that in the network economy, inequality is going to be as much of an issue as it is already and so issues of appropriation and distribution are obviously also notions we need to consider.

Case Studies

Open Content Licensing Initiatives

AEShareNET

Open Digital Rights Language (ODRL)

Youth Internet Radio Network (YIRN)

Australian Creative Resources Online (ACRO)

> PROFESSOR ARUN SHARMA, CAROL FRIPP, DENNIS
> MCNAMARA, DR RENATO IANELLA, JEAN BURGESS,
> MARK FALLU AND DAVE ROONEY

Open Content Licensing Initiatives
*This section focuses on some specific instances of people working on projects related to Open Content Licensing. The Chair for this session at the conference was **Professor Arun Sharma**, Deputy Vice-Chancellor of Research at QUT.*

AESharenet
***Carol Fripp** and **Dennis McNamara** discuss the AESharenet open licensing project for educational institutions and material.*

Open Digital Rights Language
***Dr Renato Ianella** looks at the use of Rights Expression Language in Digital Rights Management Technologies, and in particular the Open Digital Rights Language and its use in relation to the Creative Commons licences.*

YIRN: Youth Internet Radio Network
*This section, prepared by **Jean Burgess** and **Mark Fallu**, focuses on the case study YIRN: Youth Internet*

Radio Network, which aims to establish an online network of young content providers across Queensland.

ACRO: Australian Creative Resources Online
Dave Rooney *discusses Australian Creative Resources Online (ACRO) an online database of multi-media objects.*

Professor Brian Fitzgerald
(Head, QUT Law School)

Open Content Licensing Initiatives

PROFESSOR ARUN SHARMA

I have been a spectator of open source for quite a while. The first operating system I used as an undergraduate student in the early 1980s was a form of Unix and since then I have stuck with Unix. In the early 1990s I was a post doc at MIT at the time Richard Stallman was becoming a cult figure, who in some sense was a precursor to what Linus Torvalds did in the 1990s. If you try to look at the history of open source it is replete with examples of how things have happened. But, while I have always respected, and been amused by, and admired, people working on open source, I have always felt that they have become a little evangelical, and at times, very strident. The game has to be at the intersection where you have a system that has a continuum, where people can move from one part of transacting business to the other part – sometimes it is commercial, sometimes it is something that you just want to be given away for free, and sometimes you want to give something under certain considerations.

The fact that it is good for society to have multiple ways of these things happening, some commercial, some free, some restricted free, came home to me when I was the Head of the School of Computer Science and Engineering at the University of NSW. I was the Head during the IT boom. It was a School that attracted some of the most talented students in New South Wales. We were producing more than a hundred first-class honours graduates per year during the boom and I had all these talented students and I needed to do something with them. In turn, I found that mostly they were three types of personality. One particular group was highly academic, motivated by the sheer elegance of ideas and these were the students who no matter what you did with them were going to do a PhD. There was another group, extremely intelligent, highly aggressive, wanting to make money. They really were out there to start a company, get a job, do something and get ahead in life. They were as talented as my best students, who were going to become academic stars. And then there was another group. In terms of intellectual ability they were equal to the first two groups, but they were a bit more laid back. They felt that ideas ought to be free. They looked like hippies; they had long hair. They were equally excited about doing something that was good and I pondered 'what I am going to do with them?', and I decided 'I am going to give some resources to each of the three groups'.

For the students who were talented and wanted to be academics, I gave them summer research scholarships, lots of money; so they did not have to go and flip burgers or work at the supermarket. Any job they wanted, they could just work in the University, work with researchers and be happy. With the group that really wanted to go places, I partnered with the Australian Graduate School of Management, got a bank to give $30,000 a year, and created the Business Planning Competition, which really excited them. For the open source group, a highly talented group of people, I gave them resources to create, become part of the open source movement, and even funded them to organise an international Linux User Group Conference which attracted 400 researchers from around the world.

The interesting thing was that by giving resources to all these three people, I basically said 'go out and show each other'. They hated each other. They wanted to prove the point that they were superior and I can tell you all three groups achieved. The thing that came back to me is that the world is not going to be coloured by a single commercial way of doing things or a single way of the intellectual elegance of ideas, nor is it going to be something where everything is going to be free. It will always be a continuum. There is a place for talented groups of people of different personalities and we need to support each of them.

Another experience with this kind of thing is that I was once co-opted into working with a project coming out of Carnegie Mellon University in the US, the Million Book Visual Library Project. It is being driven by computer scientists and librarians and the aim is to digitise as a demonstration case one million books that are out of copyright. From the computer scientist perspective it is to create a demonstration for extremely interesting software search engine techniques. If everything that has been written is digitised and also can be scanned in text form, it provides a test-bed for doing a more interesting search, where we can search the history of the development of a certain idea (that the software can do for us). It will provide a significant research tool that can take the web from being a search engine to a discovery engine. That is the motivation from the computer scientist perspective. The librarians have the perspective that if this happens then they will be able to provide higher value added services to the users of the library by helping them become their research assistants. The project is very interesting; the pilot was funded by the National Science Foundation. Minolta provided scanners at very low cost, some of the US research universities provided the books and the Governments of India and also China provided the labour for scanning. The books are being shipped to India and they are being scanned. There are lots of logistical problems in this but the good thing is that it is close to 100,000 books that have now been scanned.

The challenge is: what you are doing is great; you are creating new content and you are going to put this thing over the Internet and have an open content licensing scheme, but it is about the legacy. What do we do with all these books, which are still in copyright? The author has died, and the relatives own the copyright but no one cares. This team is working on ways where people can surrender their copyrights, or if you cannot find the author or the owner of the copyright, you can at least place the book on the web with the caveat that if the owner of the copyright comes in, you will take it off. Whether that is legally kosher or not is a different question and the lawyers are working on these ideas. And that will provide a very interesting perspective on how these ideas will develop. At the end of the day it will be a combination of open content licensing and also the commercial solution. These are some of the influences that I have had in dealing with these issues.

Computer scientists tend to build systems that are very generic. We say we will build a machine learning system that will learn anything. We will design a software development tool that will design any kind of software tool. Very soon we find out that it does not work. What we then do is find two ways to constrain our problem. One is we look at a specific domain; we say I am only going to develop software in the area of business or I am going develop software in the area of mining or in the area of educational software, and then the problem becomes manageable. The alternative approach is the very large project, and I am doing it in a very informal way. Can I do it in a more formal way? We start resorting to the language of mathematical logic to specify the problem, to find the proof checking mechanisms so that the semantics of our intentions can be verified. And that leads to things like Digital Rights Management.

This session is representing both these constraining mechanisms. The first topic about AEShareNet is taking the ideas of open content licensing into the educational content software, in the educational content areas. The second topic is about Open Visual Rights language and applying it to the subject of Creative Commons.

AEShareNET

CAROL FRIPP AND DENNIS MCNAMARA

CAROL FRIPP

I could not agree more with Tom Cochrane. I never thought I would be 'Copyright Carol' in the last vocational aspiration that I have ended up in. If I look at my own children, who probably reflect society, two of them have absolutely no understanding of what I do, and do not want to. The other two are mortified that I would be involved in copyright control because they download everything. I live in the world that represents society.

The session we are talking about this morning is in summary. We do want to talk about open content and you have already heard that Roger Clarke as Chair of our Board has been writing articles since being involved with this company on open content, and they are worth reading. They are on his website and if anyone wants to follow up some of the research in that, I am sure you would find that debate. There are quite a large number of articles emerging as we go through the journey.

We want to talk about the licence templates and for those who think they know something about us we hope to add some new things to our presentation this morning, because we are changing. We are really about finding other peoples' resources. That is one of the primary purposes that we exist. We are set up for education. We started in vocational education but we do go across all the areas where there is any form of vocational education occurring. It takes us across the secondary and right through to higher education and into the enterprise and corporation area and we are finding those are expanding as we go on the journey.

The challenge is quick access and even though the technologies are advancing, it is very difficult to get some of these accesses working. This audience is probably familiar with Google, currently working on a new project to catalogue large numbers of university resources which will change the way people start looking at how they want to find material, because we are finding people do like the Google approach. I do not know if it happens in the libraries in your organisation, but are you happy with the control vocabularies and specialist search engines any more? Or do you want to type in one or two words and *hey presto* it is up in front of you?

Most of our search capacities are really not set up like Google and I am wondering how long before we will be challenged. Users want easy assurance of the copyright clearances. That is still a very difficult one when a lot of educators work the night before they start delivery the next day (or in the world that I work in, that is certainly the case) and sometimes getting clearances the night before is challenging if you have not done your homework. And they are always mortified you cannot download it and use it without going through some long and protracted process that some bureaucrat in their organisation put in there for them.

Inexpensive learning resources – you have heard about that – continue to be an enormous debate. We get everything from zero dollars through to thousands or multi-thousands. People have varying expectations of what those resources are worth and in the marketplace sometimes they are not worth anywhere near what people think. They often have accountants in their organisations that are driving their competitive and commercial agenda. And the methodology to avoid the duplication of effort is one of the biggest challenges I see. We still have a culture in many areas that believes they cannot take someone else's work and build on it very well because it is something about yourself. It is about your portrayal of your image to the world and sometimes you look at someone else's work and think, 'they have not quite got it right; I think I will do it my way'. Trying to get people to re-use is sometimes a challenge and we are finding that certainly is not as easy as we had hoped.

What is ShareNet? Yes you know it is a company set up by Ministers. We would say that we are probably the first working model that we know of that has tried to set up a marketplace for both sharing and trading, and it is online. It was put online before online was even there, and it was a very brave and visionary thing to do in a world that, at that time when this concept was put together, was not working online. We still struggle with systems where people still are not online enough to take advantage of what we have to offer. We are still in front of many of the clients that we work with. Yes, we are a trading marketplace and that does not always mean money, but we operate as a broker and, if you have had experience of brokers in any form you might have views of what brokers should and should not do. That is what our webpage now looks like if you have not seen us for a while, slightly different. The main interest there is the search engine because that is really the core of our business, finding the resource, and connecting you to a player.

What do we provide? We provide, as you can see, material to anyone. We are on the Internet. Anyone can discover us anywhere in the world and anywhere in the world often does. You can acquire a licence online to use and adapt the resources and we have several of those. If you are the owner of a resource you can make that available. We do not hold the resource; we never have and we really do not want to unless people have a particular case and obtain permissions for use, so that people are clear about what they can and cannot do – a bit like Creative Commons – clarifying some of the ownership issues so people know what is going on.

The model: we have six trademarks called protocols and I am not a lawyer either, I am a practitioner, so protocols are often a strange word for people to get their head around. Four of those particular licences can be used within the system, or without the system. What we do offer is probably a little different in that we have standardised or consistent templates that simplify things for people.

It is like going to a real estate agent. You are used to getting a standardised contract. You know where to look for things, so we try to make it easier by getting people familiar with the copyright contract. Most people, in my experience, do not want to read a copyright contract. We have consistent meta-data that is used by the education sector, so the terms are familiar to people. They are used to coming up with certificates, diplomas, certain vocabulary that they work with in their, hopefully, most of their working time, and we have the online brokering system which you can see if you go through the site.

What we do is link to repositories that are evolving. We link to large numbers of collections. They might be a very small number; they might be half a dozen, or they can be very large bureaucracies where there could be something like 11-15,000 available resources. We are starting to see people play around with that repository idea as they try to link things and figure out how to use the trade marks across those repositories, which is quite exciting. If you are trying to look at your own work and make a choice that is the first place to start. One of the differences you will see on ours that may not be in many of the others, is there is capacity to vet any changes made (if you want to action that option), where some of the others do not give you a vetting option. Not all people take that up but it is there if they need it.

The 'Free for Education' protocol was developed as a response to the marketplace, and it was quite a radical change to everything else we were doing at that time. Everything else went through our system. This is one where you put the logo on a piece of work and there are series of conditions that apply to that, so it does not go through our system at all. Much like Creative Commons, you can go into a search engine and put in 'Free for Education' and see what is available. We had this developed through the Government Solicitor Office because people were wanting a lot more information and education about copyright and simplifying what copyright really means. They do not use the word 'contextualisation' in their daily work place generally or 'enhancement' or 'compilation', so we help people come to terms with working with particular material, what they are doing or want to do with that, and that helps them then find some way to get through the copyright maze.

We are refining that search engine because, like all search engines, it has its limitations. Part of this recent work is to play around with certain concepts. What we are finding useful is on the website. The other thing that we are changing (this is fairly new and we will be putting out more information) is what we call our other free or sharing protocols – the 'U' for 'Unrestricted', the 'P' for 'Preserve' and the 'S' for 'Standard'. They are all about sharing your content, usually with no money involved, and we intend to free them up and get them out there into the market place for much wider use. The licences that we broker for those people who do want to commercialise material are our 'C' and our 'E' – the 'Customisable' (or some people call it 'Commercial') and the 'E' for the 'End User Licence' and they are the ones that we are finding there is a lot more interest in because people do want, in many cases, to play around with conditions and play around with money.

What can you do? You can search; you can find; you can preview. We have various degrees of sophistication although some of it is not sophisticated. This is not Amazon. It is very much an educational organisation or an Ebay, but some of the previews are getting a lot better and available for purchase. You can access our database and find a resource that will link you to the copyright owner through standard internet protocols. If you find something you like, you press a button and you have a licence. We have examples where that takes 2 minutes from beginning to end. At the other side where people want to talk a lot more it can take a longer period of time.

Dennis McNamara

This is the schizophrenic part of the company where you think about charging for open content (it is probably heretical in this conference to say we should charge for licences). We have found in working, particularly, with vocational education but also with education generally, that if you wanted to open up IP, wanted to open up content for maximum use, sometimes you had to have money changing hands, otherwise it was not going to work. I was thinking yesterday when we heard about the Smart State in Queensland, it is quite difficult even to get a Queensland public education organisation to give any content to a New South Wales public education organisation because the Queensland public education organisation will think, 'why should we use Queensland's taxpayers' money to subsidise New South Wales'? In fact, if you want to get sharing happening across even state borders, let alone between private and private, and public and private, if you do not have money changing hands it just will not happen as easily as we would like. One example is a 3-D animation of a body part, owned by a multi-media company in Sydney, and produced for the medical industry at great expense. The company licences this animation to education for a very small sum of money. Medical courses, science courses, all sorts of courses, would make very good use of them, but education could never probably afford to produce those resources. The fact that they can get them fairly cheaply is an advantage.

Why would anyone want to charge for open content? Because they think it is part of their business to do so. Why would anyone pay for open content? Because you get it a lot cheaper than you would if you produced it yourself, so it is a win/win situation. We believe that in the open content space there needs to be room for both share-ware, allowing things to be freely given, and as our Chair has said, also for charging for content to change hands. We think both need to happen and we would like to do both for education.

In November 2004 we ran a conference on 'Unlocking Intellectual Property' where a lot of issues were made about the cost of transactions. What we are trying to do by being a broker of open content is to make it easier for organisations to trade without too much cost to them and that is a typical way of brokers working the share industry and any other industry. We have a system when we broker a licence. We also collect all the money and we reimburse people. We do all the accounting functions, all the GST functions and handle all Ebanking. If you own content and you want to charge for it but you do not want to charge too much, you only want to charge for example 10, 20 or a hundred dollars and you do it yourself, the cost of a transaction makes it counter-productive to even think about doing. But if you work through a broker, you can have money changing hands in a reasonably efficient way. Whether that is sustainable long-term remains to be seen. At the moment that seems to be a reasonably efficient way for people to proceed. The way it works is basically: you cannot obviously use our system, our brokerage, without being an AEShareNet member, but you put your stuff up, someone requests a licence, you can negotiate the conditions of the licence, or you can just accept the conditions as they are, that negotiation happens online.

To give you an example, you might put a material up and say this resource is only available for use in Australia. Someone may come along and say 'can I use it in New Zealand or India?' and you can say yes or no. Depending on if you have any embedded copyright restrictions in the resources, you can make that happen online through an online transaction. At the end of the day, we collect the money and reimburse the owners. It is a typical brokerage offering, which we think is adding value in the education sector to allow people to move resources between institutions, between public and private and so on.

You can glimpse our changing resources and see the status of the licences, in terms of whether they are draft, under negotiation, payment pending, on our site. Notice that I deliberately use the words 'sell site' and 'buy site' to show that there is a lot of business activity there. A variety of organisations that put resources up such as TAFE South Australia, have both 'licences in' resources and 'licences out' resources and they think they are better off by doing that. They make money on some of the resources they have developed. They pay money out for resources they access from elsewhere, but a lot less than if they developed it themselves. That is the kind of basic philosophy of our open content for money approach.

There are just a couple of things I want to say about some of the challenges we face in making this work. Once we develop and review resources we work out where the copyright might lie if we have not cleared it first, and then work out what can be done. This is more of a cottage industry model. You may finish up under that model with two teachers, two academics in the same institution at the same time working on producing learning resources and they may not have collaborated or know each other was doing it. If we are going to make maximum use of resources, without suggesting we go into a McDonald's model where you get the same hamburger everywhere, there might need to be more organisational faculty decisions about what programmes are run, what resources are developed and to think about what resources exist that we can build on before we start developing them. Rather than always take material and build it from scratch and then licensing resources from outside, keep records of what you have done and then licence out products to others whether for free or for money. My contention is that even if you want to give stuff away, you cannot give it away if you do not know that you own it, so it is important to get those things right.

I suggest there is a lot more to open content licensing than just developing the templates. We need business models and transaction platforms. Learning resources need to be accessible but they do not always need to be free, as we have been suggesting. The trick is to get the balance right for sharing and trading in what can be a competitive educational environment. You might be bidding for the same funds, bidding for the same students, or in straight competition between public and private providers.

I want to mention the licence template 'Free For Education' that we put up for those people who would like to licence their products, content, systems, whatever, for educational use but not other people. This is an example of one that has gone live today. I got a phone call this morning about this. It is educational software produced by an organisation that mainly works in the finance industry – training and doing professional development for financial people – and this organisation is happy to licence this to educational organisations for nothing but they would not want to give it away to their competitors. They would not want to go as far as open source software on this but they are happy for educational organisations to use their software for free. That is a good example of where the 'Free for Education' fills a particular need for educational organisations in the open content space.

Open Digital Rights Language (ODRL)

DR RENATO IANELLA

Note: this paper has been updated for December 2007

Let me start with a few words about Digital Rights Management (DRM). As usual, it was mentioned in other talks in the negative, which is fair because DRM does have some negative aspects about it. But I want to give you a different view from the DRM world. Then I will look at the Open Digital Rights Language (ODRL) Initiative. I will then look at the Creative Commons' semantics in more detail, how we mapped them to ODRL and some of the issues that we found when we were doing the mapping exercises that we feel are quite significant and should be raised. Finally, briefly, I will look at the potential to do a similar thing for the AEShareNet licences.

Creative Commons licences are represented in three ways: there is the legal code, the human code and then there is the machine code. All three are very critical to the overall licences, but what I will be presenting here is more aimed at the machine code. I will ask: how have the licences been represented at the computer level and how can they best be represented?

DRM covers two main areas. There is the information about the rights - the rights information management - and that is about who the rights holders are, what the licences are, what the royalty payments are, etc. Then there are is the enforcement/security side, or the technical protection measures, including the trusted environments. This is usually that area that gets DRM bad press as it is squarely at the consumer end. The consumer sees the way the content is encrypted and the way that limits the end user experience or changes the way the end user has to interact with that content. A lot of current DRM systems really do just focus on the security side and do not care about rights information management.

There are positive examples of DRM working, such as Apple's iTunes/iPod service. Most of the consumers who buy and download songs to their iPods have no idea that DRM is in there because it is well hidden, which it should be. And it still allows the consumer to do what they normally expect to do with their music, which is just play it an unlimited amount of times and also, in some cases, to make copies for a fixed number of times to different devices.

The technical view of DRM also needs to be balanced with the social, legal and business sides. The DRM value chain needs to support both of the two DRM areas as the rights management information normally has to travel from the beginning to the end of the value chain (ie from when content is created to when it is being used) and at the end, we need to have the rights information there. The enforcement is usually at the consumer end, so it is downstream, the last thing that happens. Usually, the content is encrypted or somehow encoded so that only a particular consumer or device can consume it.

The key here is in the rights management information metadata that is being captured in what is now called 'Rights Expression Languages' (REL), a new sub-discipline, if you like, of DRM. In terms of standards, there are basically two standard bodies that deal with DRM at the international level. There are others, but the main ones are the Open Mobile Alliance, which is the mobile sector, and then there is the MPEG-21 standard, which is the audio/video sector. In MPEG-21, Parts 4, 5 and 6 deal with DRM. There is at the moment up to fourteen parts, but those three deal with DRM. Since 2000, we have seen a bit of a standards "war". There was a battle between two rights languages, XrML and ODRL, and the two different standards bodies chose two different languages. There is a lot of politics behind that, which makes life interesting, but it basically came down to the typical "Microsoft versus The Rest of the World" battle; Microsoft owning XrML and "The Rest of the World" not wanting that technology in their standards. To this date, the war is not over. In fact it is probably hotting up at the moment because there are also a lot of DRM patent claims being fought over in this area. This is going to make life very difficult for implementers of DRM systems and devices because it will make it uncertain as to what your liabilities are.

In early January 2005 the MPEG Licensing Authority issued a press release stating the terms and conditions for licensing the Open Mobile Alliance (OMA) DRM specifications. Interestingly, we have one standards group telling the other standards groups how much they are going to have to pay to implement their own DRM standard. It is fun and games in that area. ODRL and XrML are two rights expression languages, which are extensible expression languages. You can express anything you like in them, but they do come with their own dictionaries of common terms.

The scope of RELs is explored in a report which came out of the UK in

2004[42]. It looked at where rights expressions are captured in the entire value chain and it went through these processes:

- Recognition of rights,
- Assertion of rights,
- Expression of rights,
- Dissemination of rights,
- Exposure of rights, and
- Enforcement of rights.

The ODRL Initiative is an initiative that has been running since 2000, originally developed by IPR Systems. They obtained additional partners, like Nokia and RealNetworks, and incorporated their specific rights expression languages into the ODRL language. The ODRL Initiative has an independent governance board that looks over the governance issues and promotes ODRL to larger standards groups. They have had success in OMA, and have also published a World Wide Web Consortium (W3C) Note. They have also submitted ODRL Version 1.1 to National Information Standards Organization (NISO), which is the US standards body.

A number of ODRL working groups are now looking at how to develop the language further. We have one looking at Version 2 and, of course, the Creative Commons Profile working group. We are also looking at GeoSpatial data and, in early 2005, the Dublin Core Joint Working Group was announced to look at how to use Dublin Core and ODRL together. We are also planning a NISO/Library Joint Working Group that will look at joining the needs of the library community with ODRL.

The core model of ODRL is shown in Figure 1. There are three main aspects we look at: 'rights', 'parties' and 'content'. Parties and content can be further exploded into different aspects, as well as the core rights in terms of the permissions, constraints, the conditions and requirements. These are the key aspects to any rights expression language, not just ODRL.

---

[42] Joint Information Systems Committee (JISC), *JISC Digital Rights Management Study* (2004) <http://www.intrallect.com/drm-study/>

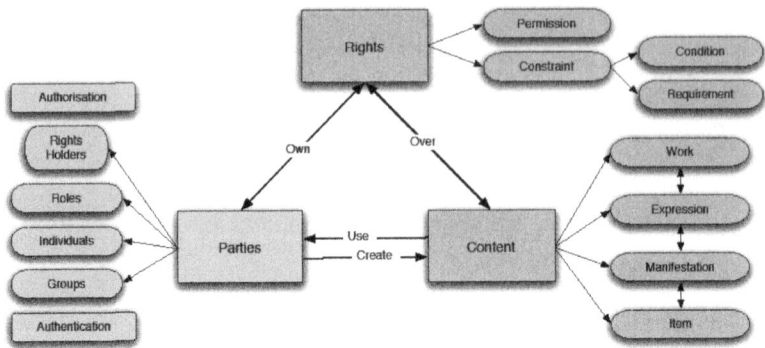

Figure 1

In a commercial example (see Figure 2), we have a famous author or retail store owning some content, having some rights holders, and able to embark upon an agreement to sell the content with a particular constraint (eg a specific country limitation). Each requirement and constraint is optional so you do not have to always have a payment attached, you can simply express the rights in that value chain, for example in the education sector. Then that person or retail store can then make subsequent agreements with other people (eg Joe Consumer) to acquire the content under different types of conditions and constraints (eg print only once).

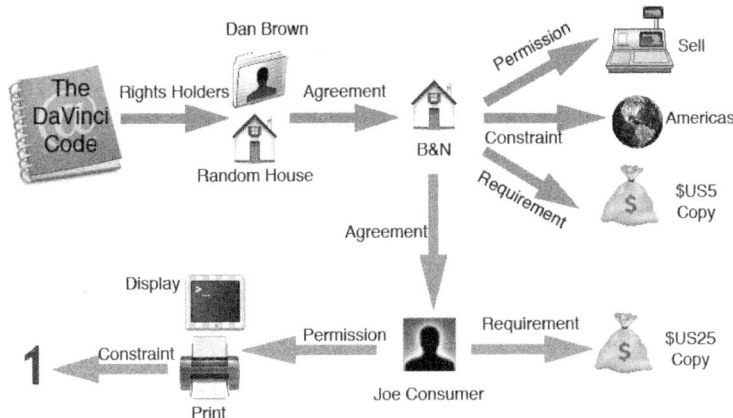

Figure 2

Creative Commons has three aspects to its licences. There are 'permissions', 'prohibitions' and there are 'requirements' – similar to the

ODRL model but not exactly the same. Each of those aspects have a number of fixed values under them and a collection of those makes up a particular Creative Commons Licence. They are technically expressed in RDF/XML, which is another issue for RELs, because the major RELs are expressed in XML Schema and not RDF/XML. That becomes a bit of an interoperability issue, but something that can be overcome.

The ODRL/Creative Commons Joint Working Group started at the end of 2004 and released the final specification in July 2005[43]. The motivation was to see how to express CC semantics in the ODRL language and the benefit of that is that it allows users to use a more expressive language – so that they can then add additional and key information to those licence terms. The actual core semantics of a CC licence includes:

- three permissions – reproduction, distribution, derivative works
- one prohibition – commercial use, and
- four requirements – notice, attribution, share alike and source code.

A combination of these makes up various CC licences.

To give you an example of some of the issues we found with the CC licences, if you look at 'attribution' for example, 'attribution' says that "credit must be given to the copyright holder and/or author". But in many cases, if you acquire content under this attribution licence, you may not know who the copyright holder is or the author. If you have a music file, or an audio file, it does not tell you who the author and the rights holders are, and how to attribute them whenever you reproduce this content for your own uses. We are still lacking some key information there. We need to be able to specify who are the authors of the content, who are the rights holders and how should you attribute them. Do you pop up a window, or do you write a bit of text on the screen? How do you do that?

Each CC licence has its own unique identity, via a URL, and is made up of a set of permissions, constraints and requirements. When we map these to ODRL, the permissions were the same as ODRL, requirements are the same, but prohibitions were not in our model because in ODRL, and other rights expression languages, we have the concept that whatever is explicit in the licence is what is only allowed. If you do not allow something, then you do not put it in licence. If you do not allow commercial use, then you

---

[43] 'Creative Commons Profile' *Open Digital Rights Language (ODRL) Initiative* (July 2005) <http://odrl.net/Profiles/CC/SPEC.html>

do not put it in the licence. It is very simple. Whatever is in the licence is what you are allowed to do.

What we had to do is map the CC prohibitions to ODRL constraints and then change them from the negative to the positive. We can have a constraint of commercial use, which is the same as a prohibition of non-commercial use, and that is what we had to do in the ODR/CC profile. The CC semantics have much broader concepts than some ODRL terms. They have terms like 'reproduction' whereas ODRL has terms like 'print', 'display', 'play', 'execute' – very specific terms that are obviously meant for a machine to interpret and manage. We decided that it was probably not a good idea to map to those four low-level terms because reproduction could include more than those four. We created new semantics for 'reproduction' and the other broader CC concepts. The same for the requirements, but we did have attribution as part of the ODRL data dictionary so we used that directly. See Figure 3 for the final mapping.

CC Licence	ODRL Permission	ODRL Constraint	ODRL Requirement
Attribution	Reproduction Distribution Derivative Works		Notice Attribution
Attri-NoDerivs	Reproduction Distribution		Notice Attribution
Attr-NonComm-NoDerivs	Reproduction Distribution	Non Commercial Use	Notice Attribution
Attr-NonComm	Reproduction Distribution Derivative Works	Non Commercial Use	Notice Attribution
Attr-NonComm-Share	Reproduction Distribution Derivative Works	Non Commercial Use	Notice Attribution Share-A-Like
Attr-Share	Reproduction Distribution		Notice Attribution Share-A-Like

Figure 3

Some of the additional features that you can use after we have created ODRL licences are that you can specify who the rights holders are, specify details of attributions, have greater fine-grained control over constraints, such as country or regions. If you want to allow distribution of your content but only within geographical bounds we can specify that.

We can also identify the asset directly as well. Creative Commons' licences do not directly identify the asset; they just assume it is been linked to from somewhere else. And, of course, we have a much richer set of permissions, constraints and requirements, etc. The other additional benefit is that ODRL has the identity of the person accepting the agreement. It does not have to, but it can allow you to be very specific about who is accepting this agreement. With CC licences, most of those licences are implicit – you just implicitly accept them – versus in ODRL we can make it very explicit. The benefit for that is, as the end consumer, I can then have a transaction that says, 'yes, I have got your content and I have got them under these conditions', so that I can use them for the conditions specified and there is no way that you can then say, later on, "well, I did not, I have changed my mind and I am withdrawing that". It gives the end consumer a bit more confidence that they can use the licences.

We found a few more examples of some of the mapping issues in some of the other licences of Creative Commons. For example, sampling licences allow people to take your work and transform it, for any purpose other than advertising. The problem we found was that there were no new semantics defined in the CC machine code for these licences. There are other prohibitions, like commercial use, but they did not define the semantics for prohibiting advertising, which is clearly part of a licence, but does not appear in the machine semantics. There are a few issues like that we are feeding back to the Creative Commons team to see whether they can update their machine semantics to make it clearer what you can and cannot do in the licences. The same problem exists in the music sharing licence. This licence says it has the same semantics as the "attribution, non-commercial, no derivatives" licence, which says you are free to copy, distribute, display or perform the work. But the music sharing licence says legally you can "download, copy, file, share, trade, distribute and publicly perform it". Trade is part of the licence description and could be misinterpreted in many ways. It could mean selling it – which is against the non-commercial term - so there are some semantics that need to be seriously tightened up.

Another final example is in the CC developing nations licence. They have created new licence semantics because the developing nation licence allows your work to be used royalty free in any nation that is not classified as a high income economy by the World Bank. The semantics include the standard permissions and requirements, and they have added a new semantic called 'high income nation use', which is a prohibition. They have added this extra prohibition in the licence description, but it does not appear in the machine code.

The ODRL/Creative Commons profile will show how you express CC licenses in the ODRL language. As another example, we are looking at potentially doing the same process for the AEShareNet licences - to be able to take their semantics and represent them in machine code. It will be very interesting because we will then be able to mix some of the AEShareNet concepts of vetting and consolidation with some of the Creative Commons concepts of notice and attribution, with some of the additional ODRL semantics. It is a good example of mixing different semantics together for different licence profiles.

There are other aspects of the licences that we need to develop further and ODRL Version 2 is still evolving. But one of the things we always had feedback on was how you support copyright exceptions in these licenses, because most other agreements will exclude the copyright exceptions. In ODRL Version 2 - that we are currently working on at the moment - we will allow people to put in an explicit part of the licence that says that the copyright exceptions from a particular jurisdiction have to be honoured as part of the licence terms. We cannot get into the specific details of what those exceptions are because it depends on the content and the jurisdictional laws, but we will be able to put that in the licence - so that you can make available to people agreements that allow them to preserve the copyright exceptions for use in the traditional areas.

To sum up, we notice that rights expressing languages are, in many cases, too expressive. That is why a number of community profiles are now being developed. Creative Commons is a very good example of that because we need to focus on what is needed by the end consumers and by the content providers and express those licences only. One of the interesting ideas is whether there is a potential to consolidate the ODRL language with the Creative Commons machine language. The more times you create additional machine languages, the more programming is required and software will not interoperate, etc. so this could be a potential to try and consolidate the two languages together.

Youth Internet Radio Network (YIRN)

JEAN BURGESS AND MARK FALLU

JEAN BURGESS

The Youth Internet Radio Network (YIRN) project is an Australian Research Council funded incorporation with industry partners including, the Office of Youth Affairs, Department of Communities, Arts Queensland, Brisbane City Council, and QMusic. The research team is Professor John Hartley, Greg Hearn, Jo Tacchi and Tanya Notley. Jo and Tanya are the two most active researchers. I have been involved with some of the content creation and training workshops as part of the first year of the development of the network.

Briefly, the Youth Internet Radio Network project uses a methodology called Ethnographic Action Research to develop and investigate a network of young content creators and youth oriented organisations from across Queensland. The most visible aspect of the network will be a website, which is going to be called not YIRN but sticky.net.au. Its aims include establishing a network of young content providers across Queensland, identifying opportunities for youth enterprise development, providing and facilitating training to young people in new media content development and considering policy level implications for the establishment of online youth networks and for enabling young people in different contexts to participate.

There are two core principles that relate to my interests in the democratisation of technologies and in how that might assist us to build a broader base of cultural participation in general. The first of these is intercreativity, which is a term that is used by the YIRN research team, most specifically to highlight the conceptual shift to inter-creativity from the older idea of interactivity. Interactivity was one of the buzz words of the early 1990s. With the advent of the World Wide Web, there is the suggestion of a more powerful sense of user engagement with media texts, individualised personalised media use and greater user choice.

For the Internet, Graham Meikle believes that the term interactivity implies greater autonomy and agency for its users, but it is often loosely defined and loosely deployed. He gives the example (often it boils down to really just an increasing array of consumer choices) in his book, *Future Active,* of going to the Republican Party website and clicking on a link marked 'On

Line Activism' and being taken straight to the Gift Shop. Building on Tim Berners-Lee's concept of intercreativity, Meikle makes this important distinction between interactive use, choosing between options already mapped out for us, and intercreativity: the potential not only to interact but to collaborate, communicate and create, and that is very much a core principle and guiding motivation for the Youth Internet Radio Network in general.

There is a plan for three content creation workshops at each of the regional sites in Queensland over a two year period and we have just finished the first series of those content creation workshops, using a methodology called 'Digital Storytelling'. Digital stories can best be understood as short, personal, multi-media tales. In a group workshop, participants collaborate together with each other and with trainers to develop a personal narrative, which they record as a voice-over and then they combine with images that they may have scanned from their own photo albums, or have captured digitally. They put all this together in a video editing program and end up with a two-minute short film. The three stories I am going to show highlight the type of content that is going to be on the network, although there will be many others.

The actual content of the film gives some idea of what types of creative content multimedia and interaction we might expect to see on the network. That is really exciting. The other important point I want to make about the film is that the first two stories are very much the kind of creative showcase stories where young people are using the medium, the opportunity to make a digital story which they know will be available eventually to the general public. They used this opportunity to showcase a particular creative pursuit that they are really interested in, hopefully, having some kind of entrepreneurial outcome.

The first story is entitled *Photography*. Here the creator actually came to this interest in photography through her participation on the Internet in the first place, and that is really interesting. The second story, *Gemma*, is about a musician who uses a recording she has made of a song that she has written herself as the soundtrack for her story. The third story is a work by a boy called Nathan, who we met at the Ipswich workshop, and he was very quiet in the session when we were developing scripts, but he said, "I know what I want to make my story on – I have a philosophy about life and death", and he had these quotes from ancient Greek philosophers and we were, like, where did this 13-year old boy get this stuff from? It turned out that he got these little quotes musing on how to live a good life, and basically the fundamentals of ethical philosophy, from a trading card from a computer game. He really wanted to use lots of rich imagery from the computer game in his story. Because none of us really know what we are doing with copyright at this stage, we made all these compromises. First, we were not going to let him do it, but he was very upset and he was very angry when we explained to him some of the basics of copyright and he made a really good argument, which was, that this game is really important and that it is really good and that I have learned something from it, so why can't I refer to it in my story?

I will just finish by pointing out that, with the Youth Internet Radio Network, all the kinds of content that are generated through the use of the network we consider to be important in understanding creativity, not just singular texts that you can attribute to one author but the kinds of discussions that might grow up on a bulletin board around a film – 'my favourite film', say – and even emails. The participants are going to be given, by default, the option to attach a Creative Commons Licence to any demonstrably original content that they are uploading to the network.

MARK FALLU

I would like to digress a little bit from our project and talk about some of the technological antecedents that make it possible and the environment in which it is occurring. I am going to talk a little bit about disruptive technologies, particularly in relation to the broadcast industry.

What is a disruptive technology? Well, you know movable type words are disruptive technology. The steam engine, telegraph and telephone are disruptive technologies. All technologies, devices, gizmos, tools, pieces of software that put an end to the good life that existed for the technologies that preceded them are examples of disruptive technologies. Steam supplanted wind and animal power. Landline phone numbers in the United States and Australia are now dropping in number in comparison to mobile phone telephone numbers. This presents interesting opportunities in places like India and China. There are going to be these divergent devices, things that are MP3 Players, mobile phones all in one. That is a whole exploding new market for us to distribute content that did not exist here.

We assume that in other parts of the developing world they will go through the same technological progression that we have gone through here, that they will start with land line telephones, they will have dial-up Internet access and, maybe if they are lucky in a few years' time, they will have broadband. Well, they are going to skip a few steps and go straight to what we are developing now.

I am going to be quite bold here and suggest that the age of broadcast is about to suffer from more than just a disruptive technology but an environment where disruption is the permanent state of being. Where we will no longer have periods of radical change and then balance, but the environment will, in fact, be characterised by continuous radical change. One of the tools that I would like to talk about here is being made with a precursor to the end of the age of broadcast: 'BitTorrent'.

BitTorrent was invented by a single individual, Graham Collin, who took some time off from the dot-com boom because he was dissatisfied with producing products for companies that never went to market because they kept on collapsing before the product actually was finished. He used his own savings and the savings of some friends and family to sit down and produce this tool that allows you to chunk up really large media files and distribute pieces of these files to people who are requesting them. And then, as soon as that person gets that piece of the file, they can start distributing that to everybody else. The audience can start to share the cost of distributing content.

I tend to think that holders of large amounts of copyrighted material and broadcasting networks must tend to view Graham Collins similarly to the way that the Pentagon views rogue biochemists and nuclear scientists, except he is not producing weapons of mass destruction, he is producing a weapon of mass distribution, a weapon where the barrier to entry for becoming a broadcaster is now conceivably so low that anyone can do it.

We have heard a lot of talk about the documentary *Outfoxed*. What has not been mentioned today is that large portions of the original content of that documentary have actually been released to the public under Creative Commons Licences to be reimagined, to be remixed for use in new documentaries. This is not the news footage, rather interviews and things like that that were done to support that material. This was not done by the production company that put together the documentary. It was not even done by the original creator of the documentary. It was done by a fan of the documentary who approached the makers with an idea, and the idea was that they would take not all of it but just a portion of the documentary and release it by this peer-to-peer network of BitTorrent.

There have been seven or eight thousand people who have downloaded it in the first three or four weeks of this material being released. That is 750 gigabytes of content. This is an enormous amount of material, far more than any one person could afford to pay, but because of the use of BitTorrent, that tool allowed the audience who were consuming the content to also distribute it in the very act of their receiving it. It meant that that 750 gigabytes was distributed in little, small parcels amongst the entire audience.

This presents a really radical, new opportunity where you already had very low barriers of entry to production. Five or six years ago a laptop that you could do word processing on was nowhere near adequate to do video editing or music production. Today it is one and the same device. Tomorrow the console gaming unit or the mobile phone that you get will have a megapixel resolution suitable for broadcast quality film captures. The barrier to entry to production is quite low but it has been distribution that has been the real problem.

What really excites me about Creative Commons is that it takes the existing production capacity and this new distribution capacity and brings them together in a legal context that allows for entirely new markets of content to develop where you do not have producers and consumers of content. You have active consumers – people who are reconfiguring, choosing exactly what they want to see, what they want to listen to when they want to do that. You are getting things like Podcasting. This is where tools from blogs, the syndication and aggregation engines (RSS – Really Simple Syndication or site summaries), allow you to subscribe actively to content. To say, 'this is what I am interested in' and then whenever new content is released, using these peer-to-peer distribution mechanisms, that content can be downloaded to your computer. That way, you do not have to click and wait to listen to something; you can subscribe to it in advance. It gets downloaded automatically and then, at some later point, you play broadcast quality material on your iPod, phone, or computer, and you timeshift it so that you are listening to it exactly when you want to. If you get home from work and you want to listen to publicly broadcast material that has an appropriate legal licence, you can do that.

This is the environment that the YIRN project, or the 'sticky' web site as we are calling it, exists in, an environment where people expect to have the right to publish content, to actively consume content when and where they want, and to be able to have discussions with their peers about this content. We have tried to cherry pick technology from a whole range of open source projects to allow us to do that. We are using largely open source software in almost every area of our project, except for one, and that is in the transcoding of video files from one format, that the producer might have made them in, to the format that they will be distributed in. The reason that we are not using open source software there is because content producers tend to use proprietary codecs – compressors and decompressors that crunch big pieces of content down into much smaller more amenable-for-transfer size pieces. Because of the proprietary nature of the codecs, we have to use proprietary software at this point to be able to turn them into stuff that we can distribute more freely. We are actively looking at getting around that, but that is a problem that lots of people are dealing with.

So what technologies are we using? We are using an open source content management system called Plone, which is built on an open source programming language called Python. This allows us to add extra functions, like RSS, which is a syndication technology which allows people to subscribe to feeds of information based on their interests. We are also using Trackback functionality from blogs. We are using it slightly differently though. One of the things about Creative Commons is that there is attribution. It tends to be in one direction, like you create a music file, someone takes a sample from it, puts it into a new music file that is put online. The notification that someone has used your piece of content does not necessarily come back to you, so we are using Trackback functionality to allow users of Creative Commons material to voluntarily let the original authors know about the secondary uses of their content. We will see these branching networks of content, where you might be a big fan of one track, see a sample that you like, and want to see all of the other uses of that sample, or what happened to that song and if anyone else liked and used it.

This is the great thing about open source: you can collaborate, if not on a programming level, even on a conceptual level. There is riffing, the backwards and forwards, a conversation about the use of material. One of the other interesting things that we are doing is allowing conversational threads to be attached to content objects. A film might inspire you to want to talk about it, go to its website and write your thoughts in a discussion thread attached to that content. But that thread of discussion does not only appear in the context of that object, it also appears in a centralised, threaded discussion board. And they are kept in locked step with each other so that, that way, people do not have to go hunting down the discussion thread; they can see what are the active ones in a central location and that will actually drive them back to the original pieces of content. They can click on the author of that piece of content and see all of the other content. You have got these constellations, these vistas, of new content that people can explore and browse. They have all got single URLs so that you can always go back. You can bookmark those pieces of content; you can go back to them; you can refer other people to them. All of these technological advances will make it really quite a rich and, hopefully, very easily understood environment for creativity.

The interesting thing about this project for me as a relatively technical person has been that the biggest challenges we have faced have not necessarily been technical; they have been the legal and the administrative challenges, and technical approaches to dealing with them. For that I am exceptionally grateful to the Creative Commons because it has provided an avenue where someone else has done a lot of the work of dealing with licensing issues. In the technical world there is a metaphor that if the only tool you have is a hammer, then every problem starts to look like a nail. It is amazing the number of solutions to problems that I have managed to apply Creative Commons to, even down to the level of the categorisation of content. Our target audience ranges from the age of 12 to 25. There are very different life experiences between those groups of people and the sort of content that would be appropriate for one sub-group will not be appropriate for another. Rather than us heavily vetting and moderating and soul searching what the content is and whether or not it is appropriate, one of the approaches that we are investigating is community-based moderation, community-based classification. What is a community standard of decency if not one decided by the community? It is not necessarily up to the curators of content to make those arbitrary decisions on behalf of the community. These are philosophical approaches that are very much informed by the openness of Creative Commons-style licensing.

I guess some of the challenges that still remain are how we can take this pool of Creative Commons enabled content and allow it to sit alongside, in an active sense, fully copyrighted content. How can we allow a 13-year old who has produced their first song to program that song alongside the works of their favourite copyrighted artists? This has been an area where we have been working with APRA in order to develop licensing that covers the broad range of usage in our system, not just the Creative Commons licensed material. When there is a stream and it has Creative Commons meta-data attached to it, the content management system will allow you to download that content to your computer. Then you are able to remix it and upload your version. We are aiming to also to allow you to include copyright material alongside that. The content management system is smart enough to report back to APRA that we have used it, so that royalties can be paid. It knows that that copyright material can only appear in live streams and if it appears in an on-demand stream then it has to have different meta-data attached to it and send different information back to APRA.

What we were hoping to see is that there will be some sort of arms race that will develop between the copyright material and the Creative Commons licensed material. And we will get to see as a research outcome exactly how our users choose to use that material. Whether the flexibility that is embodied in the Creative Commons licensed material means that it will receive a greater focus of attention from our users. That is the research project and you will have to come to the website to see it all in action. The web site will be sticky.net.au.

Australian Creative Resource Online (ACRO)

Dr David Rooney

I am going to talk to you a little bit about our experience with Australian Creative Resources Online, or ACRO as we call it. As I go along I will mention a few reflections that I can make about our experience in trying to get this project going. ACRO is essentially a database, accessible through the Internet, which is full of multi-media objects, mostly music and video, which have either been digitised or was born digital in the first place. Our basic philosophy when we began was that we wanted to create what Neeru Paharia called *the digital junkyard*. The observation by my colleague, Phil Graham, whose brainchild this is, was that in the production process a lot of stuff gets edited out and gets left on the floor. While some of that stuff is edited out and left on the cutting-room floor for very good reasons, some of that stuff is still actually quite usable and is also of broadcast quality. We thought that it would be a good idea to create some sort of infrastructure in which that kind of resource could be made more widely available. And, of course, as soon as we thought about doing that there were a whole set of questions that arose in our minds about copyright. Then we discovered Brian Fitzgerald just down the river and we began talking about Creative Commons and eventually we met Carol Fripp from AEShareNet and we began to talk about free-for-education software.

That is the background to this project and in my talk I just want to talk a little bit in general terms about copyright in the creative industries, then the creative industries in the knowledge economy, or perhaps knowledge society. I also want to talk about this project in relation to cost barriers or barriers to entry for grass-roots producers into the creative industries. The use of the word 'industries' is slightly problematic here because in my own thinking I do not see that necessarily our purpose is only to provide resources to grass-roots producers who want to make money. We certainly are quite happy for people to use our resources to make a living out of being creative, but also to people who want to work in a completely non-economic context – people like me who just do it for fun, for personal fulfilment.

I was up at five o'clock this morning mixing some music on my computer while the rest of my family was asleep and I do that for the sheer enjoyment of it. I never expect, because of my lack of talent, to make any money out of it and as someone pointed out this morning, academics already get paid anyway, so I have quite a comfortable life.

I want to finish by adding on a little bit about education and legally safe environments within which students at primary school, secondary school, TAFE colleges and universities, can work in terms of multi-media of film, television production, music and all of that kind of stuff.

It is unproblematic to say that copyright is a foundation stone of the creative industries, and that the large media corporations absolutely depend on copyright for their revenues and their existence. As Peter Drahos points out so clearly in his book *Information Feudalism: who owns the knowledge economy?*,[44] one of the problems with copyright for grass-roots producers is that copyright protects the rights of financiers rather than the rights of creators. And, of course, alternative copyright regimes, like Creative Commons and FFE (Free for Education) licences come into play when you start thinking about not protecting the rights of the people who finance the production or the distribution of both, but the producers or the creators themselves. Those are the sorts of issues that ACRO is seeking to address.

A book I read recently while I was in Taiwan was arguing that all the literature on intercultural management in the management literature was wrong because it's not intercultural management; it is cross-cultural management, and it is fundamentally a knowledge management issue. It reinforces my idea that the real fundamental base to the knowledge economy is not biotechnology, it is not information technology but it is really the media or communications generally. As a person who is something of an expert in the sociology of knowledge and the political economy of knowledge, it is fairly clear to me that one of the best sources of knowledge – and we also include culture in this – is testimonial knowledge.

Most of the knowledge that we all have of the world is not something that we have discovered empirically ourselves; it is something that we have discovered because someone has told us. We have read about it or we have seen it on TV or in the movies or whatever. We all know, for example, that viewed from space, the earth is a greeny-blue ball in the universe and it is quite pretty and it induces profound thoughts about the nature of being and existence and everything in people who see. We all know that but none of

---

[44] (2002) Earthscan, London.

us in this room have actually been out there and seen it ourselves, so we know that from testimony.

A lot of that testimonial knowledge that we all have these days we get from the media and the media is a very large part of the creative industries. Therefore we can say that the knowledge economy, if that is where we are going or indeed if that is where we already are it is a creative economy. It is an attention economy, or an economy in which people are competing to get our attention, and a communication economy. I have written extensively about this in any number of publications, including *Public Policy in Knowledge-Based Economies*,[45] which Greg Hearn is a co-author on, if you want to chase that up.

The media or the creative industries play a fundamental role in the distribution of this particular kind of knowledge, testimonial knowledge. And cultural and creative producers therefore are going to be fundamental to that. I began to think about this, to talk of the news media, but it is not just the news media. Our fundamental understandings of the world are also communicated to us culturally and artistically through drama, through novels, through music and poetry and so on, and we need to begin to take all of these things more seriously in the context of becoming a knowledge society, a knowledge economy. This is why creating ease of access to cultural producers or grass-roots cultural producers, or grass-roots testimonial knowledge producers, is very important and why having access to these kinds of resources through the Internet is also very important.

One of the things we did when we were initially trying to ground ourselves was talk to some advertising agencies. One of the things they told us time and time again was that one of the toughest bits for the ad agencies, assuming that they are doing television ads, is the actual shooting of footage just to do a pitch, which can cost up to $50,000 a go. And then you may not get the business. They have their own archives, of course, but most of that material is largely inaccessible. What that made us think about was that it is really the cost of production, rather than the cost of post-production, which is expensive in this digital age.

You can get software to edit music or video or whatever for free if you want from places like SourceForge. I certainly have some of that technology at home. But the same set of issues arise again when you start

---

[45] David Rooney, Greg Hearn, Thomas Mandeville, Richard Joseph *Public Policy in Knowledge-Based Economies* (2003) Edward Elgar Publishing, Cheltenham.

talking about grass-roots producers. These are just the ordinary producers who are struggling to make a living, people who are averaging $14,000 annual income, or less, or people who are just doing it for the sake of enjoyment, or people who are doing it as part of a learning process at school or college or university. And, of course, having a set of IP licensing arrangements that actually enable people to do this is very, very important. This again is where Creative Commons comes in, because copyright, or intellectual property protection practices, are another barrier to successful entry into this kind of work.

My final point here really is the way we are going now and where we will end up in the future, is to be focused more on education than anything else. One of the things we are acutely aware of in universities is that various copyright agencies and multi-national media corporations are systematically looking at university students and seeing what they keep on their university server accounts in terms of music and video and that kind of stuff and then trying to take them to court and sue them.

I also had the opportunity to have a look at some work done in a high school here in Brisbane, where students were making either 90 second or 3 minute documentaries or dramas or ads or whatever. On nearly every single work that I looked at, I would say at least 80 percent of the time that you spent looking at that video material, you were looking at a copyright breach. Mostly it was because the students had taken bits of music from their CD collection or whatever, but also because they were raiding their home DVD collection, or they were going down to Blockbuster on the weekend and ripping bits of scenes out of that. It also became apparent that what happens is when those students leave that school they take the video with them. There is absolutely nothing to guarantee that once those students go away from that school, that they will not somehow manage to get that broadcast and publicly shown and expose themselves, and probably the school and the Education Department to some kind of liability under copyright law.

It also became fairly obvious to me that the teachers and the students knew very, very little about copyright law and the potential trouble that they could get into. I think one of the projects that we need to get involved in, with ACRO, is not just providing the multi-media resources for these students to use, but to actually get into the schools and put some knowledge in place in those schools among the teachers and the students about what is really going on here. Also to explain to them the virtues of Creative

Commons and Free-for-Education style licensing, in order to create a legally safe environment for students to work in.

Reflecting on the comments made in the last panel about the different sorts of attitudes that different people in different sectors of the creative industries have about copyright, I do not think we actually know very much at a sociological or cultural level about what those attitudes are. In terms of having these particular licences, just because we have written them up in three different forms and we have made them available on the Internet, does not mean that they are accessible to people in real terms. I do not think we really understand the attitudes that the kinds of people that we are trying to sell this idea to have about copyright in general. Some of those ideas that they have, which form a barrier to them taking up these kinds of licences, are legitimate. They are fair enough. I agree with some of them. But some of them are not. Some of them are quite destructive attitudes that these cultural producers hold and hold very dearly and do not necessarily want to give up.

Policy Issues

Internet and Innovation

Digital Sampling and Culture Jamming in a Remix World: What does the law allow?

> PROFESSOR JOHN QUIGGIN, PROFESSOR BRIAN FITZGERALD AND DAMIEN O'BRIEN

The following two papers reflect the significant challenges that face intellectual property in the digital world.

Internet and Innovation

*In this paper **Professor John Quiggin** of the University of Queensland discusses the impact the internet has had on innovation in modern society, and in particular networked innovation and the rise of social capital.*

Digital Sampling and Culture Jamming in a Remix World: What does the law allow?

***Professor Brian Fitzgerald** and **Damien O'Brien** examine the extent to which the law restricts the use of the cultural environment as part of modern discursive practices.*

Professor Brian Fitzgerald
(Head, QUT Law School)

Internet and Innovation

Professor John Quiggin

We have had worldwide significant acceleration of productivity in the market sector of the economy in the past decade or so, a lot of different factors coming together there, with a lot of the innovation coming from the Internet and from associated things. That contrasts with a long period when transport was the focus of innovation. When we talked about periods in the nineteenth and twentieth centuries, where we talked about the steam or railway age, the jet age, and so forth – it was modes of transport that were really distinctive. The last major innovation in transport that made a big difference was the Jumbo jet pioneered by Boeing in 1967 and in 2005 we saw the next big innovation in travel, A380 Jumbo jet, produced by Airbus of Europe. That is what 40 years or so of progress in transport has produced. If we look at the other things, railways and motor vehicles, we will see even more incremental changes over that period. The important thing about transport is first, it is the embodiment of innovation. It is the jet itself that matters and the process that produces it is a traditional one – of getting lots of people and a traditional organisation to work together to produce a collective outcome.

One of most important things that the Internet has given us since 1980, both in terms of economic and non-economic activity, like email and the Web, is electronic commerce. Just as important, is the capacity to find what is out there in the world of knowledge, represented most obviously by Google, but also by all sorts of other tools now associated with things like RDF and RSS. Ways of distributing information that are not as passive as putting up a page and waiting for Google to find it, and the ideas of the Semantic Web and so forth that are associated with that.

Importantly, most of these innovations were pioneered outside the market sector. The Internet was entirely non-commercial up until 1992 and remained predominantly non-commercial for a few years after that. Of course in the late 90s it was discovered by business and literally hundreds of billions of dollars were poured into various forms of innovation. What is striking is that that really did not produce very much. The new exciting ideas, to me at least, are things that continue to be done in the background during the dot com boom – things like blogs and wikies which highlight the economics of networks and the economic concept of public goods.

First, innovations on a network are naturally non-rival. That is, if I improve a network naturally the improvement for me is improvement for everybody else. There is no sense, unlike ordinary goods where more cake for me is less cake for you. The other feature of a public good in economics is excludability. That is, can I stop somebody from getting access to it? Those are just two different things. A song is non-rival: my listening to it does not affect your ability to listen to it. But if I have got the right sort of copyright regime I can say only somebody who buys the record can have the song.

In general it is hard to exclude users without losing access to the full scope of the network, and we saw this with the rise of the Internet itself. The Internet was not the only network that was set up to tie computers together. There were a whole bunch of commercial networks set up at the same time which tried to keep people out, people who had not paid Delphi and others. The only one of those that survived the modern day even as a name is AOL (America On Line) and the only reason America On Line survived is because it took the decision in the mid-1990s to connect up to the Internet, and it still tried to wall its own little bits off. It tried to get the best of both worlds and maybe for a few years did so, but in the end has largely given up, so that these days there are not many walled off sections of the Internet because the attempt to do that cut you off from too much.

In the world of newspapers, lots of people tried subscription models. The only people who have done it successfully are financial papers, where there are plenty of people with a willingness to pay to access the content and not that much interest in the network as a whole. Now, this was one of the reasons I was very keen to come here was to hear Larry Lessig talk. One of the things that I really liked in his books is the distinction between centralised and end-oriented networks. They are both very important and we can see important examples of both of them and they have different sorts of properties for innovation.

Traditional telephony is a centralised network; everybody gets a connection to the central switchboard. They are then switched through to the person they want to talk to and if you improve it, what you do is make that central switchboard work better. You get rid of the operator who spoke to you and plugged in the number you wanted. You replace that with an automatic switch. You put in additional services that you can access by pressing the right numbers. The network as a whole is a public good and the important feature of this is that the innovations in a centralised network are automatically available to all. No particular effort is required on the part of the telephone company once it is made the service, to make that service available to every single user. Sometimes there might be some need to improve the connections in the network but in a symmetrical network there is no problem. This can be seen as exclusivity – the network owner can say only people who pay can get the improved functionality – but in essence the process is largely automatic and the cost can be recovered through pricing systems because excludability is typically relatively feasible.

The other sort of network is end-oriented network, where most of the action is going on at the end. Most of the intelligence is at the end and the network itself does nothing more than the bare bones of connecting people and the Internet is the paradigm example of an end-oriented network. At the centre of it, to the extent there is a centre, there is nothing more than a set of protocols that turn generalised bits of signals into, or transmit generalised signals from, one part of the network to another. All the action of turning those signals into web pages is done at the end. It can disseminate distributed innovations from widely separated sources. The most famous example of this, but in some ways a misleading one because various particular sorts of motives come into it (it opens all software), is the paradigm instance: Linux.

More interesting to me, because I am not a programmer although I am a writer, are things like newsgroups, weblogs and wikies in which text information from a wide variety of sources is combined, circulated and remixed. In the process, new ways of handling that information, new ideas about how to do things, are also disseminated. People come up with different ideas for what will be a nice way of organising blogs for example, web logs. Should we have group web logs? How should we run comments, and so forth. Those things are distributed around the network but this is not nearly so much an automatic process.

First, it is generally impossible to recover costs. If I am work hard on writing code that will make my web log look prettier, I cannot as a general rule get much of that effort back, certainly not from other people who might want to copy my innovation. I can keep it a secret to some extent. The methods of trade secrecy are still out there, although they do not usually work much. In this whole area it is fair to say that patents have done more harm than good.

We heard about IBM licensing a bunch of its patents. When a patent in this kind of area, like a company like Scode, that has supposedly got a few lines of its code allegedly has snuck into generalised code, not stuff that is of any importance, just stuff that happens to be there. They are then using that to essentially try and extract rent from a wide variety of people who have contributed their effort for nothing.

Or, when I think of copyright, I think of the Church of Scientology trying to prevent its activities being publicised by use of copyright control over its works. It is fair to say they are not trying to get money. It is fair to say that these traditional methods of IP in this text area have not done any good whatsoever. There is much more of a trade off in, say, music and film than there is in these text-based areas.

This notion of social capital has been very big for the last decade or so with economists and social science, popularised very much by Robert Putnam. First of course, capital, physical capital, is machines and so forth. Economists analogised that to knowledge in peoples' heads, human capital, around about the 1960s and the old economic category of lands has been churned into natural capital, stuff that nature provides us. Unlike these things though, there is no clear characterisation of investment in social capital. Second, social capital itself is a type of distributed network. If we think about human capital, my human capital is the knowledge in my head. That is pretty straightforward. If I walk out and get hit by a truck, my human capital is gone. Social capital is not like that; social capital is to do with my relationship with other people. It is not me. It is not them. It is in the relationships. It is very much a network kind of good.

It has been something which economists and social science has been tearing their hair out about. We have recognised the importance – it makes a big difference to economic performance. But trying to measure it is incredibly difficult. One of the features of the Internet is that we can, in important respects, measure it because connection is what the Internet does. I can tell you right now how many people linked to my web log, how many people did so in the last day, what those links said, whether they gave me good or bad social capital. That kind of measurement and observable creation is much more pleasant in the Internet context than it is when we talk about, do I trust people in the street? Am I, is my community, socially working or not?

There are lots of different reasons why people might invest in social capital. Some of them are much more pleasant in, for example, open software, for example, a desire to exhibit your technical mastery. That is a very specialised field. This notion of gift exchange is very big there, whereas in other areas it is something like self-expression. It is much more important, or altruistic. The important point I want to make about these distinct motives is that most of them are compatible or mutually reinforcing. If I am thinking about writing a piece of code for Linux, or I am thinking about a way to improve a web log and making that available. Partly I want everybody to admire me and think how clever I am, partly I want to help my fellow bloggers or Linux fans, and partly because I just like doing it and, having done it, so I might as well share it. Those things all fit together pretty well. On the other hand I would argue most of the time market rationality is antagonistic to these motives. If I am doing this and thinking what I am going to do is come up with this idea and then sell it, if I am a good businessman, I do not let considerations like altruism or gift giving get in the way of doing business. If I do, I will be exploited. I need to calculate exchange values carefully because otherwise I will persist with money losing lines of business and I need to be worried about arbitrage.

One of the magic features of markets, as opposed to small scale communities, is that if you can find a way of making ten cents and repeat it a zillion times, you have got 0.1 of a zillion dollars. What that means is that if I am behaving in a non-market rational way when there are other players out there who have the market in mind, I can be taken down very easily and I need to guard against that.

We commonly say, "that is business". You are expected to a large extent to feign your motives in business. The person who sells me a car is expected to treat me as if they like me, regardless of what they might think about me. I would be offended if they honestly said, "you are the stupidest person I have met today", or the ugliest, or something. Even if they showed us by the normal ways in which a polite person would say, "well, I do not really like you, but I have got this car, you have got money, let us get this over with". Now bureaucratic rationality is also problematic, in some ways for the opposite reason. Although we do not like it, it is not so much there that we do not want these kinds of motives used against us. The last thing I want to see is the person in front of me walking up to the bureaucrat who says, "you have a pretty face" or "you are a member of the same club as I am. You will get your request approved", and then I do not get my request approved. We do not want notions like gift exchange in bureaucratic processes. It has another name: corruption. These kinds of motives are very hard to fit into this world of creating social capital.

What are the implications? Well first, the one we have heard about already is the Commons versus intellectual property, that there is a conflict here. The implication is we need to move, that the changes in technology need to dictate a move more towards the Commons and away from intellectual property. The second, a vague sort of term, but some content can be given to it – we need to focus more on creativity and less on rationality. As a professional dealer in rationality that is maybe not such a good thing for me. There is the implication that the kind of rational processes that have dominated public debate, particularly in Australia, in the past 20 years, are not going to be well suited to promoting creative innovation. A supporting rather than a leading role for the State is implied. The state, after all, funded the creation of the Internet and did lots of good things, but it's unlikely that state, that centralised state activity, is going to play a leading role.

Finally, a relatively peripheral role for market activity, is to see the market sector retreating from being the centre of so much innovation and instead picking up on innovations that have been generated outside the market sector, or to a lesser extent, users, rather than being generated within firms.

Digital Sampling and Culture Jamming in a Remix World: What does the law allow?

PROFESSOR BRIAN FITZGERALD AND DAMIEN O'BRIEN

Introduction

The purpose of this article is to examine the extent to which we are lawfully allowed to draw upon our cultural environment as part of our discursive practices. To what extent are we 'free' to access and reutilise that which surrounds us?

At the Straight Out of Brisbane Arts Festival in December 2004 a participant explained that they could go out into the forest and paint a picture of the trees without breaching any intellectual property laws, yet to paint a picture of the human made environment of billboards that line the M1 Highway between Brisbane and the Gold Coast could breach the law. They explained that sampling their environment was like using the English language in the process of talking and billboards as much as the trees were part of their cultural environment. What right did they have to 'jam' with these artefacts of modern day life? What right did they have to sample music or culture more broadly as part of their creative activity?

The fact that people want to utilise their environment in their creative activity is not the only point to note here. Nowadays technology is making this even easier to achieve. New digital technologies along with the Internet have opened up enormous potential for what has become known as 'remix' – cutting, pasting, mashing, sampling etc. No longer are end users or consumers seen as passive receptors of information, but rather in the process of distributed and peer production, consumers can take on the role of producers to become what Creative Commons legal counsel Mia Garlick calls 'content conducers'.[46]

Specifically, this article will consider the legal issues that arise in relation to the distinct yet related creative and social practices of remix known as digital (music) sampling and culture jamming. The picture is not particularly encouraging. There appears little scope for sampling music without the permission of the copyright owner under fair dealing

---

[46] Lawrence Lessig, *Free Culture: How Big Media Uses Technology and the Law to Lock Down Culture and Control Creativity* (2004) New York, Penguin Press, 283-4.

(Australia) or fair use (USA) doctrines, especially in relation to the sound recording and especially where there is no 'transformative' use.[47] While Australian law will still consider whether a 'substantial part' of the original material has been reproduced through the sampling, the approach in the recent US decision of *Bridgeport Music Inc v Dimension Films Inc*,[48] applying a somewhat similar quantitative/qualitative test is to suggest that any copying of the sound recording will amount to an infringement. It is unclear to what extent Australian courts would follow this decision and decide that copying any amount of a sound recording is a reproduction of a substantial part of the original material. The suggestion is that Australian courts should not adopt the *Bridgeport* approach as a rigorous 'substantial part' doctrine informed by an understanding of the creative innovation system[49] - especially in its digital and remix aspects – is vital to allowing flexibility in our copyright system and innovation in our information society. The limitation of fair dealing doctrine in promoting innovation makes this even more apparent. The implementation of a more tolerant doctrine of fair use so as to facilitate creative innovation (through the current review of fair use by the Commonwealth Attorney-General)[50] and widespread use of modalities such as permission in advance Creative Commons styled licences provide hope for the creative class that some sampling will be allowed. The expectation that every second or note of recorded music must be paid for and therefore cannot be utilised without permission is too rigid and ignores the fact that the creativity of today builds on that of the past quite often without any compensation being paid.[51]

In relation to culture jamming and copyright and trademark law, once again Australian law is deficient in providing clear guidance as to the extent to

---

[47] On the notion of "transformative use" see *Campbell v Acuff-Rose Music Inc* 510 U.S 569 (1994).
[48] 401 F 3d 647 (6th Cir, 2004), *en banc* rehearing and revised opinion 410 F 3d. 792 (6th Cir. 2005).
[49] On this notion see A Fitzgerald and B Fitzgerald, *Intellectual Property in Principle* Chapter 1; John Howkins, *The Creative Economy: how people make money from ideas*, (2001) London, Penguin; John Hartley (ed.), *Creative Industries* (2005) Oxford, Blackwell, 2005; DCITA, *Creative Industries Cluster Study* Volumes 1-3 (2004) ww.dcita.gov.au.
[50] See further, B Fitzgerald "Fair Use for "Creative Innovation": A Principle We Must Embrace. A Submission in Response to the A-G's Issues Paper on Fair Use and Other Copyright Exceptions" (2005)
http://www.law.qut.edu.au/about/staff/lsstaff/fitzgerald.jsp
[51] *Emerson v Davies* 8 F. Cas 615 at 619 (C.C. Mas. 1845); W Landes and R Posner, "An Economic Analysis of Copyright Law" (1989) *J. Legal Stud.* 325 at 332.

which creativity can draw upon the surrounding environment. US copyright and trademark law permits a degree of culture jamming by way of trade mark parody, yet Australian law is largely silent on this issue. To this end Australian law needs to clearly define the extent to which trade marks, particularly well known marks, can be utilised without the permission of the copyright and trademark owner for political, social and creative activity. In a vibrant democracy we deserve the right to remix and jam with these cultural artefacts to 'some degree'.

Music Sampling

Introduction

The term music sampling refers to the process by which a producer or artist making a recording, samples a sound or series of sounds from its original context and then makes a new use of it. In its more technical sense this process is referred to as digital sampling, which involves the use of digital technology to enable the recording and storage of sounds and their reproduction in a host of aural formats.[52] This process is achieved by breaking down the wave forms that characterise the different sounds and converting them into a precise numerical form.[53] This information is then coded into a digital synthesiser, enabling the artist or producer to manipulate the sound bites (samples) in a number of different pitches, echoes, speeds, tones and rhythmic combinations.[54] The courts have taken a similar approach to these generic industry definitions in considering what music sampling and digital sampling encompass. Most recently in *Bridgeport Music Inc v Dimension Films Inc*,[55] the United States Court of Appeals for the 6th Circuit held that digital sampling is a term of art, in adopting the definition commonly accepted within the music industry. In *Newton v Diamond*,[56] Schroeder CJ held that 'sampling entails the incorporation of short segments of prior sound recordings into new recordings.' Similarly, in *Jarvis v A & M Records*,[57] Ackerman DJ held that digital sampling involves the conversion of analog sound waves into digital

---

[52] Paul Weiler, *Entertainment, Media, and the Law* (2nd ed, 2002) 412.
[53] Ibid.
[54] Ibid 413.
[55] 401 F 3d 647, 655 (6th Cir, 2004); 410 F 3d 792, 798 (6th Cir 2005).
[56] 349 F 3d 591, 596 (9th Cir, 2003).
[57] 827 F Supp 282, 286 (DNJ, 1993).

code. Elaborating on this process Ackerman DJ described it 'as similar to taping the original composition and reusing it in another context.'[58]

This notion of sampling is not a novel or new one, indeed it may well be argued that it is something which is a part of culture and freedom of expression that has been alive for centuries. However, the origins of sampling in its current musical and digital context can be traced to the reggae musicians of Jamaica in the 1960's who in turn influenced the rap and hip-hop culture in urban New York in the late 1970's.[59] It was here that an African-American musician from the Bronx, Afrika Bambaata pioneered the practice we now know as music sampling.[60] Through sampling the electronic beats of German pop group Kraftwerk, Bambaata was able to lay the foundations for an entirely new culture of music, which embraced the use of sampling.[61] Today this practice of music sampling is not only confined to rap and hip-hop culture. Its influence can also be seen in movements like pop, funk, dance, house, techno, trip-hop and acid jazz.[62]

An ability to sample lawfully yet without the permission of the copyright owner is an important part of a dynamic creative innovation system because it allows content (e.g a portion song) to be negotiated instantaneously and without friction. Under copyright law we are entitled under certain conditions (including payment of a statutory licence fee) to record a song without the permission of the copyright owner of the song[63] but we cannot copy a sound recording of a song unless we have the permission of the copyright owner of the sound recording. If we are allowed to sample a sound recording without permission then a road block or veto power over creativity is removed and a space for re-use or free culture is opened up. Having to pay for samples might also prove expensive for an artist who merely wants to experiment with sounds in a process of creativity.[64] The focus of this article then is to ask - when can sampling be undertaken without the permission of the relevant copyright owner and without the need to pay compensation?

---

[58] *Jarvis v A & M Records*, 827 F Supp 282, 286 (DNJ, 1993).
[59] Rachael Carnachan, "Sampling and the Music Industry: A Discussion of the Implications of Copyright Law" (1999) 8(4) *Auckland University Law Review* 1033. See also *Newton v Diamond* 349 F. 3d. 591 at 593 (6th Cir 2003).
[60] Rachael Carnachan, *supra* at 593.
[61] Ibid.
[62] Ibid.
[63] *Copyright Act 1968* ss 54-65.
[64] "A New Spin On Music Sampling: A Case For Fair Play" (1992) 105 *Harvard Law Review* 726 at 727-8.

What Does Copyright Law Allow?

In determining what copyright law will allow in relation to music sampling, it is first necessary to identify the relevant rights which may exist in original material. Under the *Copyright Act* a single composition of recorded music may give rise to a number of different types of copyright. These include economic rights in the literary work (lyrics), musical work (score), sound recording and performance of the song as well as moral rights in the lyrics, score and more recently performance of the song. Each of these rights will be considered separately below.

In regards to the literary and musical aspect of recorded music, s 32 of the *Copyright Act* provides protection for an original literary and musical work. In the context of music sampling, song lyrics are recognised as a literary work and are therefore afforded protection under the *Copyright Act*.[65] There is no definition of a musical work however, it is generally accepted that this category protects the method of production, rather than any artistic or aesthetic qualities of the work.[66] Under this any combination of sounds and noises will be protected by copyright, provided it is in a fixed form.[67] Copyright infringement in either the literary or musical work will occur where the sampler does any of the acts within the copyright owner's exclusive rights.[68] In the case of music sampling this will most often occur where the literary or musical work is reproduced in a material form.[69] In order to prove infringement in either the literary or musical work the copyright owner will need to show that the infringing sample was a reproduction of the original work, and that a substantial part has been reproduced.[70] These two requirements are discussed in detail below in relation to copyright in a sound recording.[71]

---

[65] *Copyright Act 1968* (Cth) s 10(1).
[66] Anne Fitzgerald and Brian Fitzgerald, *Intellectual Property in Principle* (2004) Thomson Sydney 99.
[67] Ibid.
[68] *Copyright Act 1968* (Cth) s 36 - including the right to reproduce the work in a material form, to perform the work in public, to communicate the work to the public, or to make an adaptation of the work: s 31 (1).
[69] *Copyright Act 1968* (Cth) s 31(1)(a)(i).
[70] Fitzgerald and Fitzgerald, *supra*, 144.
[71] Note that the *Bridgeport* decision suggests that this analysis be undertaken separately for the lyrics/music and sound recording as reproduction of a substantial part of a sound recording brings into play different considerations: 401 F. 3d 647 at 655 (6th Cir, 2004). *Cf* "Amici Curiae Brief of Brennan Center for Justice at NYU Law School and EFF in *Bridgeport Rehearing*" 21 January 2005

The other right in relation to recorded music and the one which is most commonly associated with music sampling is copyright in a sound recording. A sound recording is defined to mean the aggregate sounds embodied in a record and will therefore extend to the recording of sounds on the most common medium, CD.[72] Under s 85(1) of the *Copyright Act* an owner of copyright in a sound recording has the exclusive right to make a copy of the sound recording, cause the recording to be heard in public, communicate the recording to the public and enter into a commercial rental arrangement in respect of the recording. Copyright infringement in a sound recording will occur where a person who is not the copyright owner does any of the acts within the copyright owner's exclusive rights.[73] This most commonly occurs in music sampling where a copy of the sound recording is made which embodies the original recording. In order to prove the infringement of copyright, the copyright owner will need to show that the infringing sample was a reproduction of the original material, and that a substantial part of the original sound recording has been reproduced.[74]

The first of these requirements is that there must have been a reproduction of the original sound recording. What this requires is that there must be 'a sufficient degree of objective similarity between the two works' and 'some causal connection between the plaintiff's and defendant's work'.[75] In the context of music sampling what must be shown is that the sample embodies the actual sounds from the original sound recording.[76] In order to establish this it is useful to rely upon digital sound technology, which is able to detect whether the sounds that are embodied in the original sound recording have been reproduced.[77] This is achieved by isolating the original sound recording and the sample.[78] A sampler is then used to graph the amounts of particular frequencies in the sounds, thereby establishing if there has been a reproduction of the original sound recording.[79]

<http://www.fepproject.org/courtbriefs/bridgeport.pdf> See also *Newton v Diamond* 349 F. 3d. 591 (6th Cir 2003)
[72] *Copyright Act 1968* (Cth) s 10(1).
[73] *Copyright Act 1968* (Cth) s 101(1).
[74] Fitzgerald and Fitzgerald, above n 33, 144.
[75] *Francis Day & Hunter Ltd v Bron* [1963] Ch 587, 614.
[76] Helen Townley, 'Sampling: Weapon of the Copyright Pirate?' (1993) 12(1) *University of Tasmania Law Review* 102, 105.
[77] Ibid.
[78] Ibid.
[79] Ibid.

Assuming there has been a reproduction of the original sound recording, it is then necessary to consider the second requirement of whether a substantial part of the original sound recording has been reproduced.[80] The issue which arises here and one which is particularly crucial in regards to music sampling as most cases concern the use of very short samples, is what will amount to a substantial part? The general test for a substantial part was stated by Lord Pearce in *Ladbroke (Football) Ltd v William Hill (Football) Ltd*[81] as 'whether a part is substantial must be decided by its quality rather than its quantity.' This test was affirmed by Mason CJ in *Autodesk Inc v Dyason (No 2)*[82] who held that 'in determining whether the quality of what is taken makes it a 'substantial part' of the copyright work, it is important to inquire into the importance which the taken portion bears in relation to the work as whole: is it an essential or material part of the work?'. The High Court approved Mason's CJ statement in *Data Access Corporation v Powerflex Services Pty Ltd*[83] where it was held that 'in determining whether something is a reproduction of a substantial part of a [copyright work], the essential features of the [work] should be ascertained by considering the originality of the part allegedly taken.' The High Court referred to the definition of substantial part again in *Network Ten Pty Ltd v TCN Channel Nine Pty Ltd*[84]. In this case Kirby J explained that a small portion in quantitative terms may constitute a substantial part having regard to its materiality in relation to the work as a whole.[85] More recently in *TCN Channel Nine Pty Ltd v Network Ten Pty Ltd (No 2)*[86] it was held that whether a part taken is a substantial part or not, involves an assessment of the importance of the part taken to the work as a whole.

Applying a strict approach to this test of qualitative importance, it would appear that where a recognisable portion of a song has been sampled then a substantial part will have been reproduced.[87] However, applying a more liberal approach, a substantial part will only have been reproduced where

---

[80] *Copyright Act 1968* (Cth) s 14(1).
[81] [1964] 1 WLR 273, 293.
[82] (1993) 176 CLR 300, 305.
[83] (1999) 45 IPR 353, [84]. On the approach taken in the US see *Newton v Diamond* 349 F. 3d. 591 at 594-6 (6th Cir 2003).
[84] (2004) 78 ALJR 585.
[85] *Network Ten Pty Ltd v TCN Channel Nine Pty Ltd* (2004) 78 ALJR 585, 605; see also McHugh ACJ, Gummow and Hayne JJ, 589; *TCN Channel Nine Pty Ltd v Network Ten Pty Ltd (No 2)* [2005] FCAFC 53 (Unreported, Sundberg, Finkelstein and Hely JJ, 26 May 2005) [50].
[86] [2005] FCAFC 53 (Unreported, Sundberg, Finkelstein and Hely JJ, 26 May 2005) [52].
[87] Mathew Alderson (ed), *Current Issues in Music Law* (1998) 62.

the sample takes a portion of the song which has led to its popular appeal or commercial success. This was alluded to in *TCN Channel Nine Pty Ltd v Network Ten Pty Ltd (No 2)* where Finkelstein J held that one of the determining factors is the economic significance of that which has been taken.[88] While the issue of substantial part was not closely considered in *Universal Music Australia Pty Ltd v Miyamoto*[89], as the samples in question were entire songs, the recent United States decision in *Bridgeport Music Inc v Dimension Films Inc*,[90] tends to favour the strict approach in determining what will amount to a substantial part. In this case the Court held that even where a small part of a sound recording is sampled, then the part taken is something of value and will therefore infringe copyright.[91]

Another type of right which arises in relation to recorded music is that of performers' rights. Previously under the *Copyright Act* performers had quite limited rights and did not obtain copyright in the sound recordings of their performances.[92] However, as a result of the Australia-United States Free Trade Agreement and the enactment of the *US Free Trade Agreement Implementation Act 2004* (Cth), significant changes have been made to the protection of performers' rights under the *Copyright Act*. These changes have included extending the current ambit of performers' rights by granting performers' ownership of copyright in the sound recordings of their performances.[93] This is in addition to the existing performers' rights to authorise recording and broadcasting of the performance, and the right to prevent the knowing copy, sale, distribution or importation of unauthorised recordings.[94] As a result of these changes to the *Copyright Act* the person at the time of recording who owned the record and the performer who performed the performance are now co-owners of the copyright in equal shares.[95] It should also be noted that provisions have been introduced to prevent performers claiming compensation for infringement of copyright in

---

[88] [2005] FCAFC 54 (Unreported, Sundberg, Finkelstein and Hely JJ, 26 May 2005) [12].
[89] [2003] FCA 812 (Unreported, Lindgren J, 18 July 2003).
[90] 401 F3d 647 (6th Cir, 2004); 410 F 3d 792 (6th Cir 2005).
[91] *Bridgeport Music Inc v Dimension Films Inc*, 401 F3d 647 at 658 (6th Cir, 2004); 410 F 3d 792, 801-802 (6th Cir 2005).
[92] Fitzgerald and Fitzgerald, *supra*, 124.
[93] *Copyright Act 1968* (Cth) s 22(3A).
[94] *Copyright Act 1968* (Cth) s 248G.
[95] *Copyright Act 1968* (Cth) s 97(2A).

a sound recording[96] and for infringement of performers' rights arising from the same event.[97]

The other type of right which arises in regards to recorded music and has the potential to pose a significant obstacle for music sampling is that of moral rights. Moral rights are personal rights belonging to the author or creator of the copyright work, which exist independently from the economic rights mentioned above.[98] Under the *Copyright Act 1968* there are three types of moral rights which are recognised. These are the right of attribution of authorship, the right not to have authorship falsely attributed and the right of integrity of authorship.[99] The first of these moral rights, the right of attribution of authorship involves the right to be identified as the author of the work if any 'attributable acts' are done in respect of the work.[100] The second moral right provides the author of the work the right not to have authorship of the work falsely attributed.[101] Given the nature of music sampling, it can be argued that the first of these moral rights is almost always infringed as musicians rarely credit the work they have sampled.[102] However, further questions need to be asked as to whether the sampled material adequately identifies the moral rights holder[103] or whether it was reasonable in all the circumstances not to identify the author?[104] It should also be noted that the right of attribution only applies in relation to a substantial part of the work and therefore in instances where a substantial part has not been reproduced this will not be an issue.[105]

The third moral right of integrity involves the right not to have the work subjected to derogatory treatment which would demean the creator's

---

[96] Under s 85 (1) and as distinct from performers protection, in order to prevents double dipping.
[97] *Copyright Act 1968* (Cth) s 248J(4), (5).
[98] Fitzgerald and Fitzgerald, *supra*, 118.
[99] *Copyright Act 1968* (Cth) s 189.
[100] *Copyright Act 1968* (Cth) s 193.
[101] *Copyright Act 1968* (Cth) s 195AC. Under s 195AG (1) it is an act of false attribution for a person to knowingly deal with an altered work or reproduction of an altered work as if it were the unaltered work or reproduction of an unaltered work of the author. An insubstantial alteration is not covered by this provision: s 195 (2).
[102] Nicola Bogle, 'Does Black and White Make Gray? A Critical Analysis of the Legal Regime Governing Digital Music Sampling' (2005) 61 *Intellectual Property Forum* 10, 17.
[103] Section 195 *Copyright Act 1968*.
[104] Section 195AR *Copyright Act 1968*.
[105] Section 195AZH *Copyright Act 1968*.

reputation.[106] Once again the potential for infringement (in relation to the music and lyrics, but interestingly not the sound recording) arises as sampling by its very nature involves some degree of manipulation, which could lead to the demeaning of the creator's reputation.[107] However, the critical issue to determine is the extent to which digital sampling debases an original work. Does taking a part of a sound recording and/or placing it in another context impact upon the integrity of the lyrics or the music? As there are no moral rights in the actual sound recording,[108] joined with the fact that a sound recording can be made of music and lyrics pursuant to a statutory licence (i.e. the author cannot veto the recording)[109] there seems merit in the suggestion that the moral right of integrity in relation to recorded music must permit a broad range of approaches in the face of any attempt at creative censorship, although racist or other abhorrent forms of communication would be questionable.[110] Once again it should be noted

---

[106] *Copyright Act 1968* (Cth) s 195AQ.
[107] Bogle, above n 57.
[108] *Copyright Act 1968* (Cth) s 189.
[109] Sections 54-65 *Copyright Act 1968*.
[110] See further Matthew Rimmer, 'The Grey Album: Copyright Law and Digital Sampling' (2005) 114 *Media International Australia* 40, 48-50; Elizabeth Adeney, 'Moral Rights/Statutory Licence: The Notion of Debasement in Australian Copyright Law' (1998) 9 *Australian Intellectual Property Journal* 36; Michael Blakeney and Fiona Macmillan 'Journalistic Parody and Moral Rights under Australian Copyright Law' (1998) 3 *Media Arts and Law Review* 124. The meaning of debasement (as provided for by s 55(2) *Copyright Act 1968* (Cth) – no statutory licence permitted where debasement of the musical work occurs (no equivalent provision in s 59 *Copyright Act 1968* (Cth) in relation to lyrics) - which was repealed by the *Copyright Amendment (Moral Rights) Act 2000* (Cth)) was considered by the Federal Court of Australia in *Schott Musik International GmbH & Co v Colossal Records of Australia Pty Ltd* (1997) 37 IPR 1. This case concerned whether a techno adaptation of a musical work by the group Excalibur debased the original work. The Full Federal Court held that in assessing the notion of debasement the court must take a broad approach, paying due regard to the community's wide spectrum of tastes and values. Accordingly, the techno adaptation was held not to have debased the original work. In *Morrison Leahy Music Limited v Lightbond Limited* [1993] EMLR 144 Morrit J held that the use of samples from an original work by George Michael did amount to derogatory treatment. In coming to this conclusion, Morrit J favoured the argument of the plaintiffs that the sampling of parts of the music had completely altered the character of the original work. In *Confetti Records v Warner Music* [2003] EWCh 1274 (Ch) [150] which concerned an alleged derogatory treatment of a composition in a remix by a UK garage band Lewinson J held 'that the mere fact that a work has been distorted or mutilated gives rise to no claim, unless the distortion or mutilation prejudices the author's honour or reputation.' Here, the court was unable to find that the original author's honour or reputation had been prejudiced, thus the claim for derogatory treatment failed. Would one be able to argue that the author's moral rights of integrity in relation to music and

that the right of integrity only applies in relation to a substantial part of the work and therefore in instances where a substantial part has not been reproduced this will not be an issue.[111]

It should also be noted that in accordance with *US Free Trade Agreement Implementation Act* 2004 (Cth) moral rights will extend to performers. Performers' moral rights will include the right of attribution of performership, the right not to have performership falsely attributed and the right of integrity of performership. However, these changes are yet to come into effect, as they are contingent upon Australia's obligations under the *WIPO Performances and Phonograms Treaty* entering into force.

Once it has been determined that an infringement has occurred we would then need to determine if a fair dealing exception relating to criticism, review, research, study or news reporting is applicable.[112] It is generally accepted that the scope for a fair dealing argument under the current law in the context of sampling would be very small.[113] In contrast the fair use doctrine in the US has supported some forms of 'transformative' sampling most notably in the area of parody.[114] It is also important to note that the current fair dealing provisions in the *Copyright Act* do not remove liability for the infringement of moral rights.

Sampling Case Law

In Australia we have very little case law on the issue of sampling. The closest we have is *Universal Music Australia Pty Ltd v Miyamoto*[115] a case where entire songs were sampled onto compilation style CDs and it is no

---

lyrics were infringed in the critiquing rap recasting of Roy Orbison's classic, 'Oh Pretty Woman' by 2 Live Crew, held to have the potential to be fair use by the US Supreme Court in *Campbell v Acuff-Rose Music Inc* 510 U.S 569 (1994)?

[111] Section 195AZH *Copyright Act 1968*.

[112] *Copyright Act 1968* (Cth) ss 40-43, 103A, 103B, 103C, 104.

[113] See the analysis of the fair dealing provisions below in the context of MP3 Blogs.

[114] *Campbell v Acuff-Rose Music Inc* 510 U.S 569 (1994). See further Nicola Bogle, 'Does Black and White Make Gray? A Critical Analysis of the Legal Regime Governing Digital Music Sampling' (2005) 61 *Intellectual Property Forum* 10 at 16-17; Matthew Rimmer, 'The Grey Album: Copyright Law and Digital Sampling' (2005) 114 *Media International Australia* 40 at 44-5; B Challis,"The Song Remains the Same: A Review of the Legalities of Music Sampling" www.musicjournal.org; M Heins, NYU Free Expression Policy Project, "Trashing The Copyright Balance" (2004) http://www.fepproject.org/commentaries/bridgeport.html ; "Sixth Circuit Rejects De Minimis Defense to the Infringement of A Sound Recording Copyright" (2005) *118 Harvard Law Review* 1355.

[115] [2003] FCA 812 (Unreported, Lindgren J, 18 July 2003).

surprise that the Federal Court of Australia (Lindgren J.) was not prepared to entertain any excuses based on the concept of music sampling. *Universal Music Australia Pty Ltd v Miyamoto*[116] concerned an action for copyright infringement brought by a number of recording companies against fives DJ's, who had remixed a number of tracks from different recordings and then produced a remix CD. The five DJ's claimed that they had only produced the CD's in order to raise their profiles and satisfy audience demand.[117] Nonetheless Lindgren J held that the remix CD's constituted copying of a substantial part of the sound recordings and therefore was an infringement of ss 101 and 103 of the *Copyright Act*.[118] As this case concerned infringing samples that were entire songs and not smaller parts of songs the Court did not closely consider the crucial issue of what will amount to copying of a substantial part of a sound recording in the context of music sampling.

In a later hearing for damages in *Universal Music Australia Pty Ltd v Miyamoto*[119]. Wilcox J scolded the five DJ's for their flagrant disregard of the applicant's rights.[120] His Honour found that all five respondents had deliberately infringed copyright law for ultimate financial gain.[121] He went on to further comment that there was a culture within the music industry of blatant disregard for copyright restrictions, based on an ill-conceived perception that sound recording companies were wealthy multinationals and therefore fair game.[122] However, Wilcox J did acknowledge that '[i]f the respondents' infringements of copyright had been limited to [the] creation of one or more of the compilation CDs for use only by the respondent himself, so as facilitate his presentation on a particular occasion, I would have taken a less serious view of the infringements.'[123] However, the decisive factor in this case was that the respondents went beyond the production of the compilation CDs for their own use.[124] Instead, the respondents motivated by their own ultimate financial gain knowingly

---

[116] [2003] FCA 812 (Unreported, Lindgren J, 18 July 2003).
[117] *Universal Music Pty Ltd v Miyamoto* [2004] FCA 982 (Unreported, Wilcox J, 30 July 2004) [12].
[118] *Universal Music Pty Ltd v Miyamoto* [2003] FCA 812 (Unreported, Lindgren J, 18 July 2003) [23], [26].
[119] [2004] FCA 982 (Unreported, Wilcox J, 30 July 2004).
[120] *Universal Music Pty Ltd v Miyamoto* [2004] FCA 982 (Unreported, Wilcox J, 30 July 2004) [24].
[121] Ibid.
[122] Ibid.
[123] Ibid [26].
[124] Ibid.

trampled on the applicants' rights, thereby infringing copyright.[125] Unfortunately this case does not provide clear guidance for digital sampling of smaller amounts of material.

The recent US decision in *Bridgeport Music Inc v Dimension Films Inc*,[126] has thrown the law on sampling into somewhat of a spin. For years American and UK courts have allowed very small (*de minimus*) amounts of songs to be sampled but *Bridgeport* challenges that approach.[127] In *Bridgeport* the United States Court of Appeals for the 6th Circuit overturned a District Court finding that the very small (*de minimus*) amount of sampling in this case did not amount to copyright infringement. At issue was the use of a sample from the rap song '100 Miles and Runnin' in the sound track of the movie 'I Got the Hook Up'. The allegedly infringing sample was a two second, three-note solo guitar 'riff' which was copied, the pitch lowered and then looped and extended to 16 beats.[128] This sample then featured in five places with each looped segment lasting for approximately seven seconds. In an action for copyright infringement Higgins J of the Middle District Court of Tennessee held that the infringement was *de minimis* and therefore not actionable.[129] However, this decision was overturned on appeal with the Court of Appeals for the 6th Circuit finding that 'no substantial or *de minimis* inquiry should be undertaken at all when the defendant has not disputed that it digitally sampled a copyrighted sound recording.'[130] Severely limiting the application of the notion of *de minimis* use in cases concerning music samples, their Honours held that even where a small part of a sound recording is sampled, the part taken is something of value.[131] In their view this was the only logical conclusion, since if you cannot pirate the whole sound recording there is no reason why you should be able to lift or sample

---

[125] Ibid.
[126] 401 F3d 647 (6th Cir, 2004); 410 F 3d 792 (6th Cir 2005).
[127] B Challis, "The Song Remains the Same: A Review of the Legalities of Music Sampling" www.musicjournal.org; Amici Curiae Brief of Brennan Center for Justice at NYU Law School and EFF in *Bridgeport Rehearing* 21 January 2005 <http://www.fepproject.org/courtbriefs/bridgeport.pdf>
[128] *Bridgeport Music Inc v Dimension Films Inc*, 401 F3d 647, 652 (6th Cir, 2004); 410 F 3d 792, 796 (6th Cir 2005).
[129] 230 F Supp 2nd 830 (MD Tenn, 2002).
[130] *Bridgeport Music Inc v Dimension Films Inc*, 401 F3d 647, 654 (6th Cir, 2004); 410 F 3d 792, 798 (6th Cir 2005).
[131] *Bridgeport Music Inc v Dimension Films Inc*, 401 F3d 647, 658 (6th Cir, 2004); 410 F 3d 792, 801-802 (6th Cir 2005); *TCN Channel Nine Pty Ltd v Network Ten Pty Ltd (No 2)* [2005] FCAFC 53 (Unreported, Sundberg, Finkelstein and Hely JJ, 26 May 2005) [19].

something less than the whole.[132] The message from *Bridgeport Music Inc v Dimension Films Inc*, is clear, 'get a license or do not sample'.[133]

The Court also made the point that their decision would not serve to stifle creativity as anybody was free to make a new sound recording of the composition.[134] In their view sampling acts to provide a savings in production costs and should not be allowed at the expense of the person who made the original sound recording.[135] This view to some extent underestimates the creative innovation involved in sampling and privileges the notion of the taking of value and saving of production costs.

This decision appears to show a changing attitude within the courts in regards to music sampling infringements. Previously, courts had been willing to allow the use of music samples based on the legal maxim of *de minimis*, 'the law cares not for trifles'. This was demonstrated in *Newton v Diamond*,[136] where the majority held that the unauthorised use of a music sample by the group Beastie Boys, was *de minimis* and therefore not actionable. In reaching this decision the majority was of the opinion that the use of a brief sample, consisting of three notes separated by a half-step over a background C note, was insufficient to sustain a claim for copyright infringement.[137] Admittedly *Newton* is a confusing precedent as the Beastie Boys had licenced the sound recording so what was in issue was simply the sampling of the music or score. There is conjecture over whether the strict approach of *Bridgeport* or the more flexible approach of *Newton* will become the dominant approach in the US,[138] however, it is suggested that Australian courts in determining whether a substantial part has been reproduced should blend the reasoning of both cases.[139]

---

[132] *Bridgeport Music Inc v Dimension Films Inc*, 401 F3d 647, 658 (6th Cir, 2004); 410 F 3d 792, 801-802 (6th Cir 2005).
[133] *Bridgeport Music Inc v Dimension Films Inc*, 401 F3d 647, 657 (6th Cir, 2004); 410 F 3d 792, 801 (6th Cir 2005).
[134] *Bridgeport Music Inc v Dimension Films Inc*, 401 F3d 647, 657 (6th Cir, 2004); 410 F 3d 792, 801 (6th Cir 2005).
[135] *Bridgeport Music Inc v Dimension Films Inc*, 401 F3d 647, 657-658 (6th Cir, 2004); 410 F 3d 792, 802 (6th Cir 2005).
[136] 349 F 3d 591 (9th Cir, 2003).
[137] *Newton v Diamond*, 349 F 3d 591, 603 (9th Cir, 2003).
[138] See "Amici Curiae" Brief of Brennan Center for Justice at NYU Law School and EFF in *Bridgeport Rehearing* 21 January 2005 <http://www.fepproject.org/courtbriefs/bridgeport.pdf>.
[139] See further: "Sixth Circuit Rejects De Minimis Defense to the Infringement of A Sound Recording Copyright" (2005) *118 Harvard Law Review* 1355.

MP3 Blogs

What Are MP3 Blogs?

Since their inception in early 2003, MP3 blogs have rapidly become the latest evolution in how people choose to share their favourite music in the digital environment. The concept of an MP3 blog essentially involves the combination of an online journal, with a music column that features MP3 music files that are available for download.[140] Generally, MP3 blogs contain one or two tracks from a CD album available for download. This is usually accompanied by the traditional blog which features a commentary or review on the track and the artist. Readers are then encouraged to download the music, read the accompanying review and share their thoughts online. The MP3 files that are contained on the blogs are generally either available for download directly from the blog itself or via a link to another site where the MP3 files have been uploaded. However, in most cases the MP3 files are usually only available to download for a couple of days. By their very nature most MP3 blogs tend to feature obscure 'musical nuggets', those hard to find often outdated tracks which are restricted to a particular musical sub-genre or theme. MP3 blogs tend to fall into two categories, those that provide music with the copyright owner's permission and those that do not. It is the latter which will have implications for copyright law.

What Does Copyright Law Allow?

Thus far MP3 blogs have managed to avoid the wrath of the music industry and are therefore yet to be legally challenged.[141] However, it is has been

---

[140] Rick Ellis, *MP3 Blogs Combine Reviews with Music Files* (2004) NBC13 Technology < http://www.nbc13.com/technology/3369203/detail.html#> at 8 April 2005.

[141] Cf. *Commonwealth Director of Public Prosecutions v Ng, Tran and Le* (Unreported, Sydney Central Local Court, Henson DCM, 18 November 2003) where Peter Tran, Charles Ng and Tommy Le ran a website called MP3 WMA Land. The website essentially provided free MP3 music downloads to 390 commercially available CD albums and 946 singles. The site was said to have received some seven million hits during its operation, with an estimated loss to copyright holders of up to $200 million. The Court found the three defendants guilty under s 132(2)(b) of the *Copyright Act 1968* (Cth) for knowingly distributing copyrighted work, to an extent that prejudicially affects the owner of copyright. Tran and Ng both received prison sentences of 18 months, suspended for three years; in addition to this Tran was fined $5000 and Ng and Le ordered to perform 200 hours community service. See also *Universal Music Australia Pty Ltd v Cooper* [2005] FCA 972 (Unreported, Tamberlin J, 14 July 2005);

well documented that they exist within a so called legal grey area, and it may only be a matter of time before the law turns its attention to MP3 blogs. Recently the Recording Industry Association of America stated that in terms of piracy MP3 blogs are an issue which they are closely monitoring and that at any time they could decide to make enforcement a priority.[142] The main reason for the survival of MP3 blogs is their relatively low profile, with even the most popular MP3 blogs having only a few thousand regular visitors.[143] This is a far cry from the millions of people who engage in peer to peer file sharing through programs like WinMx or Kazaa. In addition to this most MP3 blogs tend to feature music which is no longer termed as mainstream, and has often been out of the public eye for a long time.[144]

However, despite these factors while MP3 blogs continue to feature tracks without the permission of the copyright owner they run the risk that they will infringe copyright law. Under the *Copyright Act* bloggers will infringe copyright when they do any of the acts within the copyright owner's exclusive rights.[145] In the context of a sound recording, this will most often occur on MP3 blogs where the host blogger makes a copy of the sound recording or where they communicate the recording to the public by posting it to the blog.[146] In this scenario – that is posting by the host blogger – there will also most likely be a copyright infringement of the musical and literary work, as well as the sound recording. This infringement in the musical and literary work will occur where the copyright owner's exclusive rights are infringed, by either reproducing the work in a material form, communicating the work to the public or performing the work in public.[147] In light of the recent decision in *Universal Music Australia Pty Ltd v Cooper*[148] host bloggers also need to

---

Universal Music Aistralia Pty Ltd v Sharman License Holdings Ltd [2005] FCA 1242 (Unreported, Wilcox J, 5 September 2005).
[142] Bill Werde, *The Music Blog Boom* (2004) Rolling Stone <h ttp://www.rollingstone.com/news/story/_/id/6478068?rnd=1095273257416&pageid=rs.Home&has-player=true&pageregion=single1&> at 18 April 2005.
[143] Wikipedia, *MP3 Blog* (2005) <http://en.wikipedia.org/wiki/Mp3_blog> at 8 April 2005.
[144] Ibid.
[145] *Copyright Act 1968* (Cth) ss 36(1), 101(1).
[146] *Copyright Act 1968* (Cth) s 85(1)(a), (c). The posting of the sampled work on the Internet might also infringe the copyright owner's right to allow the recording to "be caused to be heard in public": s 85 (1) (b).
[147] *Copyright Act 1968* (Cth) s 31 (1)(a).
[148] [2005] FCA 972 (Unreported, Tamberlin J, 14 July 2005).

be mindful of authorisation liability for facilitating copyright infringement through hypertext linking.

Assuming an action for copyright infringement can be made out against an MP3 blog, one issue which does arise is whether MP3 blogs fall within the defence of fair dealing under the *Copyright Act*. In particular, it may be argued that MP3 blogs come within the fair dealing defence of criticism or review.[149] Under this provision a musical or literary work or a sound recording may be fairly dealt with, without infringing copyright for the purposes of criticism or review.[150] There is no definition of criticism or review within the *Copyright Act*, however, it has been held that the words criticism and review are of 'wide and indefinite scope which should be interpreted literally.'[151] In *Warner Entertainment Co Ltd v Channel 4 Television Corp PLC*[152] Henry LJ stated that the question to be answered in assessing whether a dealing is fair or not is 'is the [work] incorporating the infringing material a genuine piece of criticism or review, or is it something else, such as an attempt to dress up the infringement of another's copyright in the guise of criticism'.

The issue which then arises is whether the commentary and review posted on MP3 blogs will be sufficient to constitute criticism and review under ss 41 and 103A of the *Copyright Act*. Given the differing nature of each MP3 blog it is not possible to provide one complete answer; rather each site will need to be assessed on a case by case basis. However, it is possible to identify a number of key indicators which may suggest whether the fair dealing defence of criticism or review will be applicable in a given case. The primary determining factor will be the amount of commentary which is featured on the MP3 blog itself. In the case where an MP3 blog contains quite detailed commentary, a court may be inclined to view it as a genuine piece of criticism or review. This is to be distinguished from those sites that do not contain detailed commentary and are likely to be viewed as an infringement of copyright. Another determining factor will be the number of tracks that are available for download on the MP3 blog. Where there are only one or two tracks available, a court may be more willing to allow the criticism or review defence. However, MP3 blogs which contain an entire album or a substantial number of tracks will most likely not be afforded the defence of fair dealing. In summary, it would appear that as a general

---

[149] *Copyright Act 1968* (Cth) ss 41, 103A.
[150] Fitzgerald and Fitzgerald, *supra*, 171.
[151] *TCN Channel Nine Pty Ltd v Network Ten Ltd* (2001) 50 IPR 335, [66].
[152] (1993) 28 IPR 459, 468.

guide, where an MP3 blog is prima facie nothing more than an attempt to disguise copyright infringement, the defence of fair dealing will not be allowed. However, if the MP3 blog is a genuine piece of criticism or review, and is on a small scale, then a court may be inclined to allow the fair dealing defence.

Culture Jamming

What Is Culture Jamming?

Culture jamming is part of a movement; a desire to change how the world currently operates – where individuals are replaced by corporations in a culture of consumerism. The term culture jamming refers to a form of social and political activism, a resistance movement to the hegemony of popular culture which utilises the mass media to criticise and satirise those very institutions that control and dominate the mass media.[153] Culture jammers are revolutionaries, they intend to incite and provoke social and political upheaval, ultimately for change.[154] They are discontent with the control that politicians, corporations and capitalism have taken over the mass media and society in general and wish to free the public from what they see as a propagandised world. Their technique is to take conventional forms of mass communication such as corporate advertising and imitate the visuals, either logos or slogans, subtly altering the intended message to express dissenting opinions.[155] Culture jamming may take a number of different forms and mediums however, it is mainly restricted to the internet, posters, billboards and personal apparel like t-shirts. Some popular examples of culture jamming include:

- Subvertising – this involves undermining the authority of corporations and politicians that impose capitalism and consumerism, and sabotaging their efforts to control the minds of the public.[156]

- Guerrilla communication – this is the intervention in the more conventional processes of communication in order to grab the audience's attention and express unconventional views.

---

[153] See generally: Communication Studies University of California, *What is Culture Jamming?* (2004) Culture Jamming <http://www.bol.ucla.edu/~nsajous/ > at 12 April 2005; Kalle Lasn, *Culture Jam: How to Reverse America's Suicidal Consumer Binge – and why we must* (1999) Eagle Press.
[154] Ibid.
[155] Ibid.
[156] For an example of subvertising see http://www.subvertise.org.

- Google bombing – this involves the manipulation of search engine results to link search keywords with negative or humiliating phrases and websites.
- Billboard liberation – this is a practice used against corporate and political advertising, whereby critical and often cynical messages replace the original message while still remaining visually similar.[157]

What Does The Law Allow?[158]

It impossible to define all of the legal issues associated with culture jamming, as these will largely depend upon the medium or form in which the culture jamming takes. However, by using 'billboard liberation' as an example it is possible to identify a number of legal issues which may arise in similar cases of culture jamming. The first legal issue which may arise in this instance of culture jamming is the potential for the logo or slogan used in 'billboard liberation' to infringe copyright. Under the *Copyright Act* copyright infringement will occur where the culture jammer does any of the acts within the copyright owner's exclusive rights.[159] Using the example of 'billboard liberation' this will most likely occur where the culture jammer either reproduces in a material form or communicates to the public an artistic work.[160] An artistic work is defined to mean a painting, drawing or photograph, whether or not the work is of artistic quality.[161] This definition will therefore incorporate the images and drawings which feature heavily in 'billboard liberation'. Where there is also accompanying text, this will also infringe copyright in the literary work when it is reproduced in a material form or communicated to the public.[162] The text featuring in 'billboard liberation' will be classed as a literary work as it is a particular form of

---

[157] For an example of billboard liberation see http://www.billboardliberation.com.

[158] Culture jamming may also lead to criminal charges or property based actions: see *Pat O'Shane v John Fairfax & Sons* [2004] NSWSC 140 (Unreported, Smart AJ, 16 March 2004) [29] referring to a recent example of this in relation to a Berlei bra billboard.

[159] *Copyright Act 1968* (Cth) ss 36(1), 101(1).

[160] *Copyright Act 1968* (Cth) s 31(b). See *Compagnie Generale des Etablissements Michelin "Michelin&Cie" v National Automobile Aeroscope, Transportation and General Workers Union of Canada (CAW-Canada) (T.D.)* [1997] 2F.C. 306; *British Columbia Automobile Assn v Office and Professional Employees International Union Local 378* [2001] B.C.J. No. 151.

[161] *Copyright Act 1968* (Cth) s 10(1).

[162] *Copyright Act 1968* (Cth) s 10(1).

expression through which the ideas or information are conveyed.[163] The scope for a defence of fair dealing based on parody is extremely limited and would most likely be unsuccessful.[164] This form of culture jamming also has the potential to infringe the creator's moral rights of attribution of authorship, the right not to have authorship falsely attributed and the right of integrity of authorship.[165]

Another legal issue which arises in relation to 'billboard liberation' is the infringement of registered trade marks. In Australia protection is conveyed upon those trade marks which are registered under the *Trade Marks Act 1995* (Cth). Trade marks are defined as 'a sign used, or intended to be used, to distinguish goods or services dealt with or provided in the course of trade by a person from goods or services so dealt with or provided by any other person'.[166] This definition of a trade mark will therefore convey protection upon any 'letter, word, name, signature, numeral, device, brand, heading, label, aspect of packaging, shape, colour, sound or scent' providing it is distinctive.[167]

---

[163] *Victoria Park Racing and Recreation Grounds Co Ltd v Taylor* (1937) 58 CLR 479; *Blackie & Sons Ltd v Lothian Book Publishing Co Pty Ltd* (1921) 29 CLR 396. Note that copyright will not usually subsist in very short titles, slogans or phrases although the law is inconsistent on this issue: Anne Fitzgerald and Brian Fitzgerald, *Intellectual Property in Principle* (2004) Thomson Sydney 88-9; Jill McKeough, Andrew Stewart and Philip Griffith *Intellectual Property in Australia* 3rd ed (2005) LexisNexis Butterworths Sydney, 164-5.

[164] See *Compagnie Generale des Etablissements Michelin "Michelin&Cie" v National Automobile Aeroscope, Transportation and General Workers Union of Canada (CAW-Canada) (T.D.)* [1997] 2F.C. 306 holding that "criticism" under the Canadian fair dealing provisions does not include parody; *TCN Channel Nine v Network Ten* (2001) 50 IPR 335, [2001] FCA 108 at [66]; *AGL Sydney Ltd v Shortland County Council* (1989) IPR 99 at 105-6. cf. *TCN Channel Nine v Network Ten* (2002) 118 FCR 417, [2002] FCAFC 146 at [98]-[104], [116]; See generally Ellen Gredley and Spyros Maniatis, 'Parody: A Fatal Attraction? Part 1: The Nature of Parody and its Treatment in Copyright' (1997) 7 *European Intellectual Property Review* 339. On the application of fair use doctrine in these circumstances see *Leibovitz v Paramount Pictures* 948 F Supp 1214 (SDNY, 1996).

[165] *Copyright Act 1968* (Cth) s 189; Ellen Gredley and Spyros Maniatis, 'Parody: A Fatal Attraction? Part 1: The Nature of Parody and its Treatment in Copyright' (1997) 7 *European Intellectual Property Review* 339, 341, 344.

[166] *Trade Marks Act 1995* (Cth) s 17.

[167] *Trade Marks Act 1995* (Cth) ss 6, 41.

Prior to the introduction of a dilution styled provision into Australian trademark law[168] in 1995 the trademark holder would have had to prove that culture jamming created consumer confusion as to the source of goods or services leading to an action for trademark infringement[169] or passing off.[170] Since the enactment of section 120(3) of the *Trade Marks Act 1995* (Cth) which provides protection for well known trade marks, which are typically owned by multinational corporations or national companies with a high market share,[171] a registered trade mark will be infringed where a person uses a mark that is the same or deceptively similar to a well known mark as a trade mark (regarding unrelated goods or services) where use of the mark is likely to indicate a connection with the well known mark and thereby adversely affect the interests of the registered owner.[172] Interestingly the Canadian case of *Compagnie Generale des Etablissements Michelin "Michelin & Cie" v National Automobile Aeroscope, Transportation and General Workers Union of Canada (CAW-Canada) (T.D.)*[173] suggests s 22 of the *Canadian Trade Marks Act* – a dilution provision broadly similar to the Australian provision - would not be enlivened in parody situations as in such circumstances there is no "use of the mark as a trademark".[174] In the *Michelin Case* the NAATGW Union in seeking to recruit workers of the Michelin company depicted the Michelin man or 'Bibendum' (a marshmallow rotund figure composed of tyres) on leaflets distributed to workers in a manner so as to suggest he was just about to step on and squash a Michelin worker. The Canadian Court of

---

[168] On this notion see: B Fitzgerald and E Sheehan, "Trademark Dilution and the Commodification of Information: Understanding the "Cultural Command"" (1999) 3 *Mac LR* 61; *TRIPS* Art 16.

[169] Sections 120(1) and (2) Trade *Marks Act 1995* ; Fitzgerald and Fitzgerald, supra, 369-75; *Mattel Inc v NCA Records Inc* 296 F 3d 894 at 900 (9th Circ 2002) Cert. Denied 537 U.S. 1171 (2003); *Elvis Presley Enterprises v Capece* 141 F 3d 188 (5th Cir 1998).

[170] See generally: Mark Davison, Kate Johnston and Patricia Kennedy, *Shanahan's Australian Law of Trade Marks and Passing Off* (3rd ed, 2003) 571; *Clark v Associated Newspapers Ltd* [1998] 40 IPR 262 at 268.

[171] Fitzgerald and Fitzgerald, *supra*, 370.

[172] *Trade Marks Act 1995* (Cth) s 120(3). To determine whether a mark is well known, it is necessary to consider the 'extent to which the trade mark is known within the relevant sector of the public, whether as a result of the promotion of the trade mark or for any other reason': s 120(4).

[173] [1997] 2F.C. 306

[174] See further *British Columbia Automobile Assn v Office and Professional Employees International Union Local 378* [2001] B.C.J. No. 151; M Bibic and V Eatrides, "Would Victoria's Secret Be Protected North of the Border? A Revealing Look at Trade-Mark Infringement and Depreciation of Goodwill in Canada" (2003) 93 *The Trademark Reporter* 904.

Appeal held that this was not trademark infringement of any kind but was a substantial reproduction of copyright material and therefore an infringement of Canadian copyright law. The *Michelin Case* would suggest that in Australia in most instances using a trademark for the purpose of parody would not infringe s 120 (3) as it would not be "use of a mark as a trademark."[175] This would allow some forms of 'billboard liberation' but copyright infringement could still be an issue. However as dilution laws aim to protect the value of the well known mark and ridiculing potentially devalues a mark, arguments for infringement will continue to be made and until there is a clear ruling on this issue there can be no certainty that the Canadian approach will be fully adopted in Australia.[176]

As well known trademarks become part of our constructed reality and cultural environment one school of thought suggests we should have a broader right to access and utilise them as part of cultural discourse.[177] A number of US cases have considered the issue as to what extent a well known trade mark may be reproduced or re-used as a medium of expression or a part of free culture. In *Lucasfilm Ltd v High Frontier*,[178] George Lucus unsuccessfully tried to bring an action for trade mark infringement against public interest groups who had labelled Ronald Reagan's plans for outer-spaced weaponry, 'Star Wars'. The court held that despite the fact that the original meaning derived from the trade use, courts cannot regulate descriptive non-trade use, without becoming language police. The court further held that trade marks laws are designed to regulate unfair trade competition, not the development of the English language in everyday human discourse. This case can be contrasted with *San Francisco Arts & Athletic Inc (SFAA) v US Olympics Committee (USOC)*,[179] where the US Supreme Court held that SFAA's promotion of an event called the 'Gay Olympic Games' was in breach of the *Amateur Sports Act* which allowed USOC to prohibit commercial and promotional

---

[175] Fitzgerald and Fitzgerald *supra*, 372-5; *Philmac Pty Ltd v Registrar of Trademarks* [2002] FCA 1551; *Coca-Cola Co v All-Fect Distributors Ltd* [1999] FCA 1721; *The Australian Steel Company Operations Pty Ltd v Steel Foundations Ltd* [2003] FCA 374.
[176] E Gredley and S Maniatis, "Parody: A Fatal Attraction? Part 2: Trade Mark Parodies" [1997] 8 *European Intellectual Property Review* 412 at 419-20.
[177] P. Loughlan, *Intellectual Property: Creative and Marketing Rights* (1998) LBC Information Services, Sydney 168ff.; R. Dreyfuss, 'Expressive Genericity: Trademarks as Language In the Pepsi Generation' (1990) 65 *Notre Dame Law Review* 397; B Fitzgerald and E Sheehan, "Trademark Dilution and the Commodification of Information: Understanding the "Cultural Command" (1999) 3 *Mac LR* 61.
[178] 622 F Supp 931 (1985).
[179] 483 US 522 (1987).

use of the word 'Olympic'. In this instance free speech and cultural discourse reasoning, that the word was now part of the common language, was rejected by the US Supreme Court.

In relation to parody the US courts have tended to allow trademarks to be reproduced on goods and even sold so long as it is a 'take off' and not a 'rip off'.[180] However the introduction of a federal trademark dilution law has brought some uncertainty in the case law as to the legality of parody, yet there seems to be a clear argument that 'non commercial speech' (in essence social commentary) involving a mark is protected by the First Amendment and such use will not amount to dilution.[181] The critical question will be whether parody devalues the mark? And if the answer is yes, the further question will be whether the parody devalues the mark in its ability to draw consumers or only within a broader social consciousness?[182]

In terms of 'billboard liberation' which features a political message, it is necessary to consider the implied guarantee to free political speech. The courts have held that there is an implied freedom to communicate on political matters under the *Commonwealth Constitution*.[183] The implied freedom to communicate on political matters protects individuals against laws that would otherwise restrict this freedom. This body of law may therefore provide a defence to any action against a form of culture jamming which contains a political message.

---

[180] *Nike Inc v "Just Did It" Enterprises* 6 F3d 1225, 1227-8 (7th Cir, 1993); *The Coca Cola v Co v Gemini Rising Inc* 346 F. Supp. 1183 (E.D.N.Y. 1972); *Anheuser-Busch Inc. v L & L Wings Inc* 962 F. 2d 316 (4th Cir. 1992); G Mayers "Trademark Parody: Lessons from The Copyright Decision in Campbell v Acuff-Rose Music Inc" (1996) 60 *L & Contemp. Probs.* 181.
[181] See *Mattel Inc v Walking Mountain Productions* 353 F. 3d. 792 (9th Cir 2004); *Mattel Inc v NCA Records Inc* 296 F 3d 894 (9th Circ 2002) Cert. Denied 537 U.S. 1171 (2003); *Dr Seuss Enterprises v Penguin Books USA* 109 F 3d 1394 (9th Cir 1997); E Gredley and S Maniatis, "Parody: A Fatal Attraction? Part 2: Trade Mark Parodies" [1997] 8 *European Intellectual Property Review* 412.
[182] *British Columbia Automobile Assn v Office and Professional Employees International Union Local 378* [2001] B.C.J. No. 151 at [165]-[168]; *Mattel Inc v Walking Mountain Productions* 353 F. 3d. 792 at 812 (9th Cir 2004); *Mattel Inc v NCA Records Inc* 296 F 3d 894 at 902-7 (9th Circ 2002) Cert. Denied 537 U.S. 1171 (2003).
[183] *Nationwide News Pty Ltd v Wills* (1992) 177 CLR 1; *Australian Capital Television Pty Ltd v Commonwealth* (1992) 177 CLR 106; *Theophanous v Herald & Weekly Times Ltd* (1994) CLR 104; *Lange v Australian Broadcasting Corporation* (1997) 189 CLR 520.

It is suggested that a clearer principle needs to be embodied in Australian copyright and trade mark law to allow broader social and cultural use of trademarks and reduce the threat of being sued.

What Does the Future Hold?

Introduction

The great dilemma that faces the spirit of social or cultural innovation in Australia is the degree to which the law can respond to iron out these apparent roadblocks. One group – the owners - would feel happy having an enormous power of censorship and control over 'appropriation' or at least a statutory licensing scheme providing some remuneration while creatives and social innovators seek to harness the power of 'remix' to build out the future. One of the most powerful concepts that has arisen to assist creativity and social innovation is that of the Creative Commons. The CC movement asks copyright owners to consider sharing copyright material where appropriate and for stated purposes and aims to set up a mechanism for clearly articulating such a process of sharing in the Internet world. On the back of this the Australian government has realised that copyright law is too inflexible and has sought to re-examine the way in which certain re-uses of copyright material without permission of the copyright owner should be facilitated. CC gives permission in advance and a more flexible fair dealing doctrine morphing into a fair use doctrine would provide a space where creatives and social innovators could harness to 'some degree' the existing store of knowledge and culture without permission of the copyright owner. This ability to negotiate copyright material upon the instance of seeing it and to innovate upon it and republish/distribute it provides a dynamic that the digital environment sponsors in a process of creative and social innovation. In terms of trademarks we need to consider reform of the law to more clearly articulate what type of re-use should be allowed.

Creative Commons

In 2004 the Creative Commons (CC) project was launched in Australia: (http://creativecommons.org.au). Creative Commons aims to build a distributed information commons by encouraging copyright owners, where appropriate, to licence use of their material through open content licensing protocols and thereby promote better identification, negotiation and reutilization of content for the purposes of creativity and innovation. It aims to make copyright content more 'active' by ensuring that content can be reutilized with a minimum of transactional effort. As the project highlights, the use of an effective identification or labeling scheme and an easy to understand and implement legal framework is vital to furthering this purpose. This is done by establishing generic protocols or license terms for the open distribution of content that can be attached to content with a minimum of fuss under a CC label. In short the idea is to ask copyright owners – where willing - to 'license out' or distribute their material on the basis of four protocols designed to enhance reusability and build out the information commons.[184]

Through the Creative Commons licences a copyright owner of content, be it text, music or film, can place that material in the commons. These base licences have been 'ported' or adapted to Australian law as they have in a number of other countries throughout the world.[185] The CC licences provide that anyone can use the content subject to one or a number of the following conditions[186]:

- **attribution** of the author;
- **non-commercial** distribution;
- that **no derivative** materials based on the licensed material are made (i.e. all copies are verbatim); and
- share and **share alike** (others may distribute derivative materials based on the licensed material under a licence identical to that which covers the licensed material).

It is also important to point out that moral rights are asserted under the core terms of the current Australian version of the CC licence. While this presents a challenge for remix culture it is anticipated that further options regarding moral rights will be presented in future versions.[187]

---

[184] On the key motivations for sharing content see: B Fitzgerald *'Structuring Knowledge Through Open Access: The Creative Commons Story'* in C Kapitzke and B Bruce (eds.) *New Libraries and Knowledge Spaces: Critical Perspectives on Information Education* (2005) Lawrence Erlbaum and Assoc.

[185] <http://creativecommons.org/international> <http://creativecommons.org.au>

[186] All of the conditions are presented as options which the licensor may choose, except for the attribution condition which is now a default condition in each Creative Commons licence.

[187] B Fitzgerald, "Creative Commons (CC): Accessing, Negotiating and Remixing Online Content", in J. Servaes and P. Thomas (eds), *Communications, Intellectual Property and the Public Domain in the Asia Pacific Region: Contestants and Consensus* (forthcoming 2006) Sage New Delhi.

The licence can be presented in common, legal or digital code language – by simply going to creativecommons.org and choosing a licence online. This is then linked to the work that you wish to give or licence out through the commons. Creativecommons.org reports there have been over 53 million 'link-backs' to Creative Commons licences (including over 20 000 to the Australian licence) in ways that has further promoted creativity, innovation and education.[188]

Like the free software movement, Creative Commons uses intellectual property rights as the platform on which to structure downstream user rights. By claiming copyright in the content that will go into the commons the owner can determine how that content can be used downstream e.g. to further develop the commons. However, unlike copyleft free software licences, Creative Commons does not *require* utilisation of material in the commons to carry with it an obligation to share further innovations back to the commons – this is only one of the four conditions, known as 'share and share alike', the copyright owner might employ.[189]

Creative Commons cannot solve all of the legal issues associated with digital sampling and culture jamming. However, what it will enable is the 'building of active and distributed repositories of copyright content that can be utilised by creatives to build the next layer of creativity.'[190] It is through the building of these repositories that Creative Commons will enable music samplers to sample and culture jammers to jam freely, without the fear of litigation.

In relation to music CC has developed three different types of sampling licences (which are yet to be ported or translated into an Australian licence):

1. **The Sampling Licence** - This licence allows users to use part of the licensed material for any purpose other than advertising, but does not allow users to perform, display or distribute copies of the whole of the licensed material for any purpose.

---

[188] For example see <http://www.onlineopinion.com.au> <http://www.vibewire.net.au> <http://creativecommons.org.au>

[189] See generally Anne Fitzgerald and Brian Fitzgerald, *Intellectual Property in Principle* (2004) Thomson Sydney 455.

[190] Brian Fitzgerald and Ian Oi, 'Free Culture: Cultivating the Creative Commons' (2004) 9(2) *Media and Arts Law Review* 137 at 140; Brian Fitzgerald, 'Creative Choices: Changes to the Creative Commons' (2005) 114 *Media International Australia* 83.

2. **The Sampling Plus Licence** - This licence allows users to use part of the licensed material for any purpose other than advertising. It also allows users to perform, display and distribute copies of the whole of the licensed material for non-commercial purposes.
3. **The Noncommercial Sampling Plus Licence** - This licence allows users to use the whole or a part of the licensed material for non-commercial purposes[191]

In November 2004 Wired Magazine released a CD containing a collection of 16 songs all distributed under the Creative Commons sampling licenses – thirteen under the sampling plus license and three under the non commercial sampling plus license. The CD jacket encouraged readers to 'rip, mix, burn and swap till you drop',[192] activities which would otherwise have been prevented under the 'all rights reserved' copyright regime normally associated with the distribution of CDs. The release of the Wired CD symbolised more than just the free sharing of music, with 16 high profile artists recognising by 'doing' that sharing digital culture can be an advantage and not a threat.[193]

It must be noted that in Australia musicians that are members of certain collecting societies will not have the ability to utilise CC licences without the permission of the relevant collecting society. The Australian Performing Right Association[194] (APRA) takes an assignment of the rights of public performance and communication to the public, which subsist in musical works and lyrics.[195] The Australasian Mechanical Copyright Owners' Society (AMCOS) takes an exclusive licence over mechanical rights in relation to music and lyrics, including the right to make recordings.[196] The rights granted to both APRA and AMCOS cover all present and future music and lyrics owned by the member.[197] Accordingly, a member of APRA is generally not the owner of the right of public performance or communication to the public in his or her music and lyrics,

---

[191] <creativecommons.org>
[192] Thomas Goetz, *Sample the Future* (2004) Wired Magazine <http://www.wired.com/wired/archive/12.11/sample.html > at 15 April 2005.
[193] Ibid.
[194] <http://www.apra.com.au>
[195] Australasian Performing Rights Association, Constitution, cl 17 <http://www.apra.com.au/corporate/downloads/APRA%20Constitution%2005.pdf>
[196] AMCOS Membership Agreement, cl 2 <http://www.apra.com.au/writers/downloads/input_agreement-applicationformindividual5Nov2004.pdf>
[197] APRA Constitution, cl 17(a); AMCOS Membership Agreemeent, cl 1.1.1.

and is thus unable to negotiate rights under a Creative Commons licences, without APRA's permission. Likewise, a member of AMCOS is unable to give a license over the mechanical rights in his or her music and lyrics without the permission of AMCOS.[198] Both APRA and AMCOS provide methods for musicians to opt-out of collection of royalties in one or more of a limited number of categories, or to have the rights in a particular work licensed back to them for a particular purpose. 'Opt-out' means that the collecting society will re-assign a subset of the public performance, communication or mechanical rights for every work owned by the member, and will cease collecting from the relevant streams.[199] It is not possible to opt-out for a smaller number of works, and a minimum of 3 months notice is required for a re-assignment. 'Licence-back' means the creator is granted a non-exclusive license to a particular work for a particular performance or set of performances, or for a particular recording or other purpose.[200] Because the licence granted is limited in duration and scope, it is not sufficient for use with Creative Commons licences. A similar situation exists in some parts of Europe yet there is much more flexibility under the collection mechanisms established in the US.

More work needs to be done on developing a flexible mechanism for allowing musicians to negotiate rights under CC licences while still maintaining a workable model for the relevant collecting societies. This is a complex issue and CC will need to adequately address criticisms such as the interests of the musician are best met through an organised collecting mechanism, CC may not be in anybody's best interests and the existing system does not distinguish between commercial and non commercial performances.[201] Much of this criticism is a legacy of entrenched business models and consequently denies, as if it were a disruptive technology,[202] the potential of free culture.

In summary if you are a member of APRA or AMCOS the dynamic CC infrastructure is not available to you unless those organisations allow you to use it. Your American counterparts are not limited in this manner and

---

[198] Members of AMCOS are generally music publishers, but Individuals can apply for AMCOS membership if they do not have a publisher.
[199] APRA Constitution, cl 17(c); AMCOS Membership Agreement, cl 2.6.
[200] APRA Constitution, cl 17(g); AMCOS Membership Agreement, cl 2.6.6.
[201] Emma Pike, "What you need to know about Creative Commons" *M* (15 March 2005) <www.bmr.org/html/news/news53.htm>; S Faulder, "What Creative Commons Really Means for Writers" (2005) *Music Week* <www.cisac.org>
[202] See further: Clayton Christensen, *The Innovators Dilemma* (1997) Harvard Business School Press, Boston MA

many would see this as a distinct yet odd advantage in a free trade world where Australia and the US have sought to build an harmonious intellectual property law. If you are not an APRA or AMCOS member your music can be shared at *your choice* in the creative commons.

Fair Use Reform

On the 18 February 2005 the Commonwealth Attorney-General, Phillip Ruddock announced a review of copyright law to examine whether a fair use exception should be added to the *Copyright Act*.[203] In a speech outlining the Australian Government's copyright agenda for the next year, the Attorney-General acknowledged that some user groups expressed support for the introduction of 'an open ended exception to copyright similar to the fair use provision in the United States.'[204] In response to the changing nature of copyright, the Attorney-General said that 'a fair use provision may give the Copyright Act more flexibility to maintain the copyright balance in a digital environment.'[205]

There is no doubt that reform to this aspect of the *Copyright Act* is long overdue, and that the introduction of a fair use provision similar to that contained in United States law will go a long way towards solving the legal issues created by digital sampling and culture jamming.[206] The current fair dealing provisions in the *Copyright Act* are no longer capable of providing genuine fair dealing of content in the digital environment.[207] This is largely due to the fact that the current provisions are limited to a narrow range of activities which do not reflect the potential of the digital environment.[208]

---

[203] Attorney-General Phillip Ruddock, 'Copyright: New Futures, New Agendas' (Speech delivered at the Australian Centre for Intellectual Property and Agriculture Conference, Brisbane, 18 February 2005).
http://www.ag.gov.au/agd/WWW/MinisterRuddockHome.nsf/Page/speeches
[204] Ibid. at [38]
[205] Ibid. at [39]; see further Brian Fitzgerald, 'Underlying Rationales of Fair Use: Simplifying the Copyright Act' (1998) 2 *Southern Cross University Law Review* 153, 157.
[206] See further, B Fitzgerald "Fair Use for "Creative Innovation": A Principle We Must Embrace. A Submission in Response to the A-G's Issues Paper on Fair Use and Other Copyright Exceptions" (2005)
http://www.law.qut.edu.au/about/staff/lsstaff/fitzgerald.jsp
[207] *Copyright Act 1968* (Cth) ss 40-43, 103A, 103B, 103C, 104.
[208] See also *Ashdown v Telegraph Group Ltd* [2001] Ch 685 at 697-8 affirmed on appeal [2002] Ch. 149 at 171.

What is required is the introduction of a single open-ended fair use defence which is sufficiently flexible to adapt to new uses that emerge with technological developments, but also certain enough to provide guidance to copyright owners and users.[209] The harsh reality of the current *Copyright Act* is that even inconspicuous acts such as transferring music files to an iPod or making a back up copy of a CD are most likely an infringement of copyright.[210] These two common place activities while graphic demonstrations of the dire need for reform are merely the tip of the iceberg.

In implementing any doctrine of fair use the parliament needs to be mindful that fair use will not be thwarted by moral rights.[211] In a digital remix world the moral rights of attribution and integrity provide significant challenges to innovation and need to be carefully implemented. As some American scholars suggest moral rights are a transaction cost in the negotiation of culture and have the potential to stifle free speech in the spirit of censorship.[212] While acknowledging the value of moral rights we must guard against this potential in the remix world lest nothing will ever be remixed or transformed in a process of social comment and/or creativity.

Conclusion

As this article highlights the legality of the digital sampling of music needs to be clarified in order to sponsor creative and social innovation[213] by:

- clearly articulating how the notion of 'substantial part' will apply to music sampling. What amounts to a substantial part is yet to be clearly settled by the Australian courts and until this occurs this area of activity will be chilled by a lack of certainty and fear of being sued. If we are serious about creative innovation as an economic and cultural driver then we need to provide clear legislative or judicial guidance on

---

[209] Attorney-General's Department, 'Fair Use and Other Copyright Exceptions', *Issues Paper*, May 2005, 33; Copyright Law Review Committee, *Simplification of the Copyright Act 1968 (Cth) Report: Part 1* (1998) <www.clrc.gov.au>
[210] Ruddock, *supra* at [40]
[211] The the scope of "reasonableness" under s 195 AS will be important to this question: K Giles, "Mind the Gap: Parody and Moral Rights" (2005) 18 *AIPLB* 69
[212] Consider W Fisher, "Property and Contract on the Internet" (1999) 73 *Chicago-Kent Law Review* 1203
[213] On creative and social innovation see: L Lessig, *Free Culture* (2004); John Howkins, *The Creative Economy: how people make money from ideas*, (2001); John Hartley (ed.), *Creative Industries* (2005); DCITA, *Creative Industries Cluster Study* Volumes 1-3 (2004) ww.dcita.gov.au ; Ruddcok *supra* at [8].

what is allowed. A legislative solution could articulate the boundaries of sampling without permission of the copyright owner shading into a scheme where permission and compensation might be needed.

- promoting the use of permission in advance mechanisms like Creative Commons licences where appropriate and encouraging collecting societies to support these initiatives

- the introduction of a broad based fair use doctrine sponsoring parody and transformative use that does not fundamentally detract from the market of the original material. Sampling for purely private purposes should also be covered however a broad based exception for non commercial sampling would not be acceptable to many copyright owners or collecting societies as the sample could too easily be communicated to or caused to be heard by the public thereby damaging the market for the original material.

- the availability of responsive and flexible commercial licensing mechanisms, whether statutory or otherwise, for sampling that will not be covered by the suggestions above

In relation to culture jamming we need to clearly articulate what copyright and trademark law will allow. A fair use provision that covered both would be welcomed. Section 122 of the *Trade Marks Act 1995* should be amended to provide an exception for defined areas of activity such as culture jamming. This should be mirrored in the *Copyright Act.* [214]

The very heart of intellectual property law is about seeking a workable balance between the interests of many players in society – creators, owners, commercialising agents, performers, users, social commentators and the community to name a few. To this end Australian intellectual property law should allow some degree of sampling and culture jamming for no cost and without anyone's permission as this type of activity is the raw material of creative and social innovation. The time to address these issues seems to be well and truly upon us.

---

[214] See for example the French and Spanish copyright law models. Under French copyright law an author may not prohibit a parody, pastiche or caricature. However, this exemption only applies if the parody imitates the work with humorous intent and does not create any confusion, injury or degrade the original author. Similarly, under Spanish copyright law parody is exempted from the author's right of adaptation, provided it does not confuse or harm the original work: Ellen Gredley and Spyros Maniatis, 'Parody: A Fatal Attraction? Part 1: The Nature of Parody and its Treatment in Copyright' (1997) 7 *European Intellectual Property Review* 339, 343-4.

Note on developments since 2005

Since this paper was presented in early 2005 amendments have been introduced to the Australian *Copyright Act 1968* through the *Copyright Amendment Act 2006*. Some of these amendments alter the legal position regarding reuse of copyright material under Australian law.

For example, the Act now includes exceptions that permit:

- the reproduction of copyright material for the purpose of watching it at a more convenient time (ie time shifting) – s.111;
- the reproduction of copyright material in different formats for private use (ie format shifting) – ss.43C, 47J, 109A, 110AA; and
- the use of copyright material for certain specified purposes (eg by libraries and archives, by educational institutions, or for persons with a disability) – s.200AB.

One change that potentially works in favour of those wishing to remix copyright material is the introduction of new exceptions that allow fair dealings for the purpose of parody and satire (ss.41A and 103AA).

However, the amendments also make a number of changes to the criminal provisions of the Act that serve to lower the bar for the application of criminal penalties for copyright infringement in Australia (ss.132AA-AT). As a consequence, they increase the legal risk to those distributing material over the internet.

This new environment and the uncertainty it creates for those wishing to reuse existing material serves to emphasise the importance of open content licensing as a method of facilitating innovation and creativity in the digital age.

Law and Computer Games
Games History, Content, Practice and Law
The Future

> GREG LANE, PROFESSOR LAWRENCE LESSIG, PROFESSOR BRIAN FITZGERALD, PROFESSOR STUART CUNNIGNHAM, SAL HUMPHREYS, JOHN BANKS, KEITH DONE AND NIC SUZOR

The following papers were presented as part of a special 'Law and Computer Games' forum that was run in conjunction with the main conference. This forum focused particularly on the role open content licensing plays in the larger gaming landscape.

Introduction
This presentation by **Greg Lane** provides an understanding of the development and importance of the games industry.

Games History, Content, Practice and Law
Professor Brian Fitzgerald, **Sal Humphreys**, **John Banks**, **Keith Done** and **Nic Suzor** provide an overview of the history of games, the current games landscape and some immediate legal issues.

The Future
In this section, a panel of industry experts including **Sal Humphreys** and **Professors Lawrence Lessig** and **Stuart Cunningham**, each consider the challenges that are ahead for both the industry and its regulatory environment.

Professor Brian Fitzgerald
(Head, QUT Law School)

Introduction

GREG LANE

I would like to give you a little bit of a background to this session, to give you an overview of the industry generally, where it is at, and where I see it moving forward. In particular, some of the issues that we face as a developer, specifically the legal issues that arise from day to day in the general run of the business.

Auran began operation on 1 January 1995, literally in my garage, with just myself as a programmer. That is my background – programming. Over the course of the next two years we went on to develop a product called Dark Reign, which shipped in 1997, and went on to become a very big hit for us. We did a little over 800,000 copies of that product. We are now located at Teneriffe, and we have grown to about 80-odd people. That is a sizeable growth spurt. Of course, growth of that magnitude carries with it a number of interesting issues that arise from time to time, but the industry generally, coinciding with our growth, has gone through enormous changes.

When we started, you could easily write a game for $100,000 in a garage with a few people. Nowadays, if someone walked into my office and said, "I want to write a game and I am only going to give you a few million dollars", there would be no way we would even begin. We would be looking at budgets of $10million and up. Common games nowadays are 30, 40, 50 million dollars US. The record is about US$86million to date. The budgets are getting way up there in terms of scale, competing with movies. The industry has grown astronomically. Most of you would now know someone that has a game console, or probably has more than one game console. Most people have a PC or a Mac now, so the industry is enormous. I see various figures from day to day come across my desk, but the average seems to be an industry roughly the size of, or double the size of, the motion picture industry, and growing at roughly twice the rate.

During the development phase not only have the budgets and the team sizes and so on gone up but the product quality has increased astronomically as well. No longer is it possible to have someone compose a tune that is a simple little midi file that will play through their midi sound card. Now we have built a multi-million dollar recording studio. We have professional musicians come in. Everything is scored. There is a lot of emphasis and effort put into making products that are highly realistic. Going along with that is asset production: making not just the sounds but the graphics and the art files that go with the product, in addition to the coding.

It is the assets of products that are going to undergo enormous change over the coming years. There is already some really interesting information, which I know some of the presenters to follow me are going to let you in on. Just to touch on some of those, one of our key products is 'Trainz'. It is actually a model train simulator. It is surprising how many people are into model trains. We have done about 300,000 copies to date, so it is quite large. The interesting thing about Trainz is that it is a very content rich environment. There are, as you can imagine, hundreds of different styles of locomotives and carriages and so on that exist across the globe. It is almost an impossible task for us to develop that amount of content. We would need an enormous arts staff, and given the size of the project and the amount of dollars we are prepared to put into it, it would be uneconomical for us to develop a product with that amount of content.

We have taken a very different tack with that product and really opened it up to end users to add content to it. It is not a new thing. A lot of games out there do this. But there has been a general trend away from the initial environment that games were developed in whereby you had a tool set that the development team would use to make a game. They would not release the tool set to the public. Now it is very common indeed for that tool set to be released with the game, and, in fact in Trainz's case, the tool set is a part of the actual game. It exists on the main menu with the other objects of the game, and you can enter the editor as part of the normal sequence of events.

To the people who were model railroaders, the act of actually building their railroad is obviously very important. We wanted to make that part of the environment. Of course, since there is so much content out there, we wanted the ability for other people, other end users, to make trains, to make locomotives and so on. We went to great effort to embed an entire content delivery system within the actual application itself that enables Auran to host content developed by users and to actually deliver that for free to any number of users that connect to the Internet. That model has proven to be tremendously successful. We often joke about that fact that we have only ever had one main competitor to our Trainz product – unfortunately that was Microsoft – but they have dropped out of the market now and so it is just us. What is very interesting is that Microsoft, using their marketing muscle, did about ten times the number of copies that we did. They had three million copies in circulation. Yet the content that has been developed for their product is less than ours, and they still make the tools available, but their tool was very difficult to use. Ours was extremely simple and anyone who made content in Trainz could easily make it available to others, and the net result is that we now have about twice the content readily available for our Trainz product as Microsoft do for their product, even though they distributed ten times the number of copies.

That is a really good indication that good tool development can actually significantly add to the value of the product. Of course, we use this in marketing our product. On the back of the box we highlight the fact that you can get access to, literally tens of thousands of objects that have been made available by end users and are available through our download systems. We have taken a very open approach with how we make that available to people. We ask them to give us a licence to distribute their content, but we do not want that to be exclusive. We are happy for them to give us a non-exclusive licence. We simply say, "please give us a licence so that we can make your content available and you can do whatever else you like with it as well".

It is surprising to see the number of people that have put large amounts of content onto our download station and make it available. It has proven to be one of the key successes of the product. In fact we pushed it a step further recently, whereby we made all the content we developed internally, available for near cost (I think it was $9.99). We gave them every single asset that we had ever made – sounds, art assets, whatever it might be – and put it on a disc that we made available to every user. We gave them a licence that said:

> you can use all of this content to make your own things. You can make completely derivative versions using every piece of our original content, do whatever you like with it, sell it – the only exception is that you cannot use it to make an asset that goes into a competitive product.

That was widely accepted and we had literally hundreds and hundreds of sales of that product, and, of course, in turn that has meant that there has been an explosion of additional content on our site.

Looking forward, there are some radical changes going to take place in content development and we have already seen the embryonic phases of this. Going back a little bit in the creation of our Trainz product, it was fairly easy for people to make a single locomotive, or a tree, or a house, or whatever it may be, and make that available. Looking forward, as the programs themselves become more and more complex, what the assets can do within the structure of the program becomes more complex, and a good example of this would be a locomotive. Locomotives have a cabin and they have a number of controls and so on that function, and work, and they enable you to drive the train.

For months now we have been able to allow users to make a cabin, to make the locomotive and so on. We have started to embed program script associated with art assets, that extend its functionality. People can make things such as fans that turn on inside the cabin, and handles that move, along with a whole range of things that actually interact with the environment. They can write scripts that control the weather or do anything within the scene. They might have an art asset like a windmill, and that asset can have a script associated with it that reads the wind vector and then makes the windmill point into the wind and the blades rotate, based on the wind speed and so on. All these things increase the realism of the assets that have been created. But of course, to do it they need program code and this raises a very interesting dilemma because a lot of users who are artists, who are actually making assets for us and/or for themselves and distributing them, are not necessarily programmers. You start to get small groups or teams of people forming that include an artist and perhaps a sounds engineer and a programmer and, of course, now collectively they are making a single asset for distribution. The complexities that were already there with regard to distributing assets and re-using each other's content as individuals, is now significantly more complex. We now have teams of people doing this.

This is a trend I can see taking place across the board. A number of companies that we deal with, and I talk to the CEOs of these companies almost on a daily basis, are also moving in this direction whereby they are getting more and more complex art assets that are packaged as a single product. But they are composed of a number of objects made by a number of individuals. The issues associated with who owns the copyright in those products, who is going to distribute those, and the arrangements that they enter into amongst themselves, is going to be very interesting over time.

One of the things from a developer's perspective which is very important is that as we move into these products which are now becoming more and more expensive, risk management becomes a very key issue to whether or not you actually move ahead with the product. If you are going to look at it and you think we are only going to distribute so many copies, you have got to work out what your break-even point is, and in many cases, because the asset product load is so high now – it can easily consume half your budget and in some cases it can be 80 or 90 percent of the budget – lowering those costs is critical to the success of the product. If you cannot do that, in many cases, you would abandon the project.

We have often debated at Auran whether we could continue with our Trainz product if we did not have the assistance of the third party community, and the answer is probably "no". We have had a huge amount of assistance from them, and they generally make assets for us that we can include in our product and they do so for free. There could well be an argument as to whether we should be taking free product and including it in our product. We make sure that in every single case when we do these kinds of things that we offer an agreement with the people that supply this product, to provide what they deem to be an equal-value proposition for them.

In many cases it might be advertising on the box, putting their name in the credits, allowing them to say they are a payware creator and actually selling their content. They might want to put one of their objects into the program, and use it as a sales tool so that people can see the quality of their product and hopefully come to their website. We are very open to all the suggestions that the third-party creators offer, so we say to them, "what are the arrangements under which you would like to distribute this"? We get an enormous number of individuals that readily offer up their content and without that we would not be able to continue the project. I know there are a lot of smaller companies, like Auran, that really need that input. Without that we would have to abandon some projects.

The size of the asset data base is getting to be enormous. 'World of Warcraft' has 300,000 individual objects in the game, and that is an enormous number. Just imagine the asset management task of that alone and the cost associated with keeping it. I believe they are spending about $5 million a month just on maintaining and building new assets. It is an enormous cost, and of course, there are not many large companies in the world. You can probably count the number of them on one hand. Who can afford to pay those kind of prices? The vast majority of developers are Auran size – 80 staff or less – and certainly, in our case, the product would not exist without the input of third-party people, and we happily let them know that.

We regularly post on our own forums that without their input there would not be a product and I think they have a definite sense of ownership of the product. If we go and change something without consulting them, they often get very annoyed with us and tell us how they think the product should be. We generally listen and we take their input on board. A lot of features of the product are a result of user input. In fact, often is it the case that we will have an idea as to what we should put into the program, but if someone suggests it on our forums, we will let them get the credit for that, even though we might already have thought of it and it might already be in the design document. We will often say, "great idea, we will include that". When we finally ship the product there is quite often hundreds of features in there that people did suggest. More often than not they are features that we already had, but I think it really creates this sense that they own the product and that has been enormously important to the success of Trainz and to the other products that we are working on. That gives you an overview of where we are coming from and the industry size and where it is moving.

Games History, Content, Practice and Law

Professor Brian Fitzgerald, Sal Humphreys
John Banks, Keith Done and Nic Suzor

A Brief History of Games and Gaming WITH KEITH DONE

Competition has always been a key trait of the Human race. Essentially linked to the sex drive and the need to compete for a mate, competition has evolved, as we have evolved, changing from being able to beat the living daylights out of the rival Neanderthal, to being able to beat your friend with the roll of a dice or the rapid tap on a keyboard.

Once, our ancestors spent every living moment hunting and gathering food and avoiding getting eaten in the process but, as we evolved and got good at doing what Humans do – namely, organising others to do our work for us – we had sufficient time to devote to procreation and other pursuits. From the day that the first caveman played 'flint, deerskin, rock' we have enjoyed games as a diversion for the mind and entertainment to fill in our more empty days.

Ancient paintings and relics show that competitive sports such as archery, rowing and hunting evolved as early as the late Neolithic Age in 5000 BC. These were to continue to develop into many more-organized activities; events typical of the ancient Olympics, that were both individual and team-based in nature. However, this document is devoted to the evolution of tabletop gaming and I will focus on that specific area of games.

Just as games relying on physical prowess evolved as civilisation took hold, so did games requiring a combination of luck and grey matter. Archaeological diggings in Africa and the Middle East have uncovered what is considered the oldest board games, made between 7000-5000BC. Known as Mancala, the games have been found to be essentially similar in design, the concept being to move stones into specific depressions or spaces on a stone slab, according to a set of defined rules. Games that later evolved from this basic concept include the Royal game of Ur and the Egyptian game of Senet. These were all mathematical games and it is suggested that they may have been invented by early accountants or merchants, who originally used similar boards to tally numbers, count stock etc. However, tomb paintings clearly show these boards and pieces as being used for recreational purposes.

The next real 'leap' in the evolution of gaming comes between 400 – 800 AD with the appearance of abstract wargames appearing in Asia and the Middle East. These included such games as Checkers, Go and Chess. Although all of these games had earlier histories, it is the current versions that are still played today that evolved during this period. This introduced new strategies and dimensions to gaming, especially Chess, which invested the pieces with distinct moves, rather than the board dictating the strategies.

As the world moved into the medieval age, more variants on these strategic games evolved throughout Europe, each being a spin on moving pieces on a grid or checkerboard in order to seize the opponent's pieces. These games included favourites such as Fox and Geese, Alquerque and Fierges.

The establishment of Guilds from the 1300s to 1500s AD changed the economic focus of Europe from the land to the towns; requiring the provision of manufactured goods for sale. Improved technologies in the area of printing and paper manufacture resulted in the next great innovation in tabletop games – the playing card, particularly the standard 52-card deck which we use to play a diverse range of games. The 52-card deck originated in the Middle-East and was probably introduced to Europe as a result of the Crusades. Its success was primarily due to its potential as a new form of gambling instead of dice, which had been around since ancient times. The popularity of card games continued on throughout the next few centuries as the main tabletop distraction, filling in the idle hours for commoner and noble alike.

With the 1800s came the true era of industrialisation and mass-production. Up until then, most board games were made by the hands of the person who intended to play them or by craftspeople, who sold them to the wealthy; the means of production providing for a small output and the games being highly priced. Only cards and dice were games that were available to the mainstream market. Chess and other such board games were more expensive to make and stayed in the realm of the gentry.

However, as the middle-class grew during the 1700s to 1800s, many people, with increased time on their hands, invented a new and diverse range of games mainly as a form of family amusement and acceptable social interaction outside of families. These were activities that had few (or no) pieces or board; games like Charades, Blindman's Bluff and Pass the Slipper. These are typical examples of games of the era that became known as 'parlour games', usually played in the living room, or parlour.

Recognising the popularity of these social forms of entertainment, entrepreneurs saw ways to cash in by making inexpensive saleable products. Soon, people in Victorian Britain and the USA were hand-making the first generation of – what would become the first real mass-produced board games of the modern era. These were mainly chase or race games, using dice to move along a track and set dice rolls to overcome obstacles on the board.

The first truly mass-produced example was the 'Mansion of Happiness' published in 1843 by the W and SB Ives Company. It was a moralistic game that rewarded children for doing good tasks. The success of this inspired many other companies to reflect aspects of day-to-day life in their games, culminating in the release of 'The Checkered Game of Life' in 1860 by Milton Bradley. The game is still a popular product, made by Hasbro today, and simply known as 'The Game of Life'.

Travel Games, such as 'Around the World' became popular during the early 1900s as commuting about the globe became easier. However, the biggest hit of all-time was yet to come.

Lizzie Magee designed a game in 1904 that was used as a political tool to illustrate unfair capitalist activities amongst US landlords. It was published as the 'Landlord's Game' in 1910 and although it was never a best seller, it remained popular within the Quaker community throughout the 1920s. Charles Darrow, an out-of work salesman was familiar with the game, having played it when staying in a few boarding houses run by Quakers. He added a few things, changed the focus of the game to bankrupting your neighbour as being its winning objective and presented it as his own design to Parker Brothers. In 1935 the world's best-selling game 'Monopoly' was born.

The next big hit was 'Scrabble', designed by an architect and lover of crosswords, Alfred Butts. The game was an 'underground' cult classic during the 1940's with games being hand made and distributed to crossword fans across the USA. In 1950, the president of the Macy chain of stores came across a copy while on vacation and ordered stock for his retail outlets – Scrabble soon became a board game icon across the world.

The 1950s brought the mass media into our lives via the medium of television and all kinds of products associated with marketing TV shows and motion pictures began to appear. Along with owning a cup or lunch-box displaying your allegiance to your favourite TV show, you could also buy games inspired by the very same shows. Titles such as 'Video Village' and 'Concentration' were popular for Milton Bradley in the 60's and all manner of children's cartoons had their own associated game. The trend continues today, with TV and major motion pictures influencing the market. Go into any large retailer and you can buy titles such as 'CSI', 'Big Brother' and 'Star Wars'.

The majority of the games I have described so far are abstract board games. These usually have pieces and a playing board and often incorporate dice and cards as an additional or core components. However, there was another form of tabletop game that had been evolving in concert with traditional board games, also tracing its roots back to ancient times. The difference was that this genre of game was confined to the military for many centuries and only became popularised and available to 'amateurs' in the early 1900s.

For countless ages, military commanders employed miniature figures and scaled down terrain to illustrate tactics and battle plans to their subordinates. The use of these miniatures gradually began to take on the form of 'simulation games' and, during the early part of 19th century, the use of miniatures by the military became more sophisticated, with officers taking command of Lilliputian armies and fighting simulated battles, all according to sets of detailed rules; rules governing such things as the movement rate of troops, distances and range of weapons – all scaled down for the size of the figures. 'Kriegspiel', a game employed by the Prussian army, was considered the most accurate in recreating warfare on a tabletop. Soon the armies of other nations were adapting Kriegspiel to their officer training regimes and war-gaming (or simulation gaming) was born.

Still, this type of gaming, much more complex and detailed than your average strategy game, remained out of reach of the mainstream. It was the famous British author HG Wells who introduced war-gaming to the general public. Fascinated by this military pastime, he wrote and published his own set of miniatures rules, called 'Little-Wars'. However, the game did not become an instant hit. Most publishers of mass-produced games were geared up for paper-based production, with games being largely composed of cardboard, paper and wooden tokens. War-gaming required metal-cast miniatures and detailed terrain and lacked commercial support to become an overnight success story. However, the hobby continued on with a strong cult, kept alive still by the military and talented individuals capable of casting their own metal figures. It would be a number of synchronistic factors that would combine to bring war-games more into the mainstream and, at the same time, create the next leap forward– Role–Playing Games (RPGs).

The first of the contributing factors to the advent of RPGs was the release of 'Lord of the Rings' (LOTR) by British author J.R.R. Tolkien. Arguably, this tale of Hobbits and heroic quests set against a quasi-medieval world caused a renewed interest in fantasy fiction across the UK, and in particular middle-class America of the 1960's. The second factor was the chance union of two particular Tolkien enthusiasts, based in Wisconsin, USA. Gary Gygax and David Arneson were also avid medieval war-gamers and it wasn't long before they began to use war-gaming rules to recreate battles from LOTR, instead of simulations from historical sources, such as the Battle of Agincourt or Hastings.

With a number of other friends within their gaming circle, Gygax and Arneson wrote 'Chainmail' in 1969, providing rules for small unit combat in a medieval setting – battles between forces numbering a dozen or so figures aside. Soon they were down to individual soldiers fighting one-on-one combat, and the concept of unique game characteristics was introduced. In the past, a figure on the table may have represented 20 men, to which the rules assigned an intrinsic strength. There may be multiple copies of the same figure on the table but they would all normally be rated with the same generic strength. Once Gygax and Arneson got the game down to one figure actually represented by only one person, they began to rate each figure differently according to physical characteristics, such as strength, dexterity, constitution etc. This quickly led to the idea of running a game for a heroic group of characters fighting against foes; the foes being 'controlled' by a separate referee. The game was free flowing, with the referee, controlling the game through a narrative and using the rules to govern combat and tests reliant on individual character abilities. In 1979 'Dungeons and Dragons' was published as the first commercial role-playing game (and still the market leader) under the banner of Tactical Studies Rules (TSR).

The real difference with an RPG was that, in reality it needed no board or pieces, the whole game could be played out in the imagination, under the guidance of a referee or 'storyteller'. The referee described everything that the players experienced in an alternate setting, making decisions based upon probabilities and dice rolls. The game became co-operative, with players assisting each other, acting as a team to overcome adversaries and problems introduced by the referee. Throughout the 1980's, many RPG rule systems were created by rivals of TSR, drawing their inspiration, from multitude of source materials. While largely jumping on the fantasy bandwagon, they also explored alternate settings for their rule-sets, including science fiction, the wild-west, horror and espionage. In a similar vein to board games, many RPGs drew upon TV shows and motion pictures for their settings (Star Trek, Star Wars and more recently Babylon 5 and Buffy the Vampire Slayer). The RPG was a revolutionary idea in the development of entertainment, with far-reaching consequences that would heavily influence other groundbreaking technologies of the same time period.

Paralleling the emergence of RPG's, was the development of the PC and games in the virtual world. RPG's had a great influence in material that was produced for the PC (and they still do). Early games, such as Ultima and Wizardy, were highly text based with primitive graphics and were immediately embraced by the 'paper and pen' based RPG community. As the memory capacity and graphics quality of PCs grew during the 80s and 90s so did the PC audience, drawing a significant number of enthusiasts away from traditional forms of round-table gaming. There was a definite slump in traditional RPGs during the 1990s, which was related both to the rise in interest in PC Games and poor business practices amongst traditional RPG producers, particularly TSR.

Despite the dent made into the gaming community by PC games, innovators of non-electronic media were still out there. Another huge breakthrough in game design occurred in the early 1990s. Richard Garfield was the designer of a few moderately successful board games, including Robo-Rally. One day he was watching his children enthusiastically swapping baseball trading cards and came up with the idea of the collectible card game; the player would collect packets of cards and each packet would contain a different mix of common, uncommon and rare cards. The concept was that the player would use their skill in making up decks of cards (according to limitations set by the rules) that they thought could defeat an opponent's deck of cards in a game. 'Magic: the Gathering' arrived on the scene, published by Wizards of the Coast (WOTC) as the first collectible card game (CCG) and has spawned many copycats since then.

Such was the runaway success of Garfield's game and the millions in profit that was generated, that toward the end of the 1990s WOTC were able to buy up TSR, who was on the verge of bankruptcy. Vice-President of WOTC at that time was Ryan Dancey, a Dungeons and Dragons enthusiast. Prior to any take-over, he was sent to investigate reasons why the company that produced his favourite game was in so much trouble. Essentially, he found a company that was out of touch with its fan-base, producing poor quality products that nobody wanted and nobody needed in order to run a game of Dungeons of Dragons. In addition, hundreds of thousands of dollars were being used to protect the copyright on an endless cycle of products, which it really had no real need to protect in economic terms.

Basically, a resourceful referee of any RPG only needs the core rule-books that define the game setting. The actual game is like a series of stories (called adventure modules) and a creative referee can design their own adventures, using the core books. TSR invested a lot of energy into producing its own adventure modules and many of those were contrived or sub-standard. What's more, they clamped down on anyone trying to write independent adventure modules, alienating the more talented members of their fan-base. As the internet evolved in the 1990s, those former fans became e-community leaders and their criticism of the TSR product made a severe impact on sales. Add up falling sales and the high cost of retaining rights on a dead product and you've got a disaster waiting to happen.

Ryan Dancey managed to reverse all that and restore the Dungeons and Dragons product back to its place as market leader in a very short time. He took the 'bold' step of listening to the fan-base and organising a complete overhaul on the core Dungeons and Dragons source books. But even more dramatically, inspired with the emerging Open Copyright Licence (OCL) movement he created the Open Gaming Licence for WOTC in 2002, allowing amateur and independent companies to publish RPG adventures and related products, using a standard reference document of Dungeons and Dragons game mechanics.

This has created a renaissance in the RPG community, with many unpublished writers and artists finding work with small companies, establishing their particular niche in the market, often exploiting new technologies (e.g. offering product for download from the web rather than in a printed format). The existing licence has also drawn some criticism from those who think it is too restrictive in its current format, citing problems in distinguishing open content from closed content in publications and product identity requirements as the main issues. It is interesting to note that these critics have suggested a shift to using the OCL Attribute-Share-a-Like Licence.

There you have it, a brief synopsis of games from their creation in the ancient world to their design and publishing under a movement inspired by the OCL. As we move into the 21st Century, boldly going where no one has gone before, the games industry seems to have gotten a bit healthier and a bit wiser. There is a new boom in traditional board games being driven by the translation of many European favourites into the English language, Collectible Card Games seem to have taken a second wind with a second generation of gamers getting interested in 'Magic: the Gathering'. PC games are bigger than ever with a large following in diverse Massive Multi-player Online Role Playing Games (MMORPGs) and the traditional RPG industry is a hive of industry. The last two areas offer the best opportunity for creative input under the OCL movement and it will be interesting to see what challenges and directions the industries involved take to further embrace and engage their fan-bases in the near future.

Computer Games Landscape WITH SAL HUMPHREYS

Over the past six months Professor Brian Fitzgerald, John Banks, myself and Nic Suzor decided to look at what it was Auran was doing with their licensing and approach to managing IP in fan-created content. We were all interested in this and our paper on copyright is featured in *Media International Australia*.[215]

My task for today is to cater for people in the audience that might know nothing about games. Games are incredibly successful interactive applications. We hear about the term interactivity all the time – to the point that it has almost been evacuated of meaning, but games really are interactive in interesting and meaningful ways. Games are very successful at what they do, and it is worth looking at them whether you are interested in games or whether you are more interested in new media and digital environments. We can use them as an exemplar for how a really good interactive environment actually works, and for examining what the implications of that might be in terms of IP, copyright, and various other regulation issues. We need to look at how they differ structurally from other media. They are not the same as a story, or a book, or a piece of music. They do very different things and part of that difference is about the mode of interactivity that they actually employ in engaging their users.

---

[215] Sal Humphreys, Brian Fitzgerald, John Banks and Nic Suzor, 'Fan based production for computer games: User led innovation, the 'drift of value' and the negotiation of intellectual property rights' (2005) 114 *Media International Australia* 234.

Looking at their differences gives us the chance to look at what happens in the legal ecology that surrounds them. One of the things that has not really been dealt with, or rather, we keep touching on it and then we segue away from it, is about commercialisation. The thing about games is they already exist in a commercialised environment and so the issues about commercial and non-commercial that arise in other new media environments are already being encountered and dealt with in varying ways by the games industry and players.

The model implemented through Trainz gives us an opportunity to explore how the relationship between commercial and non-commercial does not have to be an either/or proposition in the way that it has been set up in a number of talks that have been given in the last day and a half. It's possible to actually work out hybrid solutions and this is one of the things that a Creative Commons License tries to do. When I think about Creative Commons Licensing I sometimes translate that to creative compromise – that it is a compromise around the rights between totally open and closed models.

I want to begin by outlining some basics about computer games before moving on to examining ownership and licensing. The size of the computer games industry is very big with sales at more than 239 Million in the US. There are no worldwide figures currently available. There are figures from the UK though, which estimate the revenue from entertainment and games to be £18.5 billion. In terms of demographics, there are a few myths around – for instance that game players are always geeky adolescent boys locked in their bedrooms in some little isolated bubble – and it is good to debunk these myths. Half of all Americans aged six and older play games, with the average age being 29 years old. We see here that the generation that grew up with games did not leave games behind as they got older, and are still playing. Also, 39 percent of game players are women, so it is not just a male activity.

We talk about videos games or computer games, as if they are all the same thing. They actually come on quite different platforms. There are consoles like Xbox and other proprietary hardware platforms, there are computer or PC games and then there are arcade, mobile phone and the mixed environment games. The console games give rise to a whole extra set of interesting issues around proprietary integrations of hardware and software. However we are not dealing with that in this presentation.

There are also quite significant differences between a single and multi player game particularly in terms of content creation. The multi player networked games mostly run in the PC environment, although the console games have begun to be networked. X Box now has a network facility for playing with other people across a proprietary network.

The types of games most people think of when they hear about computer games are first person shooters. In fact there are a lot of genres and first person shooters are small part of the market. Henry Jenkins says that Barbie Fashion Designer actually outsold Quake which is a fairly salutary kind of statistic. I imagine that Quake had a lot of 'cracked' copies circulating on the net, which probably meant that there were still a lot more copies of Quake than Barbie in existence. The point is there are a lot of genres of computer games which don't involve shooting

I want to talk a little bit about interactivity in the production cycle. Apart from their success and the size of the industry, games are implemented through a different structure and a different production cycle than most conventional media and these differences have implications for many of the institutions that surround them. When I use the term interactivity, I use it to mean that games require a meaningful input from players in order to progress. Some games, but not all, *require* players to make up their own content as they go (I'm not talking here about the third party content creation that is often generated by fans of a game, but that just the process of playing creates content). The person who is playing it has to be engaged in progressing the text, which is not the case with most other media that are not interactive. Rather than engaging with an already finished narrative, players are actors within the text itself, and the game assesses the performance of the player and gives feedback in various forms, about the performance.

In some games, which are more emergent there is a set of rules, a set of goals, but there is the scope for a fair bit of creativity and innovation on the part of the player within those parameters. When you structure emergence into a multi player environment you find that players actually create content for each other. Thus we are not talking about a product that is authored entirely by the developer. The product itself has undergone a shift in authorship and the consumers have become productive. This is a fairly major structural shift. We are not simply talking about a piece of music that has been authored and released and then someone has picked it up and remixed it. We are talking about the product itself being made by the people that are using it. It is a shared or a collaborative authorship.

While production of something as complex as a film, which can involve many hundreds of people, can still fit within a copyright framework, multi player games actually disrupt the cycle by incorporating the productivity of hundreds or even thousands of consumers into the construction of the text itself. Consumers usually reside at the end of the value chain, not somewhere at the start and in the middle. Texts such as books or a piece of music are usually created by an author, their distribution and access rights are organised by publishers, and they are consumed by audiences. There is a temporality to the process and it is quite linear. However, if the audiences start to author parts of the text, how are the distribution and access rights negotiated, and who actually owns that text? That is what the structural shift in games does: it disrupts a lot of the conventions because copyright relies on a notion of authorship that does not really fit with this production model.

If you disrupt authorship you disrupt the basis of copyright and intellectual property and this implies a whole shifting in relationships between developers, publishers and players that has many implications. We are not talking about all games – a single player console game which has a linear progression that gives you no options for creating your own pathways or content at all probably does not fit this model. But something like a multi-user network game really fits into the shifting terrain. They have a constant production cycle which is recursive. They are never finished and are collaboratively authored. More conventional media follow a linear cycle (although this is not to deny the process of cultural production which is very recursive at a meta level), but the production of the individual text has a linear structure.

My point thus far has been to highlight the difference between games and more conventional media. I want to move now to considering content creation communities. When we speak about modding communities we are moving away from the activity of playing and into the creation of extra content which becomes incorporated into the game. The games industry uses this content all the time, it is an integrated part of the industry model. It is a commonplace. The industry has recognised that the productivity of players can be harnessed and have understood the innovation and the research and development potential of their audiences. Their players have become creators who can actually be harnessed into the production of the text. That is a really exciting and new way of looking at how you would produce something in a media context. Game texts change through playing, they are changed through post release additions, and they have this recursive production cycle which incorporates player creations.

What do players create? There has been a long history of players doing this whether the company releases tools for doing so or not. Back in the early 1990s when PC games were still young and not a very well developed industry, players would always hack the code and make their own stuff because they often thought they could do it better. They would make 'skins'; objects; they would mess with the code and make their own artificial-intelligent agents or 'bots' to play against; make customised user interfaces; or they would create entire games using existing games engines. The incredibly successful game CounterStrike was developed by a team of players who decided that they could use the engine from HalfLife and make their own game. It has won all sorts of industry awards and player awards and has been commercialised and the whole thing was made by player creators. This is a fairly well developed pattern within the industry. Ninety percent of the content inside the Sims is created by players, who trade their content on the internet.

Where it gets interesting is the response from, or the ways in which this is managed by, developers or publishers. Publishers can be different from developers and so they have a different set of understandings of what they want from products. Some publishers will give you the tools and you can make mods. However, they will then claim to own the mods. So anything a player creates for the game, they can upload into the game, can share it with everybody else, but the publisher will claim all the IP on it. Others say players can upload it, can share it with each other, and do not claim ownership of it, but prevent players from commercialising it. Still others say players can create mods, can do a variety of things with them, and do not prevent the commercialising of them. Players can share mods and can choose to monetise them if they want (this is the model Auran has chosen with Trainz). This range of responses to modding practices is about harnessing the productivity and then negotiating the ownership of the IP, and that can be a very complex process.

Another aspect concerning ownership and licensing is the secondary economy surrounding games – black markets where people sell in-game items for real money in internet auction houses. This poses all sorts of interesting questions for the law because if a virtual item takes on a real world value, if money inside a game can be equated to real money, does that mean when somebody steals something inside the game it is theft that can be prosecuted under the law? Which is basically a jurisdiction issue in a funny way. Is the game actually a separate jurisdiction or is it inside the jurisdiction where the game is played? Is there a magic circle that delimits the game as fantasy, and can it be maintained in the face of player practices to the contrary?

The issues concerning property are about who owns the database of objects in the game. Major conflicts and tensions arise from this. In particular I would like to point to the issue of avatars. When you develop a character in a game, you inhabit an avatar – it is your online identity. Sometimes we are talking about people who play between twenty and forty hours a week inside a virtual world and their avatar embodies some of their identity. Can Sony Online Entertainment (for instance) own that online identity? Where is the hard line between the virtual and the real and between what is code and what is social? Is there ever any importance attached to the social if we always resort to property law? Do we erase the social significance of these things? Legal discourse often erases the importance of affect and social community when it resorts to property as its main discursive construction.

Involvement of End Users in the Production Process WITH JOHN BANKS

Both Sal Humphreys and Greg Lane have touched on some very dynamic and quite exciting areas in the game development process, with the game developer and the production process overlapping with the creativity and involvement of the end user communities, namely the fans and the game players. I will talk about the Trainz project and how we started it back in 2000 and recent releases and how over that process we have increasingly involved the end user community, or the fan community, which is basically a worldwide network of Trainz fans. Their passion and enthusiasm for Trainz is directly involved with the Trainz development process, which adds incredible amounts of innovation, creativity and value to the project. Auran has reaped a lot of benefit from the involvement of fans in the project – Auran is therefore accountable to the fans for the benefits gained. Towards the end of this presentation I will talk a little about the accountability we have towards the fans for the innovation and creativity that they bring to the project.

Game designers and developers are increasingly enlisting and involving fan communities in the creation, development and promotion of games. Involvement of the end users does not just happen when they pick the game up and buy it at the store and take it home and install it. Even the very idea of calling them end users is now a little redundant because fans are right up front increasingly participating in the games development project itself. They are creators and producers. Trainz is a perfect example of this – a distributed organisation that is physically located at Teneriffe in Brisbane and yet incorporates a peer production network of fan content creators who are based in the United States, the UK, Italy, Germany, throughout Scandinavia, etc. This very distributed team of content creators all come together and contribute to the Trainz project.

There is another way of thinking about this which was previously raised by Sal Humphreys. Professor John Hartley from QUT talks about how the value produced in these networks is drifting in such a way that the relationship between producers and consumers has become blurred. On one hand we have the Auran development team working on the Trainz project made up of software developers, artists, programmers, designers, producers, etc who are professional and paid for what they are doing. On the other hand the very success of Trainz relies on a pool of voluntary fan labour, so you are getting this blurring of the boundaries between the professional and the amateur.

One way of thinking about these networks is the phrase 'participatory culture' and I am borrowing this phrase from Henry Jenkins. The reason I am throwing it up is because there can be a tendency to think about these relationships as being new and novel, that they have just erupted upon the scene in the last few years. It is important I think to remember that researchers like Jenkins have been looking at the relationships between fans and corporate media producers for well over 10 years now. Jenkins' interests go back to looking at things like the Star Wars fan community and the involvement of Star Wars fans in creating amateur films that spin off around the Star Wars universe. In Henry Jenkins' *Textual Poachers Television Fans and Participatory Culture*[216] he talks about the fans troubled relationship to the mass media and consumer capitalism. He talks about fans lacking direct access to the means of commercial cultural production, and their limited ability to influence entertainment industry decisions.

Henry Jenkins' more recent work indicates a shift in these relations among fans and corporate media producers. He talks about three things that influence the emergence of these new relations that Trainz provides a strong example of. First, new tools allow end users to create and generate there own media content. Second, the Do it Yourself media production

---

[216] (1992) Routledge, New York.

culture which has emerged around these tools, which we can see with the Trainz fan community as they create things such as their own locomotive models. Third, Jenkins mentions economic trends favouring media convergence.

Keith Done's account of Dungeons and Dragons, and the move particularly more recently by Wizards of the Coast with open game licenses, gives you a sense of the importance of these open relationships with the fan communities. The whole Dungeons and Dragons milieu has been quite influential. Auran's CEO, Greg Lane, comes from a strong role playing background, and was influenced by the open culture that built up around role playing.

I want to move on to discuss Auran and Trainz and the process of making one of these distributed production networks work. How does it work? How do you manage it? You have a pool of very talented and creative voluntary fans, but because you are not paying them they do not necessarily do what you (the company) want them to do, or when you want them to do it. The relationship that emerges here between the commercial and the non-commercial, and the propriety and the non propriety gets quite messy. It is a messy network, as the relationships are not clearly delineated.

Trainz and the fan third party content creation community emerged when I first went to work for Auran. Greg Lane said "well John, the project you are going to be working on is Trainz which is about this model train simulator". I was not really excited about it at the time – I was thinking I would be working on some other cool game project and I was doing Trainz stuff! We discovered there was a network of Trainz fans with websites all over the world into which we could tap. We identified the leaders of these networks and invited them to Auran's website to share their ideas through the forum we had launched. We published on the forum the very early design ideas for the Trainz project, describing where we wanted it to go, and what we thought it would look like – its features and functionality The aim was to obtain the fans' feedback and input. There were heated debates with the fans about our initial design proposal

We had one guy by the name of Vern who was an influential member of the TrainSim online fan network. Vern had strong opinions about the design proposal and would hammer our team with his views. He was not happy with the direction in which we were taking the product and would hammer us with his opinions, with what he thought we should and should not be doing. Vern's feedback actually ended up being very influential on some of the key design decisions we eventually made.

Trainz was first released at the end of 2001. We have gone through a series of releases with the most recent being Trainz Railroad Simulator 2004. One of the interesting things about the graphics and art content for these releases is that it was not exclusively created by Auran artists, but rather also generated by members of the fan community and a lot of those fan created assets are now included in the retail release packages

Trainz now is a creative platform, we (Auran) create the platform and core functionality and users provide the art content. Over time we have established strong collaborative relationships with the extremely talented fan creators that have emerged. Some of these fans have formed teams and have gone semi-commercial and are now selling add-on packs for Trainz from their own websites. The fans bring innovation and value to Trainz through their creative efforts. The download repository for the fan created content on the Auran website now includes well over 26,000 individual assets, of which 2800 are locomotive models. Many of the assets for Trainz commercial release packages are now provided by the fans. There is an interesting mix here between the commercial and the non-commercial, the proprietary and the non-proprietary. It is a messy unruly network of creators generating innovation for us.

This creates complex IP issues/implications and Greg Lane has touched on that. Auran is fairly open with licensing relationships with the fans. Any content they create they retain the IP to. This is unlike other game companies where fan material cannot be commercially released by the fan creators and they often retain the right to take fan content without the creator's permission and commercially exploit it or release it in their own packages. Auran's approach is different whereby we think it is a good idea to talk to fans before commercially releasing their content and try to obtain their permission first. We negotiate out the relationship. Content that is on our download station, for example, is distributed under the terms of non-exclusive license. Fans who contribute this content are free to commercially exploit it or release it themselves elsewhere. Auran does not have an exclusive license to this content. The IP relationships and issues are messy, as the actors within these project networks have diverse and conflicting loyalties, values, imperatives and ethos. For example, Auran has a bottom-line imperative while for many of the fans it is about having fun making and openly sharing their creations for Trainz.

There are opposing and differing views within the Trainz fan community itself regarding IP and fan created content and I want to touch upon this quickly. The most interesting tensions within the networks are disputes between fans themselves who say 'Joe has ripped off my content and used it in his locomotive and I am not happy about that' and, as Greg has mentioned, these models are quite complex objects. What often happens is that one fan might think 'I quite like that texture that Joe's got on his locomotive, I want to take it and use it on mine'. 'Joe' might be happy about that as long as he gets credit and acknowledgements etc, but he might be very unhappy if he is not credited or acknowledged, or if that work of his turns up on another fan site being sold with someone else commercially benefiting from it.

We often get emails asking us to mediate between these fans who are having IP disputes. For example, a fan complaining 'X fan group is ripping off our content what are you, Auran, going to do about it? Please remove their content from your download station, please send them an email demanding that they recognise our rights'. We are often placed in these awkward situations of trying to mediate among fan groups and their IP disputes. One of the other really heated areas of debate among fans is the pay-ware versus free-ware conflict. Some fan creators believe all fan content should be free-ware, it should all have an open-source or creative commons type license associated with it, and fans should not be profiting from or commercialising fan content. They should not be profiting from selling content to other fans. The argument here is that a lot of the content that fans create benefits from the feedback and input from a quite big network of fans who openly and freely share information. For example, tips and tricks about how to create this content. For these creators to then commercialise that content and restrict it in some way is not the right thing to do, at least this is the view of some fans

Here are some comments posted to the Trainz forum by two fairly influential content creators. One is from John Wheelan, and the other is MagicLamb, that is his handle or nickname on the Trainz forum. John Wheelan asks:

> I have difficulty with copyright and Trainz. How many of our models carry a railroad or railways copyrighted logo? How may textures have been borrowed without the original copyrighter's permission? How many content creators can say that they have not looked at how someone else has done something?

John is getting at how the content creators rely on this network of collaborative peer creativity that they draw on; often without permission. But MagicLamb comes back and says:

> it is all a matter of giving credit where credit's due. There is a trend lately, and many other content creators agree with me, to just use whatever you want whether you have the rights to or not. It is not all about getting as much content out for Trainz as possible. It is about people who put in long hours for nothing to get the recognition they deserve. Some content creators do not care what you do with their work, some do. Their wishes do need to be respected.

You can see that the IP issues, the digital rights management issues, that are emerging through these peer distributed production networks are quite complex, quite convoluted, and sites of quite heated debate (I moderate the Auran forum and I often have to shut down threads and warn people who end up calling each other rather nasty names). Hopefully there are researchers here who may produce work in the not too distant future that may have some benefit for these fan creators and may provide them with models to work through these difficult IP issues and relationships.

I want to end with one more quote from a fan creator. This guy is talking about how much he loves the Trainz software and the community precisely because of its creativity and its open and collaborative mixing of materials and how it generates innovation through this process. He tells of how a particular project was undertaken by openly using each others content. He talks about it as being 'unashamed plagiarism, pretty much driving this community' and that is one way of putting it, that is his way of putting it. And yet this 'unashamed plagiarism' is generating so much creativity and innovation that companies like Auran are commercially benefiting from.

This raises a lot of issues about Auran's accountability to these networks. How we are accountable to the fans and need to work closely with them in an ethical and open way. I would argue Auran offers a best practice example of how that can be done, although there are still areas where we can improve significantly. We have got it wrong in the past in some areas and need to learn from those mistakes. At this point I will throw over to the lawyers to talk about ways of thinking through these really interesting IP issues: the commercial and the non-commercial, the proprietary and the non-proprietary and the way they come together in these very messy unruly networks.

Legal Issues WITH PROFESSOR BRIAN FITZGERALD

A starting point is the notion of virtual worlds and legal rights, and the other is user-led production and the way that we can allocate legal rights. There are key issues about constitutional-type rights in these virtual worlds. I remember in the mid-90s when lawyers started to deal with the Internet, there were arguments about the Internet being a legal jurisdiction – *Lex Internet* – that were put forward in a famous article by Johnson and Post about the Internet being its own jurisdiction.[217] And there is an interesting US case early on called *US v Thomas*.[218] Allegedly obscene material was uploaded from California but it was accessible in Tennessee and under the US law, obscenity took its definition from the local area, and these people tried to argue (California was much more liberal, Tennessee was a bit more conservative) that they had actually inhabited a sort of virtual world and where they had uploaded the pornography was really another space.

At that time it seemed a little bit remote and it was only a few people who were saying, "there is something in this argument". Today when you look at the games' environment there is certainly a strong argument coming forward that virtual worlds are throwing up real constitutional-like issues because people are inhabiting these spaces for an incredible amount of time. It is the reconciling of the real space jurisdiction with the virtual space that is difficult.

We see a process of development within a lot of these computer games environments which utilises IP relating to copyright, patent and trademark arise. When you have this sort of layered idea of authorship and user-led production, you have got this question about where the intellectual property rights, particularly the copyright, actually resides. Someone may develop a platform in which they have copyright and someone else may layer some content on top of that. We are looking at a sort of individual authorship, a joint authorship, and even depending on which one of those we say we are looking at, how are we reconciling the rights?

In a lot of the end user licence agreements that are wrapped around user rights in these games, we are seeing this idea of intellectual property rights

---

[217] David Johnson and David Post, 'Law and Borders – The Rise of Law in Cyberspace' (1996) 48 *Stanford Law Review* 1367.
[218] *United States of America v Robert Alan Thomas and Carleen Thomas* 74 F. 3d 701 (US App6th Cir, 1996).

being negotiated, or transacted. In many of these end user licence agreements we may see things like: you can come onto this platform and you can contribute to it in a manner of user production, but we want to claim all the IP rights. It is almost like an automatic assignment of copyright that is implemented through the end user licence agreement. Intellectual property law says that there is nothing wrong with a person who creates something, assigning that copyright to someone else. That happens all the time, particularly in publishing and so on.

There are some interesting arguments here and it throws up this whole issue we spoke about before: the intersection between copyright and contract – how contract can be used to restructure the rights of a copyright owner in various transactions. Some of the key legal issues that are arising here, and the points that we looked at when we wrote the article together, were how contract and IP rights in the games area are actually working together. Auran has some very interesting licences. They are beneficial and probably best practice style licences for their user producers where they give a lot of leeway to the people in terms of their IP rights and exploitation. There are other examples which are much more restrictive and are like automatic assignments where everything that is done is appropriated back to the platform company. That is a critical issue.

There is also this whole virtual economy that is thriving and people who are contributing to games are actually creating objects of worth. Recently reported in the papers here and overseas is this idea of someone selling a virtual island for US$26,000. People are actually trading in virtual property to create wealth and it is a very real economy.[219]

Recent Examples WITH NIC SUZOR

Moving away from the question of property, I want to discuss three emerging issues concerning clashes between players of games and copyright owners, whether in the game itself, or in third party material. The first two examples come out of two cases in the US, and the third is the

---

[219] Edward Castranova, 'On Virtual Economics' (2003) 3 *Games Studies. The International Journal of Computer Games Research* 2. For example, the virtual "Entropia Universe" allows users to shift wealth between the virtual and real world at an exchange rate of 10 Project Entropia Dollars (PED) = $1 US. An Australian fan purchased an island on the world of Calypso for $265,000 (PED) – a cost of $26,500 real US dollars – and has already made his money back from other users investing in his virtual property.

legal standing of the highly innovative filmmaking technique 'machinima', which uses computer games as an animation platform.

Blizzard v bnetd

Blizzard make several popular games, including Warcraft, Diablo and Starcraft. Online multiplayer in these games is limited to using Blizzard's Battle.net service. Battle.net provides a mechanism for users to create and join multi-player games, to meet and chat with other users, and to record statistics and participate in tournaments. Battle.net functionality is built into the games. Blizzard's Battle.net servers check the validity of users' cd-keys when a user connects to the service from within the game. This validation is known as the 'secret handshake' which allows only users with valid cd-keys to continue connecting to Battle.net.

Blizzard's End User License Agreements on the games themselves state that a user may not "in whole or in part, copy, photocopy, reproduce, translate, reverse engineer, derive source code, modify, disassemble, decompile, create derivative works based on the Program, or remove any proprietary notices or labels on the program without the prior consent, in writing, of Blizzard".[220]

Blizzard's Terms of Use on Battle.net state that a player may not:

1. copy, photocopy, reproduce, translate, reverse engineer, modify, disassemble, or de-compile in whole or in part any Battle.net software;
2. create derivative works based on Battle.net;
3. host or provide matchmaking services for any Blizzard software programs or emulate or redirect the communication protocols used by Blizzard as part of Battle.net, through protocol emulation, tunnelling, modifying, or adding components to the Program, use of a utility program, or any other technique now known or hereafter developed for any purpose, including, but not limited to, network play over the Internet, network play utilizing commercial or non-commercial gaming networks, or as part of content aggregation networks [...]
4. use any third-party software to modify Battle.net to change game play, including, but not limited to cheats and/or hacks;
5. use Blizzard's intellectual property rights contained in Battle.net to

---

[220] *Davidson & Associates v Jung* 422 F.3d 630 (8th Cir. 2005) 5 (at footnote 4).

create or provide any other means through which Blizzard entertainment software products [...] may be played by others, including, not limited to, server emulators.[221]

6. The defendants were frustrated by the poor performance of Blizzard's Battle.net service, as well as cheating and otherwise offensive players. They subsequently began free development of bnetd, which would act as a replacement server for Battle.net which gave users more control over the games they played online. To create bnetd, the defendants had to reverse engineer the protocol spoken by Battle.net and the Blizzard games, and they also developed a small utility which was used to modify the Blizzard games so they could connect to other multiplayer servers. Notably, the defendants had no way of enforcing the cd-key validity check, and were forced to treat any cd-key presented as valid.

The district court granted summary judgment to Blizzard, holding that fair-use reverse engineering could be excluded by terms in shrink-wrap or click-wrap contracts, and that the reverse-engineering exceptions in the DMCA do not protect reverse-engineering in order to create fully functional alternative products, or where the program is distributed for free.[222]

The Eight Circuit Court of Appeals affirmed the decision. Blizzard's EULA and ToS were enforceable contracts, and the defendants had waived any fair-use defence they may have had.[223] The 'secret-handshake' constituted an effective Technological Protection Measure (TPM), and bnetd circumvented that TPM by allowing all clients to connect. The 'interoperability' exception did not apply, on the basis that the bnetd emulator allowed unauthorised copies of the Blizzard games to be played on the bnetd.org servers. The court considered that this constituted infringement of copyright, and as such, the interoperability defence could not apply. The Court did not consider whether bnetd was a dual use technology which could have both infringing and non-infringing uses, or whether the playing of an infringing copy of a game on an internet server constituted copyright infringement at all.

---

[221] Ibid 6 (at footnote 5); see Blizzard Entertainment, *Battle.net Terms of Use* (2006) <http://www.battle.net/tou.shtml> at 4 September 2006.
[222] *Davidson & Associates v Internet Gateway* 334 F. Supp. 2D 1164 (E.D. Mo., 30 September 2004).
[223] *Davidson & Associates v Jung* 422 F.3d 630 (8th Cir. 2005).

The Australian position

In Australia, reverse engineering to make interoperable products is protected as an exception to copyright by *Copyright Act* s 47D. Section 47H provides that section 47D, which was inserted by the *Copyright Amendment (Digital Agenda) Act 2000*, can not be excluded by contract. In Australia, Blizzard could not require that its users refrain from reverse engineering.

Reverse engineering for interoperability is also an exception to circumvention of a technological protection measure, in s 116A(3), where a 'qualified person' is permitted to circumvent a TPM for a permitted purpose, which includes interoperability from s 47D. A qualified person in this case would mean the owner or licensee of the copy of the game. Section 116A(4)(b) provides a similar exception for supplying a circumvention device.

There is nothing in the text of the anti-circumvention law that prevents the right to reverse engineer for interoperability from being excluded by contract. The exceptions to infringement in s 116A are not protected in the same way as s 47D protects ss 47B(3), 47C, 47D, 47E and 47F. This case shows that this gap in Australian anti-circumvention law can have real consequences for Australian developers. Reverse engineering for interoperability is an important exception to the exclusive rights of the copyright owner, in that it provides developers with a mechanism to make competing products, or to adapt a technology product to work in new environments.

These exceptions are important – they concern not the piracy of games, but the right of players to make use of their lawfully acquired games in the way they want. A player who purchases a game which doesn't work satisfactorily with another product, like an internet game server, should not be precluded from seeking to play the game on another interoperable server. The right to use a game is a fundamental right of a purchaser of a copy of that game, and if the game must be reverse engineered in order to enable its use, then that reverse engineering should be permissible.

Both the CLRC *Copyright and Contract* report and the Philips Fox *Digital Agenda Review* recommended that the *Copyright Act* be amended so that the permitted purpose exceptions in s 116A(3) cannot be excluded by contract.[224] If these recommendations are not followed, there is a significant risk that the ability to create interoperable software in Australia will be crippled, and producers of computer games will be able to require that purchasers of their games are tied to their other software products and services in order to make use of the games.

Marvel v NCSoft

NCSoft and Cryptic Studios are the creators of a popular Massively Multiplayer Online Role Playing Game (MMORPG) in which players create superheroes and do battle with the forces of evil. Marvel are publishers of comic books, one of the two production houses credited with creating, or at least resurrecting, the superhero genre.[225]

Marvel alleged that NCSoft had "created, marketed, distributed and provided a host environment for a game that brings the world of comic books alive", not by the creation of new or original characters but, by directly contributory and vicariously infringing upon Marvel copyrights and trademarks".[226] Marvel pointed to the character creation process in City of Heroes, which allows players to design their own superheroes, and, with some work, replicate to some extent the likeness of well known protagonists of Marvel's comic books. Marvel alleged that the flexibility in the character creation system empowers users to infringe their valuable copyrights and trademarks.

The claim is alarming. For years, children have role-played with the

---

[224] Copyright Law Review Committee, *Copyright and Contract* (2002) [7.50] <http://www.ag.gov.au/www/clrHome.nsf/AllDocs/RWP092E76FE8AF2501CCA256C 44001FFC28?OpenDocument> at 4 September 2006; Philips Fox, *Digital Agenda Review* (2004) 113
<http://www.ag.gov.au/DigitalAgendaReview/reportrecommendations> at 4 September 2006.
[225] See 'Marvel Comics' on *Wikipedia* <http://en.wikipedia.org/wiki/Marvel_Comics> at 4 September 2006. The other similarly large production house is DC comics: see 'DC Comics' on *Wikipedia* <http://en.wikipedia.org/wiki/DC_Comics> at 4 September 2006.
[226] Second Amended Complaint, *Marvel Enterprises v NCSoft Corporation* (25 January 2005) *CV 04-9253-RGK* (PLAx) available at
<http://www.eff.org/IP/Marvel_v_NCSoft/> at 4 September 2006. Most of Marvel's claims for direct and indirect trademark infringement were dismissed by the District Court, except for direct infringement of a common law trademark: see *Marvel Enterprises Inc v NCSoft Corporation* (Unreported, *CV 04-9253-RGK* (PLAx), Klausner J, 9 March 2005) available at <http://www.eff.org/IP/Marvel_v_NCSoft/> at 4 September 2006.

characters that form their popular culture. Content producers have used advertising and merchandising so extensively that it is difficult for a child not to be immersed in a world populated by representations of these characters. These same companies encourage children to buy licensed merchandise in order to role-play with their favourite characters. For years children have played not only with that merchandise, but also with home-crafted representations – drawings, paintings, a handmade cape or costume, the possibilities are only limited by imagination. This sort of play is either a symptom of, or fuel for, the popularity of the characters depicted, and is encouraged by the production companies. However, once this role-playing moved into the digital environment, Marvel brought suit for copyright infringement.

It would be unthinkable for a production company to sue children for dressing up as their favourite comic book character and playing in the park. A shift in context to a digital environment is little different conceptually. If Marvel were successful, the ability to role-play online would have been removed to a large extent. It is difficult to reconcile how Marvel can on the one hand bombard children with images and merchandise of their characters, in the hopes of encouraging them to play with those characters, and on the other hand, bring suit to restrict those same children from playing with those characters in an unlicensed setting.

The case was settled out of court in the United States in December 2005. The terms of the settlement were not disclosed, but no changes to NCSoft's City of Heroes character generation process are to be made. Whilst this may be a win for NCSoft in this case, the fact remains that a similar case brought under Australian law may be significantly more difficult to defend.

Primary liability in Australia

Superhero comics, and potentially the superheroes themselves, are original artistic works for the purposes of Part III of the *Copyright Act*. Liability for primary copyright infringement will occur when a player of a game can be shown to reproduce the characters, or the characters as a substantial part of the comics, in a material form, or to communicate a substantial part of the characters or comics to the public.[227] 'Material form' includes "any form (whether visible or not) of storage of the work or adaptation, or a substantial part of the work or adaptation, (whether or not the work or adaptation, or a substantial part of the work or adaptation, can be

---

[227] *Copyright Act 1968* (Cth) ss 36, 31(1).

reproduced)".[228] This broad definition will cover the creation of a character in a game, as will the definition of 'communicate to the public' in a multi-player game (to "make available online or electronically transmit").[229]

In determining whether the characters have been reproduced, the Court will look for objective similarity between the in-game character and the original superhero, and the establishment of a causal link between the original work and the in-game character.[230] Where the two characters are objectively similar, a causal connection may be inferred by the popularity and level of exposure of the original, even if the person is copying subconsciously.[231]

Where only some features of the character have been reproduced, the plaintiff will need to show that those features are substantial. The question of substantiality with respect to Part III works is determined primarily by reference to the original features that have been reproduced. Determining whether a substantial part has been reproduced will again be determined by the qualitative value of the part taken, but the emphasis is on the originality of the reproduced portions. Reproduction of a large quantity of unoriginal features is unlikely to constitute reproduction of a substantial part,[232] but reproduction of a small portion of original material which resulted from a high degree of skill and labour is likely to be substantial.[233]

Given the recent restrictive approach taken by the Federal Court in relation to substantiality in Part IV subject-matter,[234] the features of a superhero are likely to constitute an important part, or a highlight, of the artistic or literary work of a comic book. Unless the court takes into account the type of use made of the player character, it is likely that they will be seen to infringe copyright in the original superheroes. Australian players will not be able to rely on a fair dealing exception to infringement.[235] The logical conclusion is that the players will be liable to the original owner. However, owners of copyright are understandably reluctant to sue their fans for

---

[228] *Copyright Act 1968* (Cth) s 10.
[229] *Copyright Act 1968* (Cth) s 10.
[230] *Ladbroke (Football) Ltd v William Hill (Football) Ltd* [1964] 1 All ER 465; *SW Hart & Co Pty Ltd v Edwards Hot Water Systems* (1985) 159 CLR 466.
[231] *Francis Day & Hunter v Bron* [1963] Ch 587.
[232] *Data Access Corp v Powerflex Services* (1999) 202 CLR 1.
[233] *Blackie & Sons Ltd v Lothian Book Publishing Co Pty Ltd* (1921) 29 CLR 396; *Ladbroke (Football) Ltd v William Hill (Football) Ltd* [1964] 1 All ER 465; *Fasold v Robers* (1997) 70 FCR 489.
[234] See *TCN Channel Nine Pty Ltd v Network Ten Pty Ltd (No 2)* (2005) 145 FCR 35.
[235] Reproduction for entertainment will not fit within exceptions for news reporting, research or study, or criticism or review.

copyright infringement. It is much less embarrassing and more convenient to achieve the same result by suing the producers of the game for secondary liability.

Secondary liability in Australia

Secondary liability for copyright infringement in Australia arises when a person 'authorises' the doing of any act comprised in the copyright.[236] Section 36(1A) tells us that, when determining whether a person has 'authorised' the doing of any such act, the matters that must be taken into account include:

1. the extent (if any) of the person's power to prevent the doing of the act concerned;
2. the nature of any relationship existing between the person and the person who did the act concerned;
3. whether the person took any other reasonable steps to prevent or avoid the doing of the act, including whether the person complied with any relevant industry codes of practice.

The meaning of 'authorisation' was recently considered in the Federal Court by Wilcox J in *Universal v Sharman*.[237] This case dealt with authorisation of infringement in sound recordings, but the relevant provisions in the *Copyright Act* for Part III works are worded identically. His honour considered the relevant authorities and extracted some guiding principles. 'Authorise' is to be construed according to its dictionary meaning of 'sanction, approve, countenance'.[238] Authorisation does not have to be a positive step: "inactivity or indifference, exhibited by acts of commission or omission, may reach such a degree as to support an inference of authorisation or permission".[239] Mere provision of the means of infringement is not enough.[240] Mere inactivity without knowledge will

---

[236] *Copyright Act 1968* (Cth) s 36(1).
[237] *Universal Music Australia Pty Ltd v Sharman License Holdings Ltd* (2005) 220 ALR 1.
[238] Ibid 90, citing *University of New South Wales v Moorhouse & Angus & Robertson (Publishers) Pty Ltd* (1975) 133 CLR 1 ('*Moorhouse*'), 12.
[239] *Universal Music Australia Pty Ltd v Sharman License Holdings Ltd* (2005) 220 ALR 1, 90, quoting *Adelaide Corporation v Australasian Performing Right Association Ltd* (1928) 40 CLR 481.
[240] *Universal Music Australia Pty Ltd v Sharman License Holdings Ltd* (2005) 220 ALR 1, 98; *Copyright Act 1968* (Cth) s112E.

not be enough.[241] Mere knowledge is not enough.[242] An implied general permission or invitation does not require specific knowledge.[243]

In *Universal v Sharman*, Sharman Networks was found to have authorised the mass infringement of copyright in sound recordings by providing the software for the Kazaa peer-to-peer filesharing network. The two most important factors considered were that (1) Sharman provided the facilities for infringement; and (2) Sharman had knowledge that Kazaa was being used predominantly to share copyright works.[244] Wilcox J did not accept that there was a large proportion of legal filesharing traffic.[245] It was not important that Sharman did not have actual knowledge of infringing acts, merely that it knew that a major proportion of traffic must be infringing.[246]

Next, Sharman had a financial interest in increasing filesharing, because of increased advertising revenue. Because most filesharing is infringing, Sharman therefore had a financial interest in high rates of infringement.[247] Sharman did nothing effective to curb the illicit filesharing on their networks.[248] Sharman ran some campaigns which implicitly promoted illicit filesharing.[249] Critically, Wilcox J found that Sharman could exercise some degree of control over its users.[250]

In *Universal v Cooper*,[251] Cooper operated a website where other parties could post hyperlinks directing users to remote websites where infringing sound recordings could be downloaded. The Federal Court found that Cooper had knowledge of the infringing material, his website facilitated the infringement of copyright, and he had power to exercise some control over the links, but did not do so.[252] Accordingly, Cooper had authorised the infringement of copyright in the sound recordings, notwithstanding that

---

[241] *Adelaide Corporation v Australasian Performing Right Association Ltd* (1928) 40 CLR 481.
[242] *Universal Music Australia Pty Ltd v Sharman License Holdings Ltd* (2005) 220 ALR 1, 90, citing *Nationwide News Pty Ltd v Copyright Agency Ltd* (1996) 65 FCR 399, 422.
[243] *Moorhouse* (1975) 133 CLR 1, 21.
[244] *Universal Music Australia Pty Ltd v Sharman License Holdings Ltd* (2005) 220 ALR 1, 49, 98.
[245] Ibid 49.
[246] Ibid 50.
[247] Ibid.
[248] Ibid 99.
[249] Ibid 98.
[250] Ibid 100.
[251] *Universal Music Australia Pty Ltd v Cooper* (2005) 65 IPR 409.
[252] Ibid 429.

none of the infringing material was hosted under his control, or that the links to the websites hosting the infringing material were placed on his website by other users.

Although the decisions in *Universal v Sharman* and *Universal v Cooper* were confined very tightly to the facts of the cases, we are able to see how the same principles could be applied to find a computer game manufacturer liable for secondary copyright infringement. NCSoft provides the means of infringement, could be shown to know of the infringement (depending on how prevalent it is), and have the power to stop such infringement (MMORPGs are much more tightly controlled than distributed filesharing networks). It is also possible that NCSoft could be shown to engage in tacit promotions of infringement in their advertising materials.

The fact that NCSoft's game obviously has many non-infringing players may be the crucial point in any such litigation. In this case, the game developer could probably successfully argue that it should not be held responsible for the infringing behaviour of a small number of its players.

NCSoft in this case may be able to escape secondary liability in Australia. However, we must consider whether this is the approach we want to take when we are shaping our digital environments. Are we certain that we only want people to be able to role-play with their favourite media icons in spaces which have been licensed by the appropriate publishers? If a provider of a virtual world made a space (like a park) where players could express themselves as they wanted, should they be liable when a significant portion of those players express themselves in ways that draw on copyright portions of their popular culture?

The disadvantages to such an approach are significant. Primarily, only people who have the ability to pay pop-culture creators have the opportunity to play – at least in the offline world, merchandisers cannot (completely) stop children from using their imagination or someone else's toys to role-play. Next, we lose a great potential for creative re-expression – the environment must be controlled by the owner or a licensee, meaning that the potential for expression is limited to their ideas of 'safe' playing with iconic characters. We also lose the ability for players to mix genres and media – Marvel characters will be segregated not only from DC Comic superheroes, but also dinosaurs, spacemen, and Walt Disney characters. The qualitative value of play is reduced because it is confined to the boundaries of corporate merchandisers.

The better solution is to exempt this type of play from copyright infringement, either by determining that it does not reproduce a substantial part of the original works, or that it should be excused as a fair dealing or fair use of material. Unfortunately, current Australian law does not support such an approach.

Machinima

Machinima is the art of filmmaking using computer generated graphics in real-time virtual worlds. Unlike traditional animation, machinima makes use of readily available virtual worlds, typically computer games, where "characters and events can be either controlled by humans, scripts or artificial intelligence".[253] Machinima allows filmmakers to use a pre-existing physics engine (and artwork, characters, and scenery) from a video game in order to develop a compelling story, without the high costs associated with either live-action filming or traditional animation. Essentially, the actors in a machinima film are able to use the game's controls to express themselves, bringing their characters to life through acting, rather than animation. The output of the game, from the point of view of one of the actors or a dedicated camera operator, is captured on a computer for later editing. Because the animation in a game is somewhat limited as to the expressions and movements of the characters, the voice acting and soundtrack that is added to the film plays a very important role in setting the mood.

Machinima involves the re-purposing of computer games for the creative expression of filmmakers. As a film technique, machinima has distinct advantages which are readily apparent. The equipment required is relatively inexpensive consumer hardware and software. Many of the art resources of the game can be re-utilised, meaning that the filmmakers can focus on the important aspects of acting, filming, and editing. Characters can be controlled by actors in real-time, instead of painstakingly animating each movement. Given the considerable budgets of films produced today, machinima provides an excellent avenue for filmmakers to express themselves on an extremely low budget.

The problem faced by machinima filmmakers is that there is great uncertainty as to their legal rights to create and distribute their films. Computer games are both literary works and cinematograph films in

---

[253] Machinima.org, 'What is Machinima? – The Machinima FAQ' <http://machinima.org/machinima-faq.html#what> at 4 September 2006.

copyright law,[254] and may also include original dramatic, musical, and artistic works, as well as many sound recordings. Reproduction of a substantial part of this material in a film will generally not be legal without the permission of the copyright owners. Whether a machinima film could be said to have reproduced a substantial part of the copyright cinematograph film in any given computer game is questionable; however, the copyright in the many individual elements that make up the film will almost certainly be infringed.

Most game publishers do not object to the use of their games by machinima filmmakers, and in many cases, actively encourage their development, by hosting competitions, film festivals, and even introducing features into the game specifically for filmmakers.[255] However, as machinima becomes more popular, and commercial releases of machinima films become more common place, or films which are critical or reflect poorly on the original game are created, the copyright owners may well begin to object. At that point, machinima filmmakers may find themselves in a very difficult legal situation.

Modifying the game to remove all copyright artwork is an option for filmmakers who only want to use the physics engine from the game. Many games provide developers with a way to create 'total conversions' of their game, in effect replacing all the visual elements of the game. This option, while certainly possible for some filmmakers, is generally unattractive for the majority of machinima creators. Stripping the game back to its bare physics engine is a lot of work for experienced programmers and artists. The advantages provided by the simplicity of machinima are, to a great extent lost, if in addition to directors, actors, script-writers, editors, and voice actors, the production crew must include experienced programmers and graphic designers. The game would no longer provide a ready-made framework for the creative expression of filmmakers, but would instead require many hours of intense preparatory work. A more subtle drawback

---

[254] *Galaxy Electronics Pty Ltd v Sega Enterprises Ltd* (1997) 75 FCR 8.

[255] For example, *Red vs Blue* <http://rvb.roosterteeth.com> is a popular series which is created using Bungie's Halo game. Machinima in Halo was mainly possible due to a bug in the game, whereby the character model could move his weapons and arms without his head moving. When Bungie released Halo 2, they fixed this bug, but added a feature in multiplayer modes where a player can control the head independently of the gun, a feature which has no purpose or use in actual play. See Bungie.net, 'Red vs. Blue: The Interview Strikes Back' <http://www.bungie.net/News/TopStory.aspx?story=rvbinterview> at 4 September 2006.

to this approach is that the popular significance of the game itself is lost. Machinima filmmakers are often fans of the game, and often make many references to the game and the game community in the film. It is often the community that has risen around the game that provides the immediate popular outlet for the film. Removing most of the aspects that make the game recognisable would alienate the film from its heritage, and the filmmakers from their community.

If the copyright owners in computer games begin to enforce their rights with respect to machinima creators, the burgeoning industry is likely to suffer. The greatest risk is not that machinima will not be created at all, but rather that only 'safe' machinima, which is acceptable to the owner of the copyright in the game used, will be permissible. Machinima as a genre provides possibilities for many people who would not otherwise have the opportunity to express themselves in film. Its utility quickly evaporates if it becomes merely a tool for the dissemination of advertisements for the copyright owner's game or point of view.

Machinima, as a tool which provides creators with an engine of expression and a means to represent their culture, should be encouraged. Machinima isn't about infringing copyright in computer games – it is unlikely that an expressive film of this type would substitute for the game in any way. Further, computer games are generally not designed with the aim of making money from licensing their use to makers of machinima. Indeed, the attraction of the genre seems to be that it is cheap, that license fees are not payable, and that the games are attractive to the filmmakers as games first, and become vehicles for their further expression second. This may change as machinima becomes more accepted and platforms are designed specifically for use in filmmaking, but it does not seem to be the case at the moment. To use copyright law to suppress the creation of these films seems to be counter-intuitive, particularly since it is likely that only negative portrayals will be suppressed, given the gaming industry's acceptance of current films.

Conclusion

These three examples show a theme of tension in Australian copyright law, between the interests of copyright owners, game developers, game players, and third party developers. The first example, *Blizzard v bnetd*, shows that makers of interoperable programs, which should be protected by the exceptions in Australian copyright law, are at significant risk of infringing the anti-circumvention provisions, which are not protected from exclusion by contract.

The second example, *Marvel v NCSoft*, shows that players of games who want to role-play with their favourite characters from popular culture are likely to infringe copyright in those characters when they play online, even though their corresponding offline actions would not be likely to attract the attention or suit of the copyright owners. The shift to the online environment makes it easier for pressure to be applied to the parties in control of playing spaces, and the value of playing in these spaces may be significantly curtailed by restrictions on the subject matter of role-playing. In order to avoid this homogenisation of play in online spaces, Australian law should move not only to ensure that secondary copyright liability should generally not attach to the providers of online spaces in this manner, but that this sort of play with popular culture should not constitute infringement of copyright at all.

The final example, machinima, shows a burgeoning industry in innovative filmmaking techniques. The wide availability of computer games means that these filmmaking techniques are available to a wider range of people, allowing more individuals to express themselves creatively. The manner in which Australian copyright law reacts to machinima will determine the continued viability of the genre. If machinima is held to reproduce a substantial part of the computer game it uses, and there is no open-ended fair use defence available, then copyright owners will have a significant form of control over the content and production of machinima, greatly reducing the utility of the genre as an expressive medium by subjugating it to the interests of copyright owners.

These three issues show an imminent conflict in Australian copyright law. The Australian courts and legislature could adapt copyright law to encourage these types of creative innovation and play in the digital environment, or they could prohibit them as mere interferences with the copyright owner's property. Which approach will be taken will depend on the recognition of the tension between the rights of copyright owners and the rights of players of computer games. By recognising that copyright law should exist not only to protect investment in the production of intellectual property, but also to encourage further creativity, innovation and social interaction, a balance can be sought which both protects game developers from piracy, and also protects the right of players to play, and the ability of players to express themselves, inside and outside the games.

The Future

Professor Lawrence Lessig, Professor Stuart Cunningham and Sal Humphreys

Professor Lawrence Lessig

I am happy to be on this panel because it is a little bit of a reminiscing for me. When I first started working in this area and wrote *Code and Other Laws of Cyberspace*[256], which was published the very week that I came to Australia for the first time, it was the virtual world's experience that motivated the central metaphor of the book. It was watching the way virtual worlds in the MUD and MOO context developed that made me start thinking about the relationship between technology and legal policy and that has of course been at the core of a lot of the work since. But today I want to talk about three points, none of which are really about the relationship between technology and policy, but all three come out of a course that I just taught last term with Julian Dibell who was one of the protagonists in my first book, and really come out of watching this field become a serious field in the context of both commercial and, increasingly, regulatory questions. The three points I want to make are first that this is real, despite its moniker 'virtual', second that it is common, in the sense that it's everywhere, not just in virtual worlds, and third, that commercial interests have exactly the wrong intuitions about how to think about this space.

First, that it is real. Some of the most significant work in getting people to see why this is a significant issue has been done by economists who are trying to demonstrate the extraordinary economic wealth that's being produced in these worlds, in particular Ed Castronova's work estimating the value of these very virtual worlds, and in some of them the per capita GDP is greater than per capita GDP of Romania, so these are huge economies if you use relatively sophisticated techniques to estimate the value of the stuff being produced in these spaces. And it is not just the value being produced in these spaces; there is a story, which because of legal reasons has never been published, so I am going to vaguely refer to it, breaking all sorts of confidentiality agreements, but if I am vague enough nobody will ever know.

---

[256] Lawrence Lessig, *Code and Other Laws of Cyberspace* (1999) Basic Books, New York

The story is about a gaming company that got into a lot of trouble because it changed its rules about whether you are allowed to re-sell objects and when they changed their rules, the people who had invested a lot of time making objects and re-selling them said, "you broke our contract". And somebody went to investigate these people making these claims and they turned out to be located in Mexico and it turned out a company had set up a virtual sweat shop in Mexico, where they brought Mexicans in and had them sitting in front of a computer, clicking 24 hours a day, creating the objects that were then sold on eBay and that that process was profitable. They were making a huge amount of money by taking these labourers and forcing them to play this game where they produced little objects that were sold in the real world. That is as real an economy as you are going to get anywhere. It has proved to be valuable to hire people to engage in this kind of transaction, and when you begin to add up the amount of wealth being devoted in time in these spaces, it is something that we who think about this from a policy perspective have got to consider much more generally. That is point one.

Point two, the form of creativity that is going on here, or creation that is going on here, is common in other spheres of social and economic life. Think about three examples, one the virtual games, where people spend an extraordinary amount of time investing in producing objects of wealth voluntarily. The Trainz example from the last session was a great one about people spending an extraordinary amount of time doing stuff that produces value but they do it voluntarily. They play and it turns out they have the same value as work. This is *play as work*. That happens also in the context that Eric von Hippel writes about user contributed value to ordinary production processes, as users become inputs into helping design these production processes. That is the one I do not want to talk about much.

The one I want to make the most direct link to is the free and open source software world, where there is an extraordinary amount of value produced by people playing, tinkering around with little objects, that turns out to be like work because it produces really powerful operating systems, or really powerful servers, that *ex ante* nobody would have expected could have been produced like this. They would have said it was impossible to produce it like this. Intuition would have told you it could not be done, but the lesson to be learned is that the intuitions are wrong. We had better re-think the models that drive the intuitions that show us that these massive, collaborative, voluntary projects cannot work, and we do that by beginning to link the very different contexts in which they are happening and beginning to recognise what makes them work in these very different contexts.

What makes open source or free software projects work? It is all the same kind of questions that are being asked in the context of the gaming communities. It is precisely the same issue. What do you do to both convince people that they have enough ownership of the project to make it feel like they are actually contributing to something that is theirs, while on the other hand, not allowing the feeling of ownership to translate into a commercial transaction so they begin to demand health benefits for the coding in the operating system context, or something like that. It is this weird balance that has to be struck and the fact is it is struck in the most dramatic and amazing context, for example, the new Linux operating system, and increasingly in lots of other contexts like that. If the gamers want to understand, or the game companies want to understand how to make this work, they ought to start looking at these other successful contexts, as well as at the work of Yochai Benkler and Steve Weber in his recent book about the success of open source resources.[257]

Third, about the intuitions of these commercial entities: when Julian and I taught this course we were teaching it in Silicon Valley, so we had a great opportunity to bring in the corporate geniuses who thought they were going to make billions of dollars off of these game companies. We had the President of 'There' come in. 'There' was a gaming company where people contributed a lot of energy to turning this game into something interesting and real and we had some very sharp students in the class, who were extremely sceptical of this man. In 'There', there were 'There' dollars, 'There Bucks' having an exchange value of 17.89 to 1 – $1 got you 1789 'There Bucks'. Where does 1789 come from? That is the year the Constitution was ratified in the United States. Everything in 'There' was grounded in the idea of America and how great America was.

One student in particular started asking the President of 'There' some questions about the way life was in 'There' and so she said:

> "When you produce things in 'There', who owns what you produce?"
> "Well, what do you mean?" he replied.
> "Well I create something, who owns it?"

---

[257] Steven Weber's *The Success of Open Source* (2004) is a complement to Yochai Benkler's classic essay, 'Coase's Penguin, or Linux or the Nature of the Firm' (2002) 112 *Yale Law Review* 369.

"Well the user licence says that we own it, 'There' owns it".

'There' was very famous because they were going to rent out spaces to Nike, or Sony, so she then said:

"Well when Nike and Sony make things inside of 'There', who owns it then?"
"Well, of course, Nike owns it".
"OK" she said, "so you've created a world where authors get nothing and corporations get everything?"
"Well, yeah. How else would you do it?"

And she said, "well the American way", which was exactly the opposite.

The copyright clause made so authors got it and corporations could not, that was the whole point.

The other great example she hit him with was (she is now a Prosecutor, she is perfect for this job):

"So do you have the right to free speech in 'There'"?

He said, "of course, you have the right to free speech".

"So I can put a poster up on my lands"?
"Absolutely" he replied.
"And I can buy land anywhere"?
"Sure".
"I can buy land next to a Nike store"?
"Sure".
"Can I put a poster up on the land next to my Nike store that says 'Nike uses Sweat Shop Labor'?"
"Er, no, you can't do that".

The point was that the natural tendency and attitude of this corporation was to think about these social relations in a purely corporate way, and we have to remember what the essence of a corporation is. As Ronald Coase taught us in his most famous, first, big article, a corporation is a communist organisation, right? A corporation is that space where it is just power that directs what happens inside, and the market place is outside the corporation. When you have this mentality where you own everything inside the corporation and you include your users as part of the corporation, that produces a certain reaction from your users.

Many people will say from this, "then we have to start thinking about corporate responsibility, and are they actually answering their responsibility to their users?" That was the theme of the last panel. I am less convinced that this is an issue because I am convinced there is going to be great competition between corporations here in producing virtual worlds that actually give users what they want, and the 'There-type' corporation is going to fail miserably.

'Second Life' is an alternate vision of this, which has a different sense of who owns what. I think it will be much more successful. Second Life announced early on that all owners, all users, owned their IP, and then the question was, well how were they going to enable people to share the IP? They said to us at Creative Commons, 'why don't you help us build Creative Commons licences so that inside virtual worlds you can actually share IP according to the Creative Commons licences.' And that lead to a really brilliant suggestion which they have not implemented yet but we are talking about, which is this: in Second Life, you can be video-camming and while you are video-camming what is inside Second Life the video camera can record or not record on the basis of whether the thing you are taking a picture of is under Creative Commons licence or not.

If you do not license your stuff under your Creative Commons licence as you pan across the room, it is just invisible, but if you do licence with a Creative Commons licence then it is visible, so this is a way of making the licensing stuff 'real-virtual' – I do not know what you want to call it – but as real as virtual could be by actually implementing the rules and the way the technology functions, and the expectation was that this dynamic would drive people to be much more open and communal about how they produced and did their stuff with intellectual property because that's the only way they, literally, would be seen inside this world.

A final point about that consideration: the people who are going to be most successful in these gaming worlds are the people who have been trained in PhDs of the history of liberal societies, you know people who got their PhD from Steven Holmes. Steven Holmes' whole theory about liberal societies is that societies when they became wealthier only became wealthier because they realised the government needed to exercise less and less power, that this was the paradox of power. That if the government exercised the maximum amount of power, the society was very poor, to the extent the government exercised less power, societies became wealthier. If a President of a corporation recognised the insight that Holmes et al have put forward, and built a virtual world around that insight, we would begin to see a virtual world replicating the kind of growth in wealth that the real world saw when the real world learnt exactly the same lesson.

The ultimate point here is that there is no significant difference between the real world and the virtual world, and the conclusion from that is we ought to start learning lessons in the virtual world which 500 years of history in the real world have taught us.

PROFESSOR STUART CUNNINGHAM

I am going to take a somewhat different tack. While I will end up with games, I am going to start with the question of innovation and the place of creative content, particularly cutting-edge, new media, emergent media forms and their place in national innovation agendas because this is where, from a public policy point of view in many countries, the greatest potential for growth in these emergent sectors, lies. As I say, I will end up with some comments about games and how games fits into this, but I am going to make a general set of points about the relation between creative content and the innovation agendas of international policy terms.

The first point to say is that they do not really connect at all. National innovation agendas, as constructs of public policy, conspicuously absent the whole area of creative content from their purview. At best, the humanities and creative arts areas, disciplines, are seen as mere hand-maidens, afterthought hand-maidens, to the power houses of new sciences as they drive innovation and research and development agendas. The best that the human sciences can hope for in this context is, usually, that they are seen as ways of understanding and managing the consequences, as one policy document says, "manage the consequences of moving to a knowledge-based economy" but, of course, implicit in that is that they could never be seen as a driver of that growth economy.

This hand-maiden model that is so endemic to national innovation thinking is patently inadequate to capture the growing contribution of creative content industries and the social phenomena that we have been looking at around the games phenomena, the social phenomena that have rapidly grown around them in contemporary society. Creative production and cultural consumption are an increasingly integral part of growth economies, not merely part of analysing and managing it. The creative industries, it goes without saying I suppose for this audience, are a significant sector of many, if not most, advanced economies.

In US copyright industries, as they are usually called, are worth $791B in 2001, representing 7.75 percent of GDP. They employ 8 million workers in the US. The share of US exports was $88B, almost $89B, outstripping the chemical, motor vehicle, aircraft, agricultural and electronic components and computer sector industries in the US exports. In the UK it is a little bit less, £112B, employing 1.3 million people, £10.3B in exports in 2001, over 5 percent of GDP. They are big, growth sectors of the economy, but they are also drivers of the knowledge economy in general and enablers of other industry sectors, especially through the provision of digital content, which is increasingly translating directly into competitive advantage and innovation capability.

In the light of that you would wonder why they do not occupy a much stronger place in innovation and R&D thinking in Western countries. Most R&D and innovation priorities reflect the science agenda at the expense of these growth sectors, but when we look more closely we see, as Jeremy Rifkin says in *The Age of Access*, that the broad content industry sectors that we're talking about here, business, education, leisure and entertainment, media and communications, represent 25 percent of the US economy, as an example, whilst the new science sector, the sector that has been the recipient of most innovation and R&D investment – that is biotech, fibre construction, materials, energy, pharmaceuticals – accounts for only 15 percent of the US economy.

Most OECD countries are increasingly consumption driven in their economic shape, 60 percent of GDP in Australia, 62 percent of the US GDP is consumption driven, and the social and cultural technologies that manage and stimulate consumption all derive from, or mostly derive, from these disciplines of humanities, creative arts and the human sciences. There is an argument that I am trying to make here for a very significant gap between where innovation and R&D thinking is at present in most OECD countries, and where creative content is going.

How does that relate to the games sector? I see the games sector as a proto-typical case of an innovative, R&D driven, or an R&D intensive, sector that should be integral in any country's innovation and R&D agenda. Consider, when you think about the history of electronic games from the 1970s you have had a massively rapid and intensely innovative cycle of innovation in terms of shape, architecture, inventiveness and rapidity. This has all happened in slightly more than 30 years of history.

The games sector is an intensely research and development driven, very innovative sector and some of the writing of the kinds of fields that I am familiar with, not being a lawyer, in the media, cultural studies, communication studies, areas, some very interesting work that has been done on innovation in the games sector. A writer that John Banks referred to earlier, Henry Jenkins from MIT, has written very interestingly on games and their relation to the history of aesthetic innovation in the 20th century. He says that games have been created without the safety net that inherited modernist rhetoric provides for established art forms and talks extensively about the way in which games are re-creating the template of what aesthetic innovation is, and in some of the work of JC Hertz, particularly in a piece called *Harnessing the Hive*, she brings the notion of innovation of games to centre stage, particularly emphasising the issues of collective IP, that Lawrence Lessig has just raised.

Hertz addresses collective IP at a user level, collaborating with games developers and the challenges of producing, of capturing the dynamics of collective IP. She talks about the way in which innovation is content driven rather than technology driven in games. Hertz says that innovation is anthropological rather than technological in games. It is about the network effects of social networking and that this is the most advanced example of network effects (with massive multi-player, online games) that we have seen so far in virtual environments. The case for innovation and R&D in games is, it seems to me, a very powerful one. Perhaps the biggest issue here is the way in which, particularly the online games world, is producing a new template that is highly recursive, that breaks the linear value chain, and is opening up a whole set of highly disruptive challenges and opportunities in re-thinking the relation between proprietary and non-proprietary, amateur and professional, and so on. There are huge issues that are going to become driver issues arising out of games, but impacting on a number of other areas over the next generation of innovation in this sector.

SAL HUMPHREYS

I am going to shift the focus just a little and come back to something Professor Lessig mentioned, which I don't agree with entirely. In massive multi-user online games, people are creating communities inside of proprietary spaces, and this throws up some issues that are not to do with property; they are to do with community management and they are to do with the fact that a games company that is publishing an MMOG (massive multi-user online game) has also now taken on the role of being a community manager, and that is not a role that is a familiar one to any publisher.

Most publishers do not have to manage communities. They do not have to intervene in their consumers' disputes. They do not have to manage their consumers' bad behaviour. They do not have to manage conflict resolution between their users. This is all stuff that MMOG publishers have to do. It indicates we have seen a shift here from a publication model to a services model, and that the MMOG represents a hybrid of the two. It is not so simple as to say that is an uncomplicated hybridity because publications and services operate with different institutional practices.

The institutional practices around a service industry are quite different from those around a publication industry, and I suggest that a publication industry is mostly formulated around the idea of property and so all its institutional practices and the discourses that circulate, in terms of user innovation, in terms of what players are actually doing, are about what kind of property they are generating. But we have also moved into a services environment here, and we now have the element of community inside of these proprietary spaces. We are dealing with social networks which are at the heart of the business plans of these publishing corporations, as the social networks are what drive the retention of players in games.

Usually, with a single player game, players will play until they have mastered it. Once they have cracked it, they move on to the next one. What happens with a MMOG is players become enmeshed in social networks inside the game and they will play for years beyond their mastery of the game. Because they are run on a subscription basis, and players pay a monthly fee in order to access it, the longer you can keep a player accessing the game, the longer you get their subscription fee. If you are relying on them staying inside the game because of the social networks, it means really that the social networks have become integral to the business plan. They are part of what drives profit. To say that if the contracts that determine the terms of service under which those players play, the EULAs (the End User Licence Agreements), are unconscionable, players should just leave, is to ignore the very social nature of what keeps them in the game, that the stickiness of the game is the socialness of it, and thus the switching costs are terribly high.

If you have been playing a game for three years and you decide that you have been treated unconscionably by the customer service team, it is not a matter of just upping stakes and moving to the next game, because all your friends are inside the game that you are in. So the switching costs have become very high. It is not as simple as changing products. It is not a matter of just choosing between alternative products and, "oh this game sucks and I have been treated poorly so I am going to move on to the next game". Unless you can convince all your friends to come with you, that is not a very valid proposition.

The other value involved in social networking is that if you stay inside a community for a number of years, then you build a reputation and status and you would have to rebuild that inside a new game. These social aspects are ignored by always focusing on the property elements inside games and that property is the important aspect. Property is the aspect that is associated with the publication model, but we need to start taking account of the services model and we need to start understanding these things as social with social consequences. One of the results that I see is that we need to have some kind of measure of accountability for the corporations that run these places in their community service management strategies, which are enabled through EULA contracts.

The game I studied is called EverQuest. In the EverQuest end user licence agreement it says they can ban me for any reason that they choose, and I have no recourse to any appeal mechanism. If I play against the spirit of the game, 'spirit of the game' is not defined particularly well anywhere – it is a very nebulous kind of concept – I could find myself banned from the game, and lose all my friends and lose all my in-game accumulated wealth. I have nowhere to go to actually appeal that decision, and the consequences for me are not only material, in that I lose the possible real world value of the property inside that game, but they are social. I lose the access to my community. The contracts are becoming the mechanism that determines access to social relations, and that is material that we have not yet really engaged with to any great extent, and something that I hope we soon will engage with.

Biographies

PROFESSOR LAWRENCE LESSIG

Professor Lawrence Lessig is Professor of Law at Stanford Law School and founder of the school's Center for Internet and Society. Prior to joining the Stanford faculty, he was the Berkman Professor of Law at Harvard Law School. He was also a fellow at the Wissenschaftskolleg zu Berlin, and a Professor at the University of Chicago Law School. He clerked for Judge Richard Posner of the 7th Circuit Court of Appeals and Justice Scalia of the United States Supreme Court.

More recently, Professor Lessig represented web site operator Eric Eldred in the ground-breaking case *Eldred v. Ashcroft*, a challenge to the 1998 *Sonny Bono Copyright Term Extension Act*. Lessig was named one of Scientific American's Top 50 Visionaries, for arguing "against interpretations of copyright that could stifle innovation and discourse online". He is the author of *The Future of Ideas* and *Code and Other Laws of Cyberspace*. He also chairs the Creative Commons project. Professor Lessig is a board-member of the Electronic Frontier Foundation, a Board Member of the Center for the Public Domain, and a Commission Member of the Penn National Commission on Society, Culture and Community at the University of Pennsylvania. Professor Lessig earned a BA in economics and a BS in management from the University of Pennsylvania, an MA in philosophy from Cambridge, and a JD from Yale. Professor Lessig teaches and writes in the areas of constitutional law, contracts, comparative constitutional law, and the law of cyberspace.

RICHARD NEVILLE (FUTURIST)

Richard Neville has been involved with challenging and changing the ways we think, ever since his student days in the sixties when he published and edited the magazine, *Oz*. It landed him in jail and gave Australia its nickname. Since that time, he has achieved prominence as a social commentator and best selling author, his subjects range from cyber-sex, smart drugs and serial killers, from globalization, the reinvention of work and the consciousness movement to the new role for business in the 21st century, the Creative Economy and the revived focus on human potential. In his professional life as a futurist, Richard talks with audiences in Australia and Asia on a range of issues that affect the way we work, play, learn, heal, think and decode the world. He does not try to predict stuff, except when it slips out his 'big mouth' ("Philosophers will be the Rock Gods of future"). Instead, he offers lots of tricks, tools and techniques for audiences to take away and apply, to help make their own assessment about the changing shape and feel of what's to come.

PROFESSOR BRIAN FITZGERALD
(Head, QUT School of Law BA (Griff) LLB (Hons) (QUT) BCL (Oxon.) LLM (Harv.) PhD (Griff))
Website at: http://www.law.qut.edu.au/about/staff/lsstaff/fitzgerald.jsp

Brian is a well-known intellectual property and information technology lawyer. He has published articles on Law and the Internet in Australia, the United States, Europe, Nepal, India, Canada and Japan and his latest (co-authored) books are *Cyberlaw: Cases and Materials on the Internet, Digital Intellectual Property and E Commerce* (2002); *Jurisdiction and the Internet* (2004); *Intellectual Property in Principle* (2004). Over the past five years Brian has delivered seminars on information technology and intellectual property law in Australia, Canada, New Zealand, USA, Nepal, India, Japan, Malaysia, Singapore, Norway and the Netherlands. In October 1999 Brian delivered the Seventh Annual Tenzer Lecture 'Software as Discourse: The Power of Intellectual Property in Digital Architecture' at Cardozo Law School in New York. Through the first half of 2001 Brian was a Visiting Professor at Santa Clara University Law School in Silicon Valley in the USA. In January 2003 Brian delivered lectures in India and Nepal and in February 2003 was invited as part of a distinguished panel of three to debate the Theoretical Underpinning of Intellectual Property Law at University of Western Ontario in London, Canada. During 2005 Brian presented talks in Germany, India and China and was a Visiting Professor in the Oxford University Internet Institutes Summer Doctoral Program in Beijing in July 2005. He is also a Chief Investigator and Program Leader for Law in the newly awarded ARC Centre of Excellence on Creative Industries and Innovation. Brian is also Project Leader for the DEST funded Open Access to Knowledge Law Project (OAK Law Project), looking at legal protocols for open access to the Australian research sector. His current projects include work on digital copyright issues across the areas of Open Content Licensing and the Creative Commons, Free and Open Source Software, Fan Based Production of Computer Games, Licensing of Digital Entertainment and Anti-Circumvention Law. Brian is a Project Leader for Creative Commons in Australia. From 1998-2002 Brian was Head of the School of Law and Justice at Southern Cross University in New South Wales, Australia and in January 2002 was appointed as Head of the School of Law at QUT in Brisbane, Australia.

THE HON JUSTICE JAMES DOUGLAS

Justice James Sholto Douglas was appointed to the Supreme Court of Queensland on 27 November 2003. After working as Sir Harry Gibbs' associate, post-graduate study at Cambridge and a brief period in a solicitors' firm in London he commenced private practice at the Bar in Brisbane in 1977, became a QC in 1989 and was President of the Bar Association of Queensland from 1999 to 2001. He was editor of the Queensland Reports from 1986 to 1991 and a member of the Legal Committee of the Companies and Securities Advisory Committee from 1992 to 1994. He is also a member of the American Law Institute, the body responsible for producing the Restatements of American Law, was a part time member of the Anti-Discrimination Tribunal during 2003 and a Grade 1 arbitrator through the Institute of Arbitrators and Mediators of Australia. From 1990 to 1996 he was Chairman of the Queensland Theatre Company and from 1989 to 1996 Chairman of the Queensland Symphony Orchestra's Advisory Board.

THE HON JUSTICE RONALD SACKVILLE

Justice Sackville has been a Judge of the Federal Court of Australia since 1994. Justice Sackville was formerly Professor of Law (1972-1985) and Dean of the Faculty of Law (1979-1981) at the University of New South Wales. He was Commissioner for Law and Poverty on the Australian Government Commission of Inquiry into Poverty (1973-1975); Chairman of the South Australian Royal Commission into the Non-Medical Use of Drugs (1979-1981); and Chairman of the New South Wales Law Reform Commission (1981-1984). From 1985 until his appointment to the Federal Court, Justice Sackville practised at the New South Wales bar, principally in the fields of administrative law, constitutional law and equity. He was appointed Queen's Counsel n 1991. From 1985 to 1989 he chaired (part-time) the Victorian Accident Compensation Commission. Justice Sackville chaired the Commonwealth Access to Justice Advisory Committee, which presented its report, *Access to Justice: An Action Plan,* in 1994. Justice Sackville has published articles and papers on a wide range of subjects, including migration law. In recent years he has been a Visiting Scholar at Cornell University, New York University, McGill University and Cardozo Law School. He is the Chair of the Judicial Conference of Australia.

LINDA LAVARCH MP

At the time of the conference Linda Lavarch was Parliamentary Secretary to the Minister for State Development and Innovation State Member for Kurwongbah. In July 2005 Linda was appointed the Attorney-General and Minister for Justice for Queensland. She resigned from her ministerial duties in October 2006, due to medical reasons. Linda was elected to

Parliament in 1997 as the State Member for Kurwongbah, and was appointed Parliamentary Secretary to the Minister for State Development and Innovation in February 2004, paying particular attention to the area of Innovation. In March 2005, Linda was appointed Parliamentary Secretary to the Minister for Energy and Minister for Aboriginal and Torres Strait Islander Policy before being elevated to Cabinet in July 2005. Currently Linda is Co-chair of the Queensland Parliament Diabetes Support Group. Linda has held positions on a number of Parliamentary Committees, as well as Chair of the Scrutiny of Legislation Committee, Chair of the Queensland Graffiti Taskforce, Chair of the Qld Fishing Industry Development Council, Deputy Chair of the Qld Small Business Advisory Council, Co-chair of the Manufacturing Leaders Group, member of the Qld University of Technology Council, and Chair of a Special Committee enquiring into the operation of Tenancy Databases. Prior to entering Parliament Linda was a solicitor. She holds a Bachelor of Laws and a Graduate Diploma in Legal Practice.

Tom Cochrane

Tom is the Deputy Vice Chancellor (Technology Information & Learning Support) at QUT. The position heads a large Division which combines the services of Libraries, the Information Technology Services area, Teaching and Learning Support and University Printing into one structure. Tom's external duties include Directorships with the Australian Partnership for Advanced Computing, the Queensland Cyber Infrastructure Foundation and the Australian Digital Alliance. Tom chairs the Australian Libraries' Copyright Committee and has served on the CLRC, established at the Federal level. He also serves on national committees providing advice to DEST and MCEETYA, and is a member of the CSIRO Publishing Board.

Professor Arun Sharma

Professor Sharma is the Deputy Vice-Chancellor (Research and Commercialisation) at the Queensland University of Technology. In this role, he oversees the University's research and research training programs, commercialisation activities and its multidisciplinary research institutes. He has played a leadership role in development of national research capacity in information and communication technology. He was co-founder of National ICT Australia Limited (NICTA) – Australia's new world class centre of excellence, and was the inaugural Director of its largest research laboratory where he oversaw recruitment of over 80 staff (including 40 PhDs trained at some of the world's leading universities). Prior to establishing NICTA, he was the Head of the School of Computer Science and Engineering at the University of New South Wales. During his three and half year tenure as Head, the School underwent a substantial expansion, including addition of 20 new academics, an increase of over 65 percent in postgraduate research enrolment and leading national position in competitive grant funding.

He continues to play an important advisory role to a number of research organisations. He is on the ICT Sector Advisory Committee of CSIRO, the advisory board of the ARC Special Research Centre for Ultra High Bandwidth Optical Devices and chairs the international scientific advisory committee for the Australasian CRC for Interaction Design. His board memberships include Cooperative Research Centre for Diagnostics, Cooperative Research Centre for Construction Innovation, Creative Industries Pty Ltd and the Australasian CRC for Interaction Design.

IAN OI

Ian Oi joined Corrs Canberra office as a partner in August 2005. His practice focuses on intellectual property, information technology and telecommunications, and strategic procurement. Formerly a senior attorney and negotiator with IBM in Australia and a special counsel with another large Australian firm, Ian has extensive experience advising on these areas for clients in the public and private sectors. He has acted for suppliers and customers in some of Australia's most significant technology-related projects in recent times, and has particular expertise in dealing with large outsourcing transactions, complex software development, IP commercialisation, and open source software and open content development, management and distribution.

Ian is regularly invited to speak around Australia on issues in the above areas. His recent presentations have been on topics such as government procurement after the Australian-US free trade agreement, privacy in the age of the smart card, recent developments in online contracting, open source software projects in the Australian public sector, 'digital amnesia' and electronic archives, and Creative Commons initiatives in Australia.

PROFESSOR RICHARD JONES

Richard Jones is an international award filmmaker and a national leader in research driven creative production. He has made a feature film, short dramas, documentaries, music clips, television and new media programs. Richard's work has been screened in the Melbourne, Adelaide, Berlin, Madrid, Chicago and Cannes MILIA film festivals, and at the London Institute of Contemporary Arts, the British and American Film Institutes and the New York Guggenheim Museum of Modern Art. He has recently completed a large Australian Research Council (ARC) grant with Kids Help Line and is currently leading an ARC grant developing interactive online tools for students with learning difficulties in partnership with The Le@rning Federation. Other work includes digital storytelling and photography projects with 'at risk' boys and men in maximum-security prison. Richard is also funded by VicHealth to work with *Somebody's Daughter Theatre* prison and post-release community arts programs. He was a Writer-in-Residence at RMIT, an Artist-in-Residence at Griffith University and the inaugural Production Fellow in QUT's Creative Industries Faculty. Richard is a Professorial Fellow at the Victorian College of the Arts, University of Melbourne, and works as a freelance teacher, film maker and photographer.

PROFESSOR GREG HEARN

Greg is acting Director of the Creative Industries Research and Applications Centre at QUT. Over the last ten years, his consulting and research has focused on the future cultural impacts and opportunities of global communication networks, for organisations and communities. He was a consultant to the Broadband Services Expert Group, the national policy group which formulated Australia's foundation framework for the Internet in 1994. In 2003 he completed work on framing Australia's digital content innovation framework for the Federal Department of Communications Information Technology and the Arts. As well, he has been involved in high level consultancy and applied research with organisations including British Airways, Telstra and many Australian government agencies, focusing on adaptation to new media technologies. His research on the knowledge society is published widely with his latest books being Rooney, D., Hearn, G., Mandeville, T. and Joseph, R. (2003) *Public Policy for the knowledge economy: Foundations and frameworks*, Cheltenham UK: Edward Elgar; and Rooney, D., Hearn, G. & Ninan, A. (eds) (2004), *Handbook of knowledge management* Cheltenham, UK: Edward Elgar.

DR ANNE FITZGERALD

Anne is a Brisbane-based intellectual property and e-commerce lawyer. She works as principal policy advisor in the Department of Natural Resources, Mines & Water(Qld) and is an Adjunct Professor at QUT Law School. As well as authoring several books on intellectual property and e-commerce law, Anne has served terms as a member of Australia's two principal Federal Government Standing Advisory Committees on IP, as a member of the Advisory Council on Intellectual Property (ACIP), which advises IP Australia, and as a member of the CLRC's expert advisory group for the CLRC's major review of the *Copyright Act* in the 1990s.

NEALE HOOPER

Neale is a specialist intellectual property lawyer and Principal Lawyer in the Intellectual Property, Technology and Communication Team in the Crown Law office in the Queensland Department of Justice and the Attorney-General with over 20 years experience in dealing with public sector issues arising in the intellectual property, technology and communication fields. He has extensive experience in e-government and e-commerce. Neale has been involved in many projects involving the identification, protection and commercialisation of public sector intellectual property, including biotechnology. Neale has been an active member of various cross-agency groups involved in the development of Queensland Government policy dealing with intellectual property and the commercialisation of such property in line with the Queensland Government's Smart State policy initiatives. More recently Neale has been engaged in whole of government initiatives dealing with the appropriate management of strategically important datasets and databases developed and maintained by various departments and agencies, including consideration of open content licensing models.

GREG LANE

Greg Lane is CEO of Auran which is an internationally known games developer based at Tenerife. Established in 1995, Auran first came to prominence with the hit RTS 'Dark Reign: The Future of War', which won Strategy Game of the Year in 1997. As one of Australia's oldest and largest game studios Auran has won numerous technology awards.

PROFESSOR JOHN QUIGGIN

Professor Quiggin is a Federation Fellow in Economics and Political Science at The University of Queensland. John is prominent both as a research economist and as a commentator on Australian economic policy. He has published over 800 research articles, books and reports in fields including environmental economics, risk analysis, production economics, and the theory of economic growth. He has also written on policy topics including unemployment policy, micro-economic reform, privatisation, competitive tendering and the management of the Murray-Darrling river system. John has been an active contributor to Australian public debate in a wide range of media. He is a regular columnist for the Australian Financial Review, to which he also contributes review and feature articles. He frequently comments on policy issues for radio and TV. He was one of the first Australian academics to present publications on a website. In 2002, he commenced publication of a weblog providing daily comments on a wide range of topics.

JEAN BURGESS

Jean is a doctoral candidate based in the Creative Industries Research and Applications Centre (CIRAC) at QUT. She holds a Master of Philosophy in cultural studies from the University of Queensland and previously worked as a classical musician, music teacher and electronic music producer. Her current research project investigates the democratization of technologies used to create, distribute and consume digital content, the potential for greater cultural participation, and the constraints on this participation (copyright law, for example). One of the case studies for this project is digital storytelling, a process by which ordinary people create short, personal multimedia stories for broadcast or web streaming. Digital storytelling has been a key component of the content creation training strategy for the Youth Internet Radio Network (YIRN), with which Jean has been involved as a trainer and researcher.

MARK FALLU

Mark is an IT specialist working with the Creative Industries Faculty of QUT.

PROFESSOR BARRY CONYNGHAM AM

Professor Conyngham was born in Sydney Australia. After study with Peter Scultthorpe at Sydney University and with Toru Takemitsu in Japan he has established himself as one of Australia's few international composers. In addition he also maintained a successful academic career, as teacher at the University of Melbourne and Harvard University, and with executive appointments as Dean of Creative Arts and Chair of the Academic Board at the University of Wollongong, Interim Dean of Information Technology and later School of Business Bond University and Foundation Vice-Chancellor and President of Southern Cross University. He now devotes his time primarily to composition and consultancy. He holds a MA (Hons) with the University Medal from the University of Sydney, a Doctor of Music from the University of Melbourne and a Certificate of Post-doctoral studies from the University of California at San Diego. He is an Emeritus Professor of both the University of Wollongong and Southern Cross Universities. During 2000-2001 he held the position of Chair of Australian Studies at Harvard University. In 1997 Barry's contribution to music and education was recognised when he became a Member of the Order of Australia.

Dr Terry Cutler

Terry Cutler is the Company Director of Cutler & Co, and an industry consultant and strategy advisor in the information and communications technology sector. His consulting practice has worked extensively on projects such as operator licensing, corporate strategy and commercial transactions, and government industry policy and regulation. Terry has served on numerous Government Boards and advisory bodies, taking a special interest in Government's role in the new global Information Economy. He is currently a Member of the Board of the Commonwealth Scientific and Industrial Research Organisation (CSIRO), a member of the Victorian Government's Innovation Economy Advisory Council, Chairman of the Australasian Centre for Interaction Design, and President of the Australian Centre for the Moving Image, an innovative 21st century cultural institution for screen culture.

Carol Fripp

Carol has over 27 years involvement in the Australian VET sector, from TAFE teacher through various organizational consultant and change agent roles into managing electronic service delivery options and ecommerce solutions in a rapidly changing environment. Carol has travelled widely over the last decade to keep current with new initiatives and innovations in the global marketplace. She has given several papers at national conferences through Australia and was Keynote Speaker at New Zealand eFEST2003. Her involvement with AEShareNet commenced in 1998 and continued through its evolution until appointed as inaugural Board Member in 2000 and subsequently moving into the role of General Manager in January 2002.

Dennis MacNamara

Dennis MacNamara has worked in vocational education for over 30 years in public and private institutions, including 19 years for TAFENSW (10 at the Open Training and Education Network, OTEN), and five at the Securities Institute. His main expertise is in the design and delivery of flexible and innovative learning services. He has been responsible for designing business models for the efficient organisation of education and training and is passionate about holistic approaches to the education business. Dennis joined AEShareNet in 2002, attracted to its potential to play a vital part in the infrastructure needed to facilitate flexible but efficient vocational education in Australia. It is imperative intellectual property be carefully managed in education, and that learning resources be used as widely as possible. Dennis believes AEShareNet offers an efficient global trading and sharing platform for learning materials, a world first for Australia.

Nic Suzor

Nic Suzor is a PhD student in the law school at Queensland University of Technology in Brisbane, Australia, researching Commons-based peer production in the creative industries. He has recently completed a research paper on the transformative re-use of copyright material. His background is in both law and computer science, holding undergraduate degrees in Law and IT from QUT, and having worked as a computer programmer before moving to legal research. He is involved in several research projects including Creative Commons Australia, research into legal issues of Free and Open Source Software, and computer games, with particular reference to massively multiplayer online environments and collaborative commons-based production. Nic teaches jurisprudence in QUT's undergraduate law programme, and legal issues to journalism students in QUT's Creative Industries faculty.

Dr David Rooney

Dr Rooney is Associate Director, Centre for Social Research in Communication and Senior Lecturer in Knowledge Management, UQ Business School. He has researched, taught and published widely in the areas of the knowledge-based economy, knowledge management, change management and economic structure of the creative industries. He is author of, Public Policy in the Knowledge-Based Economy. He is also one of the leading figures in the establishment of the Australian Creative Resource Archive, and the International Institute for Cultural Innovation, innovative new initiatives designed to stimulate creative industries growth in Australia and globally. Before entering academia he worked in the music and insurance industries.

Neeru Paharia

Neeru Paharia was most recently Executive Director of Creative Commons. Neeru graduated from the University of California at Davis in 1997 and received a Master of Science in Public Policy and Management with a concentration in Information Systems from Carnegie Mellon University in 2000. Neeru spent a year in the Coro Fellowship Program, a leadership program in public affairs and has worked for McKinsey and Company as an Associate Consultant. Neeru is also a filmmaker, illustrator, and blues guitar player. She has shown her work in various film festivals and publications.

DAMIEN O'BRIEN
Damien completed a Bachelor of Laws at Queensland University Technology and now works as a research assistant for the Law Faculty at QUT.

KEITH DONE
For over twenty five years, Keith has been a leader within the local Brisbane games community, devoting a great deal of his personal time to the development of games clubs and instigating the BIG Weekend in 1997, Brisbane's most successful and popular games convention. He has written over twenty RPG adventure modules for national games conventions. In December 2005 his pet project, 'Eldoria', which details the environment and cultures of a fantasy setting, was published in the US.

His efforts in the area were noticed by Auran Pty Ltd, one of Australia's leading PC game manufacturers and between 1999 and 2002 he took up a position with Auran, assisting them with the development of their Harn licence (Harn being a well-established fantasy setting owned by Columbia Games in Canada). Keith encouraged Auran to embrace the Open Gaming Licence that was being widely promoted by the major US game manufacturer, 'Wizards of the Coast'. The result was a series of RPG modules written under the OGL licence, which received international acclaim for the quality of the writing, artwork and cartography.

Keith has a long background in project management within the tertiary sector, specifically with the commercialisation offices of the Queensland University of Technology and Griffith University and, most recently, with the QUT Faculty of Law. Keith has worked intermittently in a supporting role in the QUT Faculty of Law's OAKLAW and Creative Commons research projects, including as coordinator of the OCL conference.

MICHAEL LAVARCH
Michael Lavarch is Professor of Law and Executive Dean of the Faculty of Law at the Queensland University of Technology, a position he has held since March 2004. The QUT is one of Australia's largest universities and the Law Faculty operates the largest of Australia's 29 law schools.

A QUT graduate, Michael commenced his legal career in Brisbane as a Solicitor. His time in practice was short, however, as in 1987, aged 26, Michael was elected to Australian Federal Parliament for an electorate in Queensland. He served three terms in the Parliament until 1996. Prior to his service in Parliament, Michael served from 1982 to 1987 as a Councillor on the Pine Rivers Shire Council.

In 1993 Michael was appointed as Attorney-General in the Australian national government. As such he had policy responsibility for major areas of substantive Law including the Australian Company Law, Family Law and Bankruptcy Law and for the major institutions of justice including the Australian Federal Police and the Commonwealth Courts, including the High Court.

RENATO IANELLA
Renato is a Program Leader at National ICT Australia (NICTA) Queensland Laboratory. His research covers eSecurity technologies and standards in information and rights management. Renato has extensive experience in the development of Internet, Web, and Mobile technologies and standards and was a former member of the World Wide Web Consortium (W3C) Advisory Board.

Renato also is an Adjunct Associate Professor at the University of Queensland, Visiting Associate Professor at the University of Hong Kong and was previously the Chief Scientist at LiveEvents Wireless, IPR Systems and Principal Research Scientist at the Distributed Systems Technology Centre (DSTC).

Index

AEShareNet...120-126, 127, 132, 143, 247

Auran...70, 190-191, 194, 203, 207, 208-213, 215, 245, 249

Australasian Performing Right Association (APRA)...63, 141-142, 182-184

Australasian Mechanical Copyright Owners' Society (AMCOS)...see 'Australasian Performing Right Association'

Australian Creative Resources Online (ACRO)...58, 143-147

Australia-US Free Trade Agreement...10, 25, 31-32, 35, 51, 75, 83, 163, 166, 184, 243

Autodesk Inc v Dyason (No 2)...162

BitTorrent...138-139

Blizzard v bnetd...216-219, 227

Blogs...30, 39, 139-140, 150, 152, 154, 170-173, 245

Bridgeport Music Inc v Dimension Films Inc...160, 163, 168-169

ccPublisher...56, 59

Code and Other Laws of Cyberspace...8, 229

Conger...13, 14, 25

Copyright
    Australian Law...see *Copyright Act 1968*
    History...11-17
    Term of Protection...11, 13-17, 21, 25
    and Contract...82, 225, 218

Copyright Act 1968...32, 33, 35, 80, 82, 160-166, 167, 171-172, 174, 184-185, 218, 220, 222

Copyright Amendment Act 2006...187

Copyright Amendment (Digital Agenda) Act 2000...218

Copyright Law Review Committee (CLRC)...79-84, 89, 185, 218, 244

Corporation, The...58

Creative Commons
    Australia...60-65, 179
    History...3
    Licences...46-47, 59-60, 61-65, 180-182
    Overview...3-6, 180-183
    Statistics...60
    see also 'Open Content Licensing'

Creative Industries...30, 70-72, 73, 84, 91, 95-100, 112-114, 143-147, 235

Crown Copyright...79-87, 106

Culture Jamming...157-158, 174-179, 181, 184, 186

Davidson & Associates v Jung...see '*Blizzard v bnetd*'

Digital Agenda Reforms...218

Digital Rights Management (DRM)...19, 43-44, 119, 127-128

Digital Sampling...158-169, 182, 185-186

Eldred v Ashcroft...7-25, 30-33

End User Licence Agreements (EULA)...214-215, 217

Fair Dealing/Fair Use...18, 24, 44, 83, 156-157, 166, 172-173, 175, 179, 184-187, 221, 224-225, 227

Flickr...59

Free Culture...36-49, 159, 177, 183, 185

Free Culture: How Big Media Uses Technology and the Law to Lock Down Culture and Control Creativity...3, 31, 95

Future of Ideas: The Fate of the Commons in a Connected World, The...3, 8

Games
    Copyright...214-228
    History...196-203
    Industry...190-191, 203-205

iCommons...3, 47, 51-65, 201-202

Internet and Innovation...150-155

Internet Archive, The...56, 58

Kahle v Ashcroft...21

Ladbroke (Football) Ltd v William Hill (Football) Ltd...162, 221

Lawrence Lessig...3, 7-10, 11-25, 29, 31, 36-49, 56, 57, 60, 68, 73-75, 80, 88, 94, 106, 151, 229-234, 239

Linux...119, 152, 154, 231

Lucasfilm Ltd v High Frontier...177

Machinima...225-227, 228

Magnatune...58

Marvel v NCSoft...219-220, 227

Massive Multi-user Online Games (MMOG)...237

Michelin Case...176-7

Miller v Taylor...14

Moral Rights...55, 62-64, 102-104, 107, 111-112, 160, 164-166, 175, 181, 185

Morpheus...59

MP3 Blogs...170-173

My Life...46

Network Ten Pty Ltd v TCN Channel Nine Pty Ltd...162, 163

Open Content Licensing
    Business...112-114, 151-155
    Cultural Institutions...78, 87-91
    Educational Institutions...47, 87-91, 109, 111, 120-126, 127, 132, 141, 144-147
    Film...99-108
    Games...204, 206-208, 211-213
    Government...78, 79-87
    Music...108-110
    Public Policy...74-79, 83-87, 234-236
    see also 'Creative Commons'

OpenCourseware...58

Open Digital Rights Language...127-134

Open Source Licensing...117-120
    see also 'Open Content Licensing' and 'Creative Commons'

Outfoxed...23, 97, 138

Oz Magazine...97-98, 239

Public Library of Science...58

Read My Lips...40-41

Remixing...4, 36-46, 56-57, 73, 80, 98, 139-140, 143, 158-160, 168-169, 181-182, 187
see also 'Digital Sampling'

San Francisco Arts and Athletic Inc (SFAA) v US Olympics Committee (USOC)...177

Science Commons...48, 60

Second Life...233

Smart State Strategy...69-72, 79, 86, 125, 245

Social Capital...153-156

Sonny Bono Copyright Term Extension Act 1998...10, 20, 31

SoundClick...59

Statute of Anne...11-15

Technological Protection Measure (TPM)...35, 217-218
see also 'Digital Rights Management'

Trade Marks...157-159, 175-177, 186

Trainz...191-195, 204, 207-213, 230

Uncovered...23

Universal Music Australia Pty Ltd v Cooper...172, 171, 223

Universal Music Australia Pty Ltd v Miyamoto...163, 166-167

Universal Music Australia Pty Ltd v Sharman...222-224

User Generated Content...191-195, 205-213, 215, 219

US Free Trade Agreement Implementation Act 2004...see Australia-US Free Trade Agreement

US v Thomas...214

Virtual Worlds...201, 208, 214, 224-225, 229, 233-234

Warner Entertainment Co Ltd v Channel 4 Television Corp PLC...172

Wired CD...173

Youth Internet Radio Network...135-142

Printed in Dunstable, United Kingdom